JavaScript Programming
Pushing the Limits

D1567473

JavaScript Programming

Pushing the Limits

ADVANCED APPLICATION DEVELOPMENT WITH JAVASCRIPT & HTML5

Jon Raasch

WILEY

This edition first published 2013

© 2013 Jon Raasch

Registered office

John Wiley & Sons Ltd, The Atrium, Southern Gate, Chichester, West Sussex, PO19 8SQ, United Kingdom

For details of our global editorial offices, for customer services and for information about how to apply for permission to reuse the copyright material in this book please see our website at www.wiley.com.

A catalogue record for this book is available from the British Library.

ISBN 978-1-118-52456-5 (paperback); ISBN 978-1-118-52455-8 (ebook); 978-1-118-52440-4 (ebook)
Set in 9.5/12 Myriad Pro Regular by Indianapolis Composition Services

Printed in The United States by Bind Rite Robbinsville

Publisher's Acknowledgements

Some of the people who helped bring this book to market include the following:

Editorial and Production

VP Consumer and Technology Publishing Director: Michelle Leete
Associate Director–Book Content Management: Martin Tribe
Associate Publisher: Chris Webb
Associate Commissioning Editor: Ellie Scott
Project Editor: Sydney Argenta
Copy Editor: Melba Hopper
Technical Editor: Rick Waldron
Editorial Manager: Jodi Jensen
Senior Project Editor: Sara Shlaer
Editorial Assistant: Annie Sullivan

Marketing

Associate Marketing Director: Louise Breinholt
Marketing Manager: Lorna Mein
Marketing Assistant: Polly Thomas

Composition Services

Compositor: Jennifer Mayberry
Proofreader: Wordsmith Editorial
Indexer: Infodex Indexing Services, Inc.

About the Author

Jon Raasch is a freelance web developer specializing in modern web apps for desktop and mobile devices. A user experience junkie, he builds JavaScript apps that focus on serving the user, whether through improved performance, increased usability or enhanced functionality. He believes that once users' demands are met, business goals will follow. Jon is the author of *Smashing WebKit* and the co-author of *Smashing Mobile Web Development*. He has written numerous articles for Smashing Magazine and his personal blog. A perfectionist when it comes to best practices, you can find him building sites and apps in his pajamas. He's currently based in Portland, OR. Follow Jon on Twitter @jonraasch and check out his website jonraasch.com.

Dedication

"Push it to the limit" – Rick Ro$$

About the Contributor

Kevin Bradwick has over ten years experience working in the web development industry. He's committed to building and sharing knowledge with the aim of producing high quality code. He currently works for the BBC where he builds and maintains applications that are used across the domestic and international website.

Acknowledgments

I'd like to offer a big thank you to everyone who has ever given back to the development community. That means anyone who has contributed to an open-source project, written a tutorial, answered a question, or even filed a bug report. We're all standing on the shoulders of giants, and these numerous contributions have brought web development to a wonderful place over the past few years. It's an amazing time to be a web developer, and that's all thanks to our excellent community.

Contents

Contents

Introduction

Writing JavaScript is more fun today than it's ever been before. In recent years, HTML5 introduced a wide variety of JavaScript APIs that push the boundaries of what developers can achieve in the browser. These new APIs allow you to create impressive features such as 3D graphics, geolocated data, and high performance animation. But HTML5's advancements are much more than flashy components to stun your audience. They also include a number of APIs to streamline the development process and allow you to create the next generation of web apps.

If the browser-level advancements aren't enough to get you excited, there's also server-side JavaScript with Node.js. Node isn't just some academic exercise about making a server with JavaScript. It's a production-ready server solution that caters to modern web app models, which need to relay messages to and from the user in real time.

This book teaches you how to create a next generation JavaScript app. You'll not only learn how to build the app, but I also explain the theory behind the way you should build it. By the end of the book, you'll be armed with techniques for building rich, interactive apps. But more importantly, you'll have a deeper understanding of engineering best practices. You'll be a more responsible developer whether you're writing JavaScript, or using another language to build the apps of the future.

The book is divided into four parts:

- **Part 1: A Firm Foundation**—Part I starts by covering some general best practices and drives home the book's central messages: loose coupling and the separation of concerns. It then discusses a number of development tools and teaches you how to establish a test driven development (TDD) approach using Grunt.js. Last, it compares a number of different libraries and frameworks you can use to jumpstart your development, and teaches you how to pick the best one for your individual project.

- **Part II: Building The Front-End**—In Part II, you dive in to building a foundation for an app using Backbone.js, which lets you you set up an MVC for your front-end, separating the data from the interface. You also learn to establish an Ajax-based navigation system using `pushState`. Next, Part II extends what you learned about Backbone, teaching you how to render views using a JavaScript templating engine. Templates allow you to further separate your app's data from its presentational layer.

   Finally, the section covers some best practices for form handling and validation to help you complete your app's foundation. You use a progressive enhancement approach, starting with a solid HTML5 base state, upon which you add JavaScript widgets, as well as polyfills to support older browsers. You then create a form in Backbone that automatically syncs with your app's backend.

- **Part III: Working with Serverside JavaScript**—In Part III, you learn how to write JavaScript on the server using Node.js. You start by learning the basics of Node, including how it works and when to use it. You also discover some general patterns of Node development to inform how you work with the platform.

Next, I introduce you to the Express framework, which will streamline your Node development and allow you to hit the ground running. You learn how to set up routes, render views using templates, and handle form postdata. Finally, you learn about MongoDB, a NoSQL database you can use with Node as an alternative to conventional relational databases like MySQL.

▮ **Part IV: Pushing The Limits**—In Part IV you push the limits of what your app can do. First, you learn how to build a real-time app, tying your server-side JavaScript knowledge together with the client-side techniques you learned in Part II. You discover WebSockets, and how to set them up in Node using Socket.IO. Then you walk through the creation of an example real-time app using Backbone.js, Express, and MongoDB.

Next I cover building your app's mobile components. You learn how to serve responsive content and use a mobile framework to arm your mobile development efforts. I also teach you how to set up handlers for touch gestures using Hammer.js, and take advantage of mobile-specific APIs such as geolocation. Then, you discover how PhoneGap can bridge the gaps in the browser-level APIs and create a dedicated mobile app based in JavaScript.

After going mobile, you discover one of the most exciting capabilities of HTML5: drawing graphics in the browser. You learn the basics of working with canvas and SVG, as well as how to use the Raphaël SVG library. Last but not least you learn how to render 3D graphics using WebGL and the Three.js library.

Finally, I provide a checklist of last-minute issues to handle for launch. You learn how to profile performance, as well as techniques for handling any performance issues that arise. You also discover best practices for how and where to deploy your app.

Companion Website

JavaScript Programming: Pushing the Limits has a companion website at `http://www.wiley.com/go/ptl/ javascriptprogramming`. The site includes code samples and demos from the examples in the book, as well as links to further resources. It's a great place to start if you're having trouble understanding a section, or just want to copy and paste the code samples.

Start Pushing the Limits

JavaScript Programming: Pushing the Limits provides a roadmap for building modern web apps. It includes solutions for the common problems you'll face, as well as general best practices for handling anything else. The book is geared towards advanced frontend developers as well as experienced backend developers who are interested in Node and have a solid understanding of JavaScript. Developers with an intermediate understanding of JavaScript should also be able to follow the concepts and examples in the book (by the end of which their skills will be much more advanced). While you should thoroughly understand client-side JavaScript, you don't need any previous experience with server-side JavaScript to understand the Node sections, since Part III starts from the ground up.

So get ready to dive in and start building a next generation web app!

Part I

Starting From a Firm Foundation

Chapter 1

Best Practices

A firm foundation is vitally important for any application. Before you write a single line of code, you need to spec out the app's architecture. What features will your app have, and how will these be implemented? More importantly, how will these features work with one another; in other words, what is the app's ecosystem?

Answering these questions involves a combination of research, prototyping, and a firm grounding in best practices. While I can't help you research or prototype the specific components of your app, I can pass on the wisdom I've gained on best practices.

This chapter covers the fundamental engineering concept of loose coupling, then explains one method of achieving it: JavaScript MVCs and templating engines. Next you discover a variety of development tools, such as Weinre, version control and CSS preprocessing. Finally, you learn how to set up a project in Grunt to automate tasks such as concatenation and minification. Using Grunt, you establish a test driven development pattern that runs your app through a suite of tests whenever a file is modified.

Loose Coupling

If you take only one thing from this book, I hope that it's to avoid tight coupling in your app. Tight coupling is an old engineering term that refers to separate components being too interdependent. For instance, say that you buy a TV with a built-in BluRay player. But what happens if the TV breaks? The BluRay player may still work perfectly, but is rendered useless by the broken TV. From an engineering perspective, it's better to avoid tight coupling and get a separate, external BluRay player.

This pattern also applies to software development. Basically, you should design your app with isolated modules that each handle a single task. By decoupling these tasks, you minimize any dependencies between different modules. That way each module remains as "stupid" as possible, able to focus on an individual task without having to concern itself with the other code in your app.

But it can be challenging to determine what exactly should be grouped into a module. Unfortunately, there's no one-size-fits-all solution—too few modules leads to tight coupling, too many leads to unnecessary abstraction. The best approach is in the middle: designing your app to use a reasonable number of modules with high cohesion. Cohesive modules group highly related pieces of functionality to handle a single, well-defined task.

Problems with Tight Coupling

Examples of tight coupling are all around us. If you're like me, your phone has replaced your music player, video game console, and even your flashlight. There's a certain convenience to having all these features integrated in one simple device. In this case, tight coupling makes sense. But that means that when one thing breaks, a chain of failures can occur—listen to enough music on your phone and suddenly your flashlight is out of batteries.

In software development, tight coupling isn't necessarily a bad thing—poorly designed coupling is more the problem. Apps almost always have a certain number of dependencies; the trick is to avoid any unnecessary coupling between separate tasks. If you don't take efforts to isolate different modules, you'll wind up with a brittle app that can be completely broken by even small bugs. Sure, you want to be doing everything you can to avoid bugs in the first place, but you aren't doing yourself any favors if every bug takes down your entire app.

Furthermore, debugging a tightly coupled app is extremely difficult. When everything is broken, it's almost impossible to track down exactly where the bug happened in the first place. This issue results from what is commonly referred to as *spaghetti code*. Much like pieces of spaghetti, the lines of code are all interwoven and very difficult to pull apart.

Advantages of Loose Coupling

Even if you rarely encounter bugs, loose coupling still has some pronounced advantages. In fact, one of the main reasons to build loosely coupled apps boils down to another cornerstone of classic engineering: interchangeable parts. Over the course of production, it's often necessary to rebuild portions of your app. Has Google started charging for their translation API? Better patch something else in. Has a component scaled poorly and begun to run slowly under load? Better rebuild it.

If your app is too tightly coupled, a change in one module can cause a ripple effect, where you have to accommodate the change in all the dependent modules. Loose coupling avoids that extra development time, and keeps code changes contained in individual modules.

Furthermore, loose coupling encourages easier collaboration with other developers. When all the individual components are isolated, working on different pieces in parallel becomes much easier. Each developer can work on his or her task without fear of breaking something someone else is working on.

Finally, loose coupling makes testing easier. When each piece of your app handles a separate, specific task, you can easily set up unit tests to ensure these tasks are executing correctly under any number of circumstances. You'll find out more about unit testing later this chapter.

> In an ideal world, you'd never have to refactor your codebase. But there will always be unforeseen issues, and even if you could account for every possible scenario, why would you bother? Trying to preemptively solve problems can lead to "premature optimization" and is sure to slow down development. In an agile world, you should only concern yourself with the problems you face right now, and deal with future issues in the future. Loose coupling streamlines the agile development process, and allows your codebase to evolve naturally as conditions change.

JavaScript MVCs and Templates

Continuing the theme of loose coupling, another design pattern emphasized in this book is the use of JavaScript model-view-controllers (MVCs) and templates. These provide a structure to decouple various aspects of your application.

MVCs

MVC is a design pattern that encourages loose coupling. It separates the data that drives an application from the visual interface that displays that data. Using an MVC framework allows you to change the front-end styling of an application, without having to modify the underlying data. That's because MVCs separate concerns into three related components: the model, view, and controller, as illustrated in Figure 1-1.

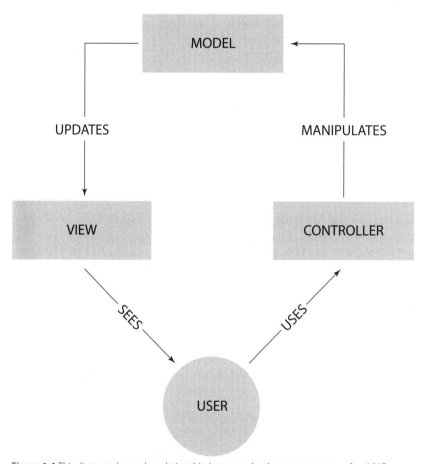

Figure 1-1 This diagram shows the relationship between the three components of an MVC.

Model

The model component of an MVC is the data that drives your application. You can think of the model layer as the domain logic of your application—it is all the data that your app will handle. On a simple brochure site, the model layer might only contain a few objects representing the content of the site: the text, image paths, and so forth. More complex apps, on the other hand, often use a large number of models to represent every individual piece of data the app needs. One example might be a model to represent an individual user (username, password, and so on).

The data in models is often saved in a database, or another data store like local storage. That way the data can persist across multiple sessions.

View

The view's sole duty is to present the user interface. In a web app, the end result of the view is markup, since it displays the content on the screen. But the view is more complicated than simple markup; it must reprocess the data from the model into a format that can be rendered as markup.

For example, dates may be stored as UNIX timestamps in the model, but you wouldn't want to display these to the user. The view takes these system time values, converts them to a readable value such as "August 4" or "Posted 5 minutes ago." Next, the view takes this cleaned-up timestamp and displays it as markup—for instance:

```
<div class="post-date">Posted 5 minutes ago</div>
```

Combine this with all the other markup you need for the page, and you've got the view.

Controller

Last but not least, the controller relays data back and forth between the model and the view. It is the component that takes in user input to modify the model and is ultimately responsible for updating the view with modified data. One example of the controller in action is a form handler. After the user posts a form, the data he or she submitted is processed by the controller, which in turn changes the appropriate data in the model. Then the change in the model is relayed back through the controller to update the view.

Putting It All Together

Alone, each of these components cannot do very much, but when the three separate pieces come together, they build an application. For example, apps commonly have a form that allows users to manage their user data: username, password, and so on. This data is stored in the model, which is typically a database. The view then takes this data from the model and uses it to render the form with all the default fields filled out (old username, twitter handle, and so on), as shown in Figure 1-2.

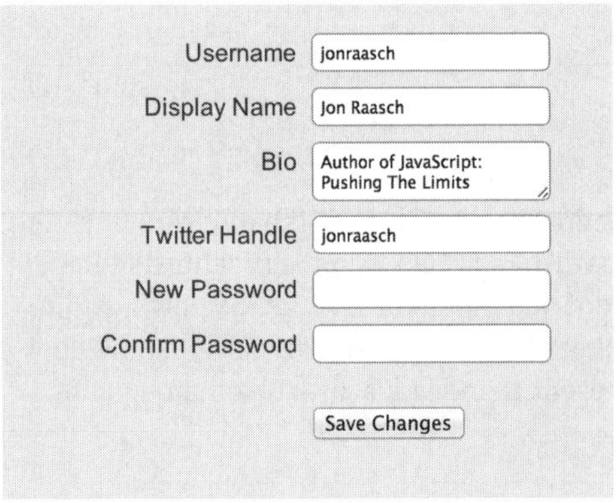

Figure 1-2 The view has displayed data from the model in a form.

The users then interact with this form, changing whichever fields they want. Once submitted, the controller handles the users' request to update the form and then modifies and optionally persists the data model. Then the cycle can repeat itself, as demonstrated earlier in Figure 1-1.

> You can find more about the MVC design pattern in Chapter 3, where I cover Backbone.js. That chapter also covers when it's appropriate to use an MVC framework: they aren't for every project.

Templates

JavaScript templates are part of the "V" in MVC: they're tools to help build the view. You don't need to use templates to follow the MVC design pattern, and you can also use templates without an MVC. In fact, I encourage you to use them regardless of whether you're using an MVC framework.

You may already be familiar with using templates in PHP or another back-end language. Then you're in luck because JavaScript templates work essentially the same.

How to Use Templates

Here's an example of a basic JavaScript template file:

```
<hgroup>
  <h1><%=title %></h1>
  <h2><%=subtitle %></h2>
</hgroup>

<section class="content">
  <p>
  <%=content %>
  </p>
</section>
```

The template is basically HTML markup with some variables enclosed in `<% %>`. These variables can be passed to the template to render different content in different situations. Don't get caught up on the syntax here— different template frameworks use different syntaxes, and most allow you to change it as needed.

> For an in-depth discussion of JavaScript templating engines, turn to Chapter 4.

Why Use Templates

Templates make it easy to represent models in the view. Their engines provide syntax for iterating though collections, say an array of products, and easy access to object properties that you want the view to render like a product's price.

Without templates, your JavaScript can get quite messy, with concatenated markup strings interspersed throughout scripting tasks. To make matters worse, if the markup ever has to change for styling or semantic reasons, you have to track down these changes throughout your JavaScript. Therefore, you should use templates anywhere you're touching the markup in your JavaScript, even if it's just one tag.

Development Tools

Part of being a good developer is using the best tools for the job. These tools speed up your development process, help you squash bugs, and improve the performance of your app. In this section you first learn about the WebKit Developer Tools. You're probably at least somewhat familiar with these tools, but we'll go more in depth and explore some of the more advanced features. Next you discover Weinre, a remote console tool you can use to get the WebKit Developer Tools on any platform, such as a mobile device or non-WebKit browser. Finally, I stress the importance of using version control and CSS preprocessing.

WebKit Developer Tools

Of all the developer toolkits available, my personal favorite is the WebKit Developer Tools. These are baked into WebKit-based browsers such as Chrome and Safari. These tools make it easier to debug issues in your JavaScript, track performance, and more.

The Chrome Developer Tools are installed by default in Chrome. You can access them through the Chrome menu or by right-clicking any element on the page and selecting Inspect Element.

> If you prefer to develop in Firefox, you can try Firebug or the baked-in Firefox Developer Tools.

Breakpoints

One extremely useful tool for JavaScript development is the Sources panel in the WebKit Developer Tools. With this tool you can set up arbitrary breakpoints in your scripts. At these points, scripting pauses and allows you to gather information about what is going on in the script. Open up the Sources panel and select a script from the flyout on the left, as shown in Figure 1-3.

Next set up a breakpoint by clicking the left margin at whatever line number you want to analyze. As shown in Figure 1-4, a blue flag displays next to the breakpoint.

Figure 1-3 First select the script you want to analyze.

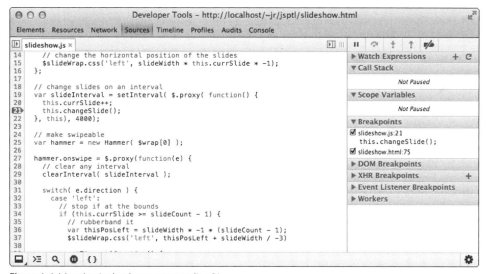

Figure 1-4 A breakpoint has been set up on line 21.

Finally, let your script run. Once it gets to the breakpoint, it pauses all scripting on the page the text, and `Paused in debugger` displays across the top of the browser window. At this point you can gather any information you need. The current variables are output in the right column in the Scope Variables section. You can also click any object in the source to see its value as shown in Figure 1-5.

Once you are done analyzing the data, simply click the play button to allow the script to continue until it hits the next breakpoint.

Figure 1-5 When the script reaches the breakpoint, you will be able to analyze the current value of any object.

Setting up breakpoints is absolutely invaluable for debugging since it allows you to pause the script whenever you want. It is especially useful on scripts that use timing functions or other features that can change before you have a chance to analyze them.

Watch Expressions

In addition to breakpoints, you can also use watch expressions from the Sources panel. Simply add an expression to the Watch Expressions column as shown in Figure 1-6.

Figure 1-6 Watching the value of an expression; in this case the sources panel tracks the value of `slideshow.currSlide`.

You can enter anything you want into the watch expression, a particular object or a custom expression. When working with watchpoints, click the reload icon to refresh the value, or use the pause button to stop scripting at any point.

DOM Inspector

The DOM Inspector allows you to click on any item on the page and bring up that element's location in the markup. It also shows any CSS styling that has been applied to that element, as shown in Figure 1-7.

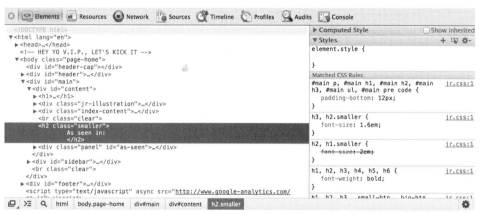

Figure 1-7 The DOM Inspector shows the element's location in the DOM and any styling.

To access the DOM Inspector, simply right-click any element on the page and click Inspect Element.

Additionally, you can use the DOM Inspector to adjust styling on the fly, changing any style rules that have been applied and adding new ones. The DOM Inspector can be instrumental both in tracking down pesky styling issues and testing new styling directly in the browser.

In more recent versions of the WebKit Developer Tools, you can also activate pseudo-classes such as :hover and :focus. Select the element you want to study, and then expand the pseudo-class menu in the right column's Styles area (by clicking the dotted rectangle icon shown in Figure 1-8).

Figure 1-8 You can also modify pseudo-classes with the DOM Inspector.

If you're using the DOM Inspector to style content as you go, be sure to save your work in a stylesheet often. Otherwise, you'll lose all your work if you accidentally reload the page or your browser crashes.

Network Panel

The Network panel allows you to track the time it takes each requested resource to be delivered to the client. It gives you a breakdown of server latency, download speed, and instantiation time for your various resources, as you can see in Figure 1-9.

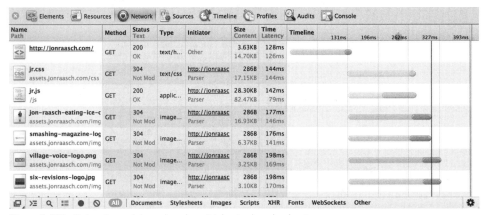

Figure 1-9 The Network panel shows how long it takes to download various resources.

The Network panel provides information for resources such as HTML, CSS, JavaScript, and images—and even allows you to filter by the type of request. This data is priceless when performance-tuning your app. Problems with slow responses are easy to pinpoint as you have access to the full request and response including the header information that was sent.

When you're developing locally, the network panel isn't useful for determining response times. That's because the browser doesn't have to download any of the resources from an external site. Upload your work to a staging server before testing.

Keyboard Shortcuts

If you use the Developer Tools as much as I do, you'll want to become skilled at using some of the keyboard shortcuts to access them quickly.

- To open or close the Developer Tools in Mac, press Cmd-Option-I, or Ctrl+Shift+I on PC.

- To open the console, press Cmd-Option-J on Mac, or Ctrl+Shift+J on PC.

- To toggle Inspect Element mode, press Cmd-Shift-C on Mac, or Ctrl+Shift+C on PC.

For more shortcuts, visit: `https://developers.google.com/chrome-developer-tools/docs/shortcuts`.

Weinre

The WebKit Developer Tools are great for working on issues in Chrome and Safari. However, often you need access to tools in other browsers, whether you're debugging an issue that affects only a specific browser or testing performance on mobile.

You could install a different set of developer tools in each browser. But these will all work slightly differently, and may be insubstantial in some cases (such as the limited tools in mobile browsers). That's where Weinre comes in. Weinre is a remote console, which allows you to access the WebKit Developer Tools in any browser or platform. It's especially ideal for mobile, since it provides a complete, robust testing suite on any device.

Setting Up Weinre

First, you need to install a Node.js server on your local machine. You can learn more about installing Node from the Node website (`http://nodejs.org/`) or turn to Chapter 6 and follow the instructions there.

Next, install Weinre using NPM. From the command line, type the following:

```
sudo npm -g install weinre
```

After the installation completes, start the Weinre server from the command line:

```
weinre --boundHost -all-
```

Finally, you need to add a script tag to your test page, to set it up as a debug target:

```
<script src="http://1.2.3: 8080/target/target-script-min.js"></script>
```

Here, replace `http://1.2.3:8080/` with the location of your local Weinre server (which is running off your desktop machine).

With Weinre set up, you can simply open the page on the mobile device you want to test (or whichever desktop browser you want to test). Then open Chrome on your desktop machine and visit `http://localhost:8080/client`. If all goes well, you should see two green IP addresses, one for the remote target (the mobile device) and one for the remote client (the desktop machine). See Figure 1-10.

Figure 1-10 Weinre is connected when the target and client IPs are both green.

Using Weinre

After you've installed Weinre, using it is a piece of cake. Simply use the Weinre console in Chrome, and you have access to all the WebKit Developer Tools you read about earlier this chapter. You can use the JavaScript console, DOM Inspector, Sources panel, Network panel, and more, as shown in Figure 1-11.

Figure 1-11 Here, I'm using the Web Inspector in Chrome to inspect elements on an iPhone. Notice how it is even highlighting DOM items on the iPhone.

Bear in mind that some data will be a little bit skewed. For instance, performance data is a little off because the device is running Weinre. Additionally, Weinre data is being relayed over the network, so network data will be off as well. There's really no way around this, and it's good to bear in mind that even native tools suffer from some of these issues.

Version Control

If you're not using version control in your development process, I can't stress its importance strongly enough. I use it on every project, even on tiny projects where I work completely alone. Version control tracks the changes in a codebase over time. Periodically, you set commit points, which you can revert to at any point, or even fold certain changes from one commit into another. It's absolutely essential for collaborating with other developers. Instead of having to figure out who changed what file, version control handles all that for you.

Even if you and another developer worked on the same file, version control can merge those changes. Occasionally, conflicts will occur—for instance, if you both edited the same line of code. In those cases, the version control system will provide a way to merge the changes manually. But even if you're working alone, I strongly encourage that you use version control. Before I used version control, I was constantly commenting out sections I wasn't using anymore, for fear that I might use them later. Now I can just revert changes whenever I want, and leave the codebase a lot cleaner. And if a client changes his or her mind on a bit of functionality, I can revert the codebase with a single command.

Of the variety of version control systems on the market, my personal favorite is Git. Git is very widely used, which is important when selecting software designed for collaboration. Most importantly, Git is distributed version control as opposed to centralized. This type of version control has a number of advantages. First it allows for each user to have their own repo, which can later be merged with the main repo (or other repos), thereby providing extra layers of versioning. Additionally, it is easier to use, because you can set distributed version control up locally without a server (and connect it to a server at a later date). You can find more about how to use Git in the free e-book, *Pro Git*: `http://git-scm.com/book`.

CSS Preprocessing

I'm not going to talk too much about CSS in this book, but your app will undoubtedly involve a certain amount of styling, and for that you should really be using a CSS preprocessor. CSS preprocessors such as SASS and LESS allow you be smarter in the way you write CSS. They provide a wide variety of scripting operations, which are all compiled to a static CSS file. That means you get advantages of dynamic scripting language, while still generating completely valid CSS files that can be read by any browser.

It's a good idea to use a preprocessor in any project with a significant amount of styling. To learn more about CSS preprocessing, turn to Appendix A, where I discuss LESS in detail.

Since CSS preprocessors generate standard CSS, you can always go back to static CSS at any time.

Testing

In order to ensure the quality of the app you're building, it's vitally important to test all the functionality thoroughly. But you shouldn't wait until the app is built in order to set up a testing framework. It's a much better idea to establish a test driven development pattern (TDD) using unit tests.

Unit tests break code into the individual tasks (units) and then ensure that the logic is working as planned. The idea is that once you set up unit tests, you can run them in a variety of different environments, browsers, and so on, to make sure that the app is working exactly as it should. This approach is the best way to weed out edge cases that may otherwise not come up until well after you've launched a product.

Yes, unit testing is more work than just coding. But if you set up a TDD approach, it can actually save you time Q&Aing and debugging pesky issues that crop up in only the rarest of cases. More importantly, having a full suite of tests will improve your confidence in your deliverables and ensure regression issues will be picked up later on in development.

In this section, you learn how to use Grunt to create a build process for your app. You use it to automatically concatenate and minify your JavaScripts, and run these files through linting to test syntax and ensure that coding conventions are being enforced. Next, you set up unit tests using QUnit. Thanks to Grunt, these unit tests will run whenever a file in your app is modified, ensuring high quality code as you write it.

Using Grunt

Grunt is a task runner that provides a number of utilities you can use when building your app. It automates many of the repetitive tasks typically associated with generating a production version of a script. In this section you use Grunt to concatenate and minify your JavaScripts, then run them through unit testing and linting. You can either run these tasks manually, or set them up to run automatically whenever a file is modified.

To use Grunt, you first have to install Node.js by following the instructions on the Node website (`http://nodejs.org/`). Grunt is a command line tool, so open up a terminal window and type the following to globally install Grunt's command line tools:

```
npm install -g grunt-cli
```

Once the command line tools are installed, open up your project's directory and install Grunt:

```
npm install grunt
```

> **If you want to use the command line tools, you have to install Grunt locally for every project. Alternatively, you can install Grunt globally and add it to your bash profile.**

Next, set up three directories for your project:

```
dist
src
test
```

These will contain the distribution and source files for the app, as well as the unit tests. Next you need to create two configuration files for Grunt: a `package.json` and a `Gruntfile.js` (both at the root of your project).

Building package.json and Installing Grunt Plugins

`package.json` stores some basic info about your app, as you can see here:

```
{
  "name": "my-project-name",
  "version": "0.1.0",
  "devDependencies": {}
}
```

This JSON simply contains the name and current version number of your app (which you should fill in), and then defines a number of dev dependencies. These dependencies are the Grunt plugins you want to use in the task runner. But rather than enter these manually, you can automatically populate this list when you install the plugins with NPM:

```
npm install grunt --save-dev
```

The `--save-dev` flag automatically enters the dependency along with its version number in your `package.json` file. Next, you install the rest of the Grunt plugins used in this example:

```
npm install grunt-contrib-concat --save-dev
npm install grunt-contrib-uglify --save-dev
npm install grunt-contrib-qunit --save-dev
npm install grunt-contrib-jshint --save-dev
npm install grunt-contrib-watch --save-dev
```

Building the Gruntfile and Creating Tasks

Now you have to create `Gruntfile.js`, which is the meat of your Grunt implementation. This file contains all the configuration and tasks you want to execute, for example:

```
module.exports = function(grunt) {

  grunt.initConfig({
    pkg: grunt.file.readJSON('package.json'),

    // concatenation
    concat: {
      options: {
        separator: ';'
      },
      dist: {
        src: ['src/**/*.js'],
        dest: 'dist/<%= pkg.name %>.js'
      }
    },

    // minification
    uglify: {
      options: {
        banner: '/*! <%= pkg.name %> <%= grunt.template.today("dd-mm-
yyyy") %> */\n'
```

```
      },
      dist: {
        files: {
          'dist/<%= pkg.name %>.min.js': ['<%= concat.dist.dest %>']
        }
      }
    },

    // unit testing
    qunit: {
      files: ['test/**/*.html']
    },

    // linting
    jshint: {
      files: ['gruntfile.js', 'src/**/*.js', 'test/**/*.js'],
      options: {
        // options here to override JSHint defaults
        globals: {
          jQuery: true,
          console: true,
          module: true,
          document: true
        }
      }
    },

    // automated task running
    watch: {
      files: ['<%= jshint.files %>'],
      tasks: ['jshint', 'qunit']
    }
  });

  // dependencies
  grunt.loadNpmTasks('grunt-contrib-concat');
  grunt.loadNpmTasks('grunt-contrib-uglify');
  grunt.loadNpmTasks('grunt-contrib-qunit');
  grunt.loadNpmTasks('grunt-contrib-jshint');
  grunt.loadNpmTasks('grunt-contrib-watch');

  // tasks
  grunt.registerTask('test', ['jshint', 'qunit']);

  grunt.registerTask('default', ['jshint', 'qunit', 'concat', 'uglify']);

};
```

To understand what's going on in this Gruntfile, let's rebuild it from scratch, starting with:

```
module.exports = function(grunt) {

  grunt.initConfig({
```

```
      pkg: grunt.file.readJSON('package.json')
    });

};
```

This snippet starts the config's initialization function by caching the settings in your `package.json` file. That way those values can be referenced elsewhere in the Gruntfile, as you'll soon see. Next, configure a task for concatenating the scripts in your app:

```
module.exports = function(grunt) {

  grunt.initConfig({
    pkg: grunt.file.readJSON('package.json'),
    concat: {
      options: {
        separator: ';'
      },
      dist: {
        src: ['src/**/*.js'],
        dest: 'dist/<%= pkg.name %>.js'
      }
    }
  });

};
```

This code configures Grunt to pull all the `.js` files from the `src/` directory. These files will be concatenated and saved to the `dist/` directory, using the name you defined in `package.json`. Next configure another task to handle minification using UglifyJS:

```
uglify: {
  options: {
    // the banner text is added to the top of the output
    banner: '/*! <%= pkg.name %> <%= grunt.template.today("dd-mm-yyyy") %>
*/\n'
  },
  dist: {
    files: {
      'dist/<%= pkg.name %>.min.js': ['<%= concat.dist.dest %>']
    }
  }
}
```

This snippet configures Uglify to minify all the files produced in the `concat` task (`concat.dist.dest`), and then save them to the `dist/` directory. Next, configure QUnit:

```
qunit: {
  files: ['test/**/*.html']
}
```

The QUnit configuration simply defines the location of the test runner files, which you'll learn how to set up later this section. Now configure a task to handle linting:

```
jshint: {
  files: ['gruntfile.js', 'src/**/*.js', 'test/**/*.js'],
  options: {
    // options here to override JSHint defaults
    globals: {
      jQuery: true,
      console: true,
      module: true,
      document: true
    }
  }
}
```

This configuration first sets the files you want to lint with JSHint, then defines a few options. Linting is a useful step in any test suite, since it checks the syntax of your JavaScript for any errors or poor formatting. Next configure the watch plugin, which runs tasks automatically whenever a file changes:

```
watch: {
  files: ['<%= jshint.files %>'],
  tasks: ['jshint', 'qunit']
}
```

This code configures the watch plugin to watch for any changes in the app's files, in which case it triggers the jshint and qunit tasks. With the watch configuration in place, any changes you make to your code will be automatically linted and unit tested. That way you can be certain that the code remains error-free and that coding conventions are being enforced.

Next, load in the Grunt plugins you installed earlier:

```
grunt.loadNpmTasks('grunt-contrib-concat');
grunt.loadNpmTasks('grunt-contrib-uglify');
grunt.loadNpmTasks('grunt-contrib-qunit');
grunt.loadNpmTasks('grunt-contrib-jshint');
grunt.loadNpmTasks('grunt-contrib-watch');
```

Finally, set up the tasks you want to run, most importantly the default task:

```
grunt.registerTask('test', ['jshint', 'qunit']);

grunt.registerTask('default', ['jshint', 'qunit', 'concat', 'uglify']);
```

To run the default task, simply type grunt on the command line. Likewise, the test task can be run using grunt test.

Using QUnit

Now that Grunt is set up, you already have a bit of testing coverage through JSHint. But linting only tests the JavaScript for syntax errors and misformatting. You still need to set up unit tests to verify the actual logic of your app. Unit tests ensure that your app behaves as expected in a variety of situations. They provide a fine-grained analysis of your app's functionality, verifying that every step executes as it should.

You got a brief glimpse of QUnit when configuring Grunt, where you set up the task runner to run QUnit tests whenever a file changes. But as it currently stands, there are no unit tests in the `test/` directory. This subsection teaches you how to use QUnit and create the tests for your app. QUnit is a JavaScript testing framework employed by jQuery and a variety of other projects. It provides easy-to-use and feature-rich unit testing capabilities.

QUnit Basics

First, download the script and stylesheet from `http://qunitjs.com`. Follow the guidelines on the homepage for setting up the markup for your unit tests page and then run the example test:

```
test('hello test', function() {
  ok(1 == '1', 'Passed!');
});
```

Here the `test()` function defines the title of the unit being tested (`hello test`) and then passes an anonymous function with the tests to run. In this example, the first argument in the `ok()` test passes (`1 == '1'`), so QUnit outputs `Passed!`, as shown in Figure 1-12.

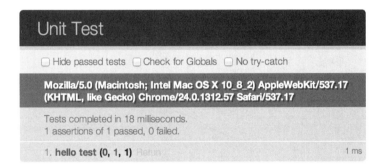

Figure 1-12 This unit test has passed. QUnit tells you how quickly it ran and allows you to rerun the test.

If you change the argument here to `1 == '2'`, the unit test fails, as shown in Figure 1-13.

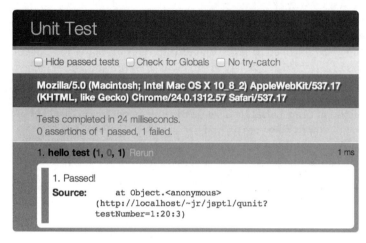

Figure 1-13 When the unit test fails, QUnit outputs a fail message and the source of the error.

Additionally, even if you have a syntax error in your code, QUnit outputs a global error, as shown in Figure 1-14.

Figure 1-14 A syntax error is throwing this global error.

Digging into QUnit

These examples have all been pretty basic. To get an idea of how QUnit works on an actual project, take a look at the QUnit tests for jQuery, which you can download here: `https://github.com/jquery/jquery/tree/master/test/unit`.

Notice that the unit tests are sequestered in a separate directory: `test/unit/`. Unit tests should never make their way into the production codebase; they're strictly for debugging and typically contain a considerable amount of extra code.

Now, open `core.js` and scroll down to `test("trim", function{ ... })`—it's at line 233 in the jQuery v1.9.1 that I'm using at the time of this writing. Here you see the following tests for the `jQuery.trim()` method:

```
test("trim", function() {
  expect(13);

  var nbsp = String.fromCharCode(160);

  equal( jQuery.trim("hello  "), "hello", "trailing space" );
  equal( jQuery.trim("  hello"), "hello", "leading space" );
  equal( jQuery.trim("  hello   "), "hello", "space on both sides" );
  equal( jQuery.trim("  " + nbsp + "hello  " + nbsp + " "), "hello",
" " );

  equal( jQuery.trim(), "", "Nothing in." );
  equal( jQuery.trim( undefined ), "", "Undefined" );
  equal( jQuery.trim( null ), "", "Null" );
  equal( jQuery.trim( 5 ), "5", "Number" );
  equal( jQuery.trim( false ), "false", "Boolean" );

  equal( jQuery.trim(" "), "", "space should be trimmed" );
  equal( jQuery.trim("ipad\xA0"), "ipad", "nbsp should be trimmed" );
  equal( jQuery.trim("\uFEFF"), "", "zwsp should be trimmed" );
  equal( jQuery.trim("\uFEFF \xA0! | \uFEFF"), "! |", "leading/trailing
should be trimmed" );
});
```

These assertions test the functionality of `jQuery.trim()` using a range of possible input parameters. These tests ensure the expected return value when these parameters are passed in: trailing spaces, leading spaces, empty strings, Boolean values, and any other unique situation you can think of. As you can see, the jQuery team has covered a wide array of edge cases in these tests. And as shown in Figure 1-15, jQuery passes all these tests.

Figure 1-15 `jQuery.trim()` passes all its unit tests.

Digging deeper into the code, the first line in the test function is `expect(13)`, which asserts that the test runs exactly 13 assertions. Then, for the first actual assertion, you see:

```
equal( jQuery.trim("hello   "), "hello", "trailing space" );
```

This line uses QUnit's `equal()` method, which determines whether the first two parameters are equal. In this case, the test expects `jQuery.trim("hello   ")` to return `"hello"`, in which case it passes.

You can do a lot more with QUnit, and I encourage you to read the QUnit docs (`http://api.qunitjs.com`) and to poke around in the jQuery tests to get a feel for how the test framework works. Or check out the tests for QUnit itself.

Setting Up Your Own QUnit Tests

Now that you know the basics of working with QUnit, you're ready to set up your own tests. It will take a little more time than coding without tests, but it shouldn't be too hard if you're already following best practices (object orientation, separating concerns, and so on).

The main place you should focus is on making your tests atomic—they should test as little functionality as possible. That doesn't mean you should test every single line separately, but rather that you should split your code into the smallest tasks possible, and test each one. The finer your tests are, the easier it will be to track down the cause of a test failure.

You should also make sure the tests are completely independent—the order you run your tests shouldn't matter, and you should be able to run any individual test without requiring another. Additionally, make sure that you document the tests with meaningful error messages. If a unit test fails the last thing you want to do is track down what the test is even checking.

Last but not least, don't wait until your app is built to write your tests—you should be writing them as you go along. Every time you add a new feature, it should be complimented with a new suite of tests. Get yourself in the mindset of TDD; a new piece of code isn't finished until you've finished the tests.

Save every test you write to the `tests/` directory of your project, so that Grunt can run them automatically. Now, whenever you save a change to your scripts, Grunt will perform a thorough sanity check and ensure that bad code never even makes it into the codebase.

Summary

In this chapter, you discovered the importance of loose coupling and separation of concerns, which I focus on throughout this book. You found out about MVCs and the different roles of the model, view, and controller. You also learned the importance of using JavaScript templates to display the view.

Next you read about the Chrome Developer Tools and how you can use them to debug your app and profile performance. You also learned how to access these tools in any browser and on any device, using the remote tool Weinre. Additionally, you discovered the importance of using version control, and also how to speed up your CSS development with CSS preprocessing.

Then you learned how to establish a test driven development pattern. You discovered the task runner Grunt and used it to automate repetitive tasks such as concatenating and minification. You also used it to automatically test the codebase whenever a file changes, using both linting and unit tests. Finally, you explored QUnit and learned how to create effective unit tests.

Now that you've learned some best practices and established a thorough testing approach, you can be confident that the code you'll write in the rest of this book will be of the highest quality.

Additional Resources

Engineering Best Practices

Separation of Concerns: `http://en.wikipedia.org/wiki/Separation_of_concerns`

Best Practices When Working With JavaScript Templates: `http://net.tutsplus.com/tutorials/javascript-ajax/best-practices-when-working-with-javascript-templates/`

Introduction to Test Driven Development: `http://www.agiledata.org/essays/tdd.html`

Chrome Developer Tools

Chrome Developer Tools Documentation: `https://developers.google.com/chrome-developer-tools/docs/overview`

Google I/O 2011: Chrome Developer Tools Reloaded: `http://www.youtube.com/watch?v=N8SS-rUEZPg`

Breakpoints: `https://developers.google.com/chrome-developer-tools/docs/scripts-breakpoints`

Weinre

Weinre Documentation: `http://people.apache.org/~pmuellr/weinre-docs/latest/Home.html`

Weinre — Web Inspector Remote — Demo: `http://www.youtube.com/watch?v=gaAI29UkVCc`

Version Control

Pro Git by Scott Chacon: `http://git-scm.com/book`

A Visual Guide to Version Control: `http://betterexplained.com/articles/a-visual-guide-to-version-control/`

7 Version Control Systems Reviewed: http://www.smashingmagazine.com/2008/09/18/the-top-7-open-source-version-control-systems/

CSS Preprocessing

LESS Documentation: `http://lesscss.org/`

Sass Documentation: `http://sass-lang.com/`

Testing

Johansen, Christian. *Test-Driven Javascript Development*. (Pearson Education, Inc., 2010)

Grunt: http://gruntjs.com/

QUnit. "Introduction to Unit Testing": `http://qunitjs.com/intro`

QUnit. "QUnit API Documentation": `http://api.qunitjs.com`

JSHint Documentation: `http://www.jshint.com/docs/`

Chapter 2

Libraries, Frameworks, and Plugins

In addition to following best practices, you should build your app on a solid foundation of libraries and plugins. Sure, you could write everything yourself, and there is indeed a time and place for that. But in most cases, it makes more sense to rely on the open-source work released by other developers.

Libraries and plugins can help speed up your development process and jumpstart your app with a boilerplate of basic functionality. Best of all, the well-known libraries have a huge community behind them, with excellent developers writing and rewriting the code, and a vast user base uncovering any bugs. With the more established, tried and tested libraries out there, you can be confident in using them in your application.

Plugins, on the other hand, are a little spottier when it comes to code quality. A good plugin saves you loads of time, while a bad plugin may end up creating more problems than it solves (and force you to spend more time debugging it than you would have spent writing it from scratch).

In this chapter, you discover how to choose the right JavaScript library for your project. I compare jQuery, Zepto, and writing your own vanilla JavaScript. Then you learn about the larger frameworks Bootstrap and jQuery UI. After briefly discussing how Modernizr can streamline cross-browser CSS issues, I show how HTML5 Shiv builds support for HTML5 elements in older browsers.

Next, I discuss HTML5 Boilerplate, which is neither a library nor a framework. It's a best-of-both-worlds template that you can use to gain all the advantages of a framework that can speed up setting up a standard HTML5 application.

Finally, I dive into jQuery plugins. You will look at good places to find new plugins, as well as a ten-point checklist you can use to determine whether the plugin is good enough to integrate into your project.

Choosing the Right JavaScript Library

One of the most important decisions you'll make at the beginning of a JavaScript project is which library to use (or whether to use a library at all). A good JavaScript library can streamline your development process, providing you with a variety of standard utilities that you can use and reuse on future projects.

Of course, this choice will be influenced by your level of experience with each library. But that said, don't be afraid of working with a new library if it's the best choice for a given project. Libraries tend to share a lot of syntax, so once you become familiar with one, it's a lot easier to adapt to another one. A number of popular JavaScript libraries are out there: jQuery, Closure, Mootools, Zepto (to name a few). My personal favorites are jQuery and Zepto, which I compare in this section.

jQuery

jQuery is arguably the most widely used JavaScript library on the web. It provides a variety of utilities and other API functions that you can use to build the components you need for your application.

Advantages of jQuery

The main advantage of jQuery is its scope. It's very robust, offering more APIs than any other library I've used. It's also really easy to use, for a couple reasons:

- The semantics of the API are very forgiving for beginners, allowing a variety of missteps without throwing JavaScript errors

- There are many convenience functions. A *convenience function* is sort of a gateway function—for instance, `jQuery.post()`, which is a proxy to `jQuery.ajax()`.

- Most jQuery methods are *chainable,* which means that each method returns itself so that you can link any number of methods on one DOM reference. For example:

```
jQuery('.my-element').addClass('my-class').fadeIn().click(myClickHandler)
```

All of these factors produce a low barrier of entry for jQuery and contribute to its overwhelming popularity. However, the scale and usability of jQuery also contribute to its main disadvantage: filesize. All the different functionality in jQuery comes at a price, which is a larger codebase. This filesize is bloated further by the convenience functions.

Fortunately, a lot of the filesize issues have been resolved in jQuery 2.0. jQuery 2.0 provides a modular build process similar to jQuery UI, which allows you to build a project-specific instance of the library which is customized for the APIs you are using. Additionally, jQuery 2.0 drops support for IE 6, 7, and 8, which contributes to a large chunk of the codebase in version 1.9. But don't worry, jQuery 2.0's API is compatible with 1.9, which means that conditional comments can be used to load jQuery 1.9 for any of the browsers that 2.0 doesn't support:

```
<!--[if lt IE 9]>
<script src="jquery-1.9.x.js"></script>
<![endif]-->
<!--[if gte IE 9]><!-->
<script src="jquery-2.x.x.js"></script>
<!--<![endif]-->
```

jQuery Community

The popularity of jQuery is also a pronounced advantage. The substantial jQuery community improves the codebase in a variety of ways:

- Several core contributors are constantly writing and rewriting different APIs—improving performance, adding to the range of functionality, and squashing bugs and cross-browser issues.

- An immense number of developers are using the library. These developers push testing to the limits, testing the library in a vast number of use cases and environments, uncovering (and hopefully reporting) any bugs that made their way into a stable build.

Whenever you encounter a problem or something you don't understand in jQuery, you can also lean on the community. The documentation on `api.jquery.com` is very complete and should be your first go-to resource. Beyond that, a ton of tutorials throughout the web describe how to tackle common jQuery problems and build larger components you may need in your app. Finally, if you can't find a way to solve a problem, simply ask on `stackoverflow.com`, and other jQuery developers will surely come to your rescue.

Including jQuery from a Universal CDN

You already found out how jQuery's popularity benefits the codebase and documentation. But did you know that it can also improve the way it's included on your site? With so many sites using jQuery, it doesn't make much sense for each of them to include it individually. Why should users have to download the same jQuery core on every site using the popular library that they visit? Fortunately, Google hosts jQuery on a Content Delivery Network (CDN), which you can leverage to improve download times for your users. CDNs are highly optimized servers designed to serve static files like JavaScript quickly. But being a CDN isn't what's important: it's the fact that this code is universal.

Although most sites still serve their own jQuery, enough sites are using Google's CDN to make it worthwhile. If your users have visited just one of these sites recently, the script is cached in their browser, meaning they won't have to download jQuery at all, even on the first visit to your site. The performance gains from this approach are substantial, and you can be proud of yourself for being part of the network of sites that leverage this CDN—the more sites that do so, the more beneficial this approach will be.

> It's important to bear in mind that using the CDN improves only download time. Instantiation time is still an issue, which is not negligible.

Using Google's CDN is a piece of cake; simply point the script source to Google's server:

```
<script src="//ajax.googleapis.com/ajax/libs/jquery/1/
jquery.min.js"></script>
```

This script requests the latest stable build of jQuery and includes it on your site. However, requesting the latest version of jQuery isn't recommended. APIs in jQuery become deprecated, and eventually unsupported, which is especially true in the transition from version 1.9 to 2.0. Thus it is a much better practice to specify the version of jQuery you want to use in your call to the CDN:

```
<script src="//ajax.googleapis.com/ajax/libs/jquery/1.9.1/
jquery.min.js"></script>
```

This script pulls jQuery version 1.9.1, since it's specified in the path.

> Omitting the http protocol ensures that your browser uses whatever protocol your page is currently using. This stops your browser from complaining about serving assets with mismatched protocols. It just won't work if you're trying to open HTML files locally using the `file:///` protocol.

Zepto

Zepto is a lightweight alternative to jQuery that was initially developed as a mobile library. But with its jQuery-like API and small filesize, it's a great choice for any project.

The majority of this book uses jQuery, but it's worth noting Zepto as a lighter weight alternative.

Advantages of Zepto

The main advantage of Zepto is filesize; weighing in at just over 8K, it's one of the smallest fully featured libraries out there. Despite its small size, Zepto is able to provide a substantial toolkit you can use for app development. Most of the common APIs and methods available in jQuery are also supported by Zepto, and those that aren't are usually easy to work around with a bit of custom JavaScript. To learn more about what is offered by Zepto, visit its documentation website at `www.zeptojs.com`.

Furthermore, since Zepto has a largely jQuery compatible API, it's incredibly easy to use, especially if you're already familiar with jQuery. You can reuse many of the methods from jQuery in exactly the same way, and conveniently chain together methods for cleaner code. This means that you can pretty much start using Zepto today, without even opening up its docs.

Finally, if you're building your app for mobile, Zepto also includes a few basic touch events you can leverage for better touch screen interaction:

- **Tap events:** `tap`, `singleTap`, `doubleTap`, `longTap`
- **Swipe events:** `swipe`, `swipeLeft`, `swipeRight`, `swipeUp`, `swipeDown`

If you're building a mobile app, there are some additional libraries you can use. You find more about these and other mobile techniques in Chapter 10.

No IE Support

But before you get too excited about Zepto, it's important to remember that it does not support Internet Explorer. This problem wasn't a cross-browser mistake by the library developer, Thomas Fuchs. Rather, it was a conscious decision to reduce filesize, much like the jQuery team's decision to drop old IEs from version 2.0.

Historically, to the pain of countless developers, IE has suffered from a slew of compatibility issues. It just doesn't adhere to standards with each major version having its own subtle quirks. Newer versions of IE have made notable efforts to close these compatibility gaps, but the fact remains that IE handles a number of JavaScript and DOM issues in a decidedly nonstandard way and is a distance behind other major browsers when it comes to HTML5 standards and features.

Most JavaScript libraries like jQuery handle these cross-browser issues with extra code so that you never have to see the problem. However, this extra code leads to a substantial amount of bloat. Zepto decided to trim that fat. That's great for mobile apps, which typically don't have to worry about IE. But it can be a deal-breaker when it comes to desktop apps.

Since Zepto uses jQuery syntax, its documentation recommends dropping in jQuery as a fallback for IE. That way your app still works in IE, while other browsers get the filesize advantages of Zepto. However, the two APIs aren't completely compatible, so use this approach with caution and test thoroughly. If you still want to go through with it, you can read up on the technique here: `http://zeptojs.com/#download`.

Vanilla DOM

Of course, you don't have to use a JavaScript library at all. Libraries can add unnecessary bloat to your app, even smaller ones like Zepto.

Pros and Cons of Vanilla DOM

The main advantage to writing all your own JavaScript is that you only include and write the things you need, and the main disadvantage is added development time. By definition, JavaScript libraries include a wide variety of functionality that is typically used in applications, but it's extremely unlikely that any individual app uses all of it. That extra, unused JavaScript falls under the category of unnecessary bloat. However, you have to weigh the filesize gains against the added development time, and if you've never written a JavaScript application from scratch, you may be underestimating the added time involved.

I'm sure you realize that you'll have to write a variety of scripts to handle all the functionality your app needs. But you may not be thinking about all the cross-browser development you'll have to do for each of these functions.

Cross-browser CSS issues are a walk in the park compared to cross-browser JS. Bizarre holdovers from the early days of browser wars keep rearing their ugly heads, forcing you to build totally different implementations for different browsers, each of which handle things slightly differently.

One familiar example is the cross-browser event handler—for instance, an `onclick` event. To bind a mouse event, all modern browsers support `addEventListener`:

```
var elem = document.getElementByID('my-element');

elem.addEventListener('click', function(e) {
  // whatever you want to do on click
}, false);
```

This will bind a click event to any element with the ID `my-element` in Chrome, Firefox, Safari, Opera, and IE9+. However, older versions of IE are notoriously poor at supporting standards. To accommodate these browsers, you'll need to use `attachEvent`:

```
var elem = document.getElementByID('my-element');

elem.attachEvent('onclick', function(e) {
  // whatever you want to do on click
});
```

Notice here how the API for the event handler is slightly different. Not only do you have to use `attachEvent`, but you also have to change the event type to `onclick` instead of `click`. Of course, you'll want to use both of these to make sure your script works for as many users as possible (older IE versions still have a depressingly large market share). To support both, you'll need to do a little feature detection:

```
var elem = document.getElementByID('my-element');

if ( document.addEventListener ) {
  elem.addEventListener('click', function(e) {
    // whatever you want to do on click
  }, false);
}

else if ( document.attachEvent ) {
  elem.attachEvent('onclick', function(e) {
    // whatever you want to do on click
  });
}
```

This basic script is just the beginning. You'll probably want to write a universal handler to take care of all types of events, like this script from NetTuts+ (`http://net.tutsplus.com/tutorials/javascript-ajax/javascript-from-null-cross-browser-event-binding`):

```
var addEvent = (function( window, document ) {
  if ( document.addEventListener ) {
    return function( elem, type, cb ) {
      if ( (elem && !elem.length) || elem === window ) {
        elem.addEventListener(type, cb, false );
      }
      else if ( elem && elem.length ) {
        var len = elem.length;
        for ( var i = 0; i < len; i++ ) {
          addEvent( elem[i], type, cb );
        }
      }
    };
  }
  else if ( document.attachEvent ) {
    return function ( elem, type, cb ) {
      if ( (elem && !elem.length) || elem === window ) {
        elem.attachEvent( 'on' + type, function() { return cb.call(elem,
window.event) } );
      }
      else if ( elem.length ) {
        var len = elem.length;
        for ( var i = 0; i < len; i++ ) {
          addEvent( elem[i], type, cb );
        }
      }
    };
  }
})( this, document );
```

If you're getting scared, that's good. Vanilla DOM is not to be taken lightly, and it gets even more complicated. Event binding is relatively simple compared to other cross-browser implementations, such as Ajax. While I can't deny the benefits of writing vanilla DOM, I also can't pretend that it's easy.

> It's worth noting that even if you write vanilla DOM, there's no guarantee that this will be smaller in filesize than a library. Popular JavaScript libraries like jQuery and Zepto have been carefully reviewed by their contributors for a variety of issues, including filesize. If you end up writing a whole lot of utility functions, you may find that they end up larger than a smaller library like Zepto (~8 K).

Adding Third-Party Utilities

That said, you still don't have to write everything yourself. Rather, you can bootstrap together a set of utility functions. One great resource for finding these functions is `www.MicroJS.com`.

You can pick and choose the scripts you need from MicroJS and build a lightweight library that fits your project perfectly.

> The MicroJS website is curated by Thomas Fuchs, who created Zepto.

Using a Framework

Recently, it has become popular to go the extra mile and use a full-on framework for your front-end development. A framework is more than a JavaScript library, because it provides styling and a variety of more in-depth features, such as form controls and other common components. I tend to steer clear of frameworks, preferring to patch together a JavaScript library, a variety of plugins and custom CSS. That way I create a custom build that suits my project's specific needs and that's styled to match design direction. But frameworks can certainly speed up development, and I encourage you to give them a try and figure out which workflow works best for you.

You can make this decision like a sculptor. Would you rather sculpt in clay, lumping together components as you need them? Or would you rather sculpt in marble, taking a complete block and chipping away the pieces you don't want? Either way, you'll end up at a similar point. The question is how you want to get there.

Bootstrap

Bootstrap offers a set of functionality and themes you can use to create your entire app. Bootstrap was first developed at Twitter for its own site and then was later released to the public. Bootstrap provides everything from a responsive grid layout to form controls. It contains a hodge-podge of different components and JavaScript plugins you can leverage to build your site quickly. Bootstrap's plugins include commonly used components such as modal dialogs, dropdowns, tooltips, and image carousels. Everything in Bootstrap is styled using a common theme, with icons, and so on.

Bootstrap is great if you want to launch a site quickly and don't need to follow a specific design direction. Of course, you can style everything in Bootstrap yourself, but its main purpose is to provide its own brand of UI look and feel.

jQuery UI

Another option, jQuery UI, isn't exactly a framework. It's more of a set of utilities you can use to enhance form elements and other aspects of your site. But because it's essentially a group of jQuery plugins that provide styling and functionality to common UI elements, I'm including it in here with other frameworks.

However, it's up to you whether you use jQuery UI as a framework. You can use all of its controls, such as tabs, accordions, and other components to build out your entire site. Or you can use jQuery UI more like a group of plugins. You can cherry-pick the components you like—for instance, using it to add a date picker to forms you're otherwise building with your own custom code. Yes, you can find individual plugins to fit each of these specific needs, but the jQuery UI core is extremely well built, and you can easily create a custom build so you don't have too much bloat from unused components.

> Personally, I use jQuery UI as a group of plugins, because I don't like to include too much styling in my JavaScript and prefer to handcode my CSS for fundamental components such as tabs and modal dialogs.

Mobile Frameworks

A number of good mobile frameworks are available, such as jQuery Mobile and Sencha Touch. You find more about these and mobile development in general in Chapter 10.

Miscellaneous Scripts

There are also a number of miscellaneous scripts and utilities you'll probably want to include in your app. Two such scripts that I include in almost every project are Modernizr and HTML5 Shiv.

Modernizr

Modernizr is a small script that can help you build modern applications, while still supporting older browsers. Basically, Modernizr is a set of feature detections you can use to determine which CSS3 and HTML5 features are available in the user's browser.

Modernizr's approach is to attach class names to the `<html>` element, describing which features are available in CSS. For instance, if `background-size` is available, it adds the class `backgroundsize` to the `<html>` element. You can then use CSS to target both cases:

```
/* no background-size */

html .my-element {
  background-image: url(../path-to/non-sizable-image.png);
```

```
    background-repeat: repeat;
}

/* supports background-size */

html.backgroundsize .my-element {
    background-image: url(../path-to/sizable-image.png);
    background-size: cover;
}
```

You can use this approach to target a variety of features, and use the class name or the Modernizr API to target HTML5 features you want to use with JavaScript. For more information about Modernizr and the types of detection it supports, visit www.modernizr.com.

> **Modernizr allows you to create a custom build that detects only the features that you care about. I encourage you to do so, because it will reduce the filesize and lessen the script's instantiation time.**

HTML5 Shiv

HTML5 Shiv is a very simple script that allows older browsers to recognize HTML5 elements such as <header>, <footer>, <nav>, <section>, and <aside>. Without a script like HTML5 Shiv, you can still use these elements; however, any CSS styling you apply to them will be lost in non-supportive browsers.

Because I like to use these semantic tags, I include this script on every site I build. To use it, first download the script from http://code.google.com/p/html5shiv. Next, include it in your site with an IE conditional, somewhere in the <head>:

```
<!--[if lt IE 9]>
<script src="dist/html5shiv.js"></script>
<![endif]-->
```

It's important to use a conditional so that you limit the browser requests for assets that are not needed. Since IE 8 and lower are the only non-supportive browsers with any significant market share, you can safely use a conditional here. Also make sure you don't include this script in the <body>. It has to exist in the <head>, ideally after any stylesheet declarations (for better performance).

> **Many other scripts and frameworks include HTML5 Shiv, so make sure you aren't including it twice.**

HTML5 Boilerplate

HTML5 Boilerplate isn't a library, and it isn't a framework. It's a template you can customize for your individual needs. Boilerplate is a base-state you can use as a foundation on which to build your apps. Noninvasive and lightweight, it's an ideal start to any HTML5 project.

HTML5 Boilerplate combines a lot of the things you've read about in this chapter; for instance, it includes jQuery via the Google CDN (with a local backup) as well as Modernizr and HTML5 Shiv. It also includes Normalize.css, a modern alternative to CSS resets, and a number of a base styles and placeholder icons. But the idea is not to use it like a framework. This base state is intended to be fully customized, and the styles are, for the most part, placeholders that are easy to switch out. Finally, HTML5 Boilerplate includes some server configurations to improve performance in Apache, Node, and other builds.

HTML5 Boilerplate is the best of both worlds. It has all the advantages of a framework in that it provides a high-water baseline you can use to jumpstart your app. But it doesn't go too far; it encourages you to replace its (very limited) styling and to bootstrap in the additional components you need.

Finding jQuery Plugins

After you have your core functionality covered by a library, framework, or boilerplate, you will most likely still need other functionality in your app. You could build each of these components yourself, but if you want a faster development process, it's better to try to find plugins. That way, you can cover most of the remaining ground for your app, all without coding a single line yourself.

This section focuses on jQuery plugins, since they are very popular. But most of the recommendations apply for any JavaScript plugins you may want to use.

Where (and Where Not) to Look

The best place to look for jQuery plugins is the official plugin registry at `http://plugins.jquery.com`. On this site, you can search, browse, and find plugins that are rated by members of the jQuery community. But jQuery's repository of plugins is hardly an exhaustive list, and you'll ultimately have to rely on a search engine to find what you're looking for. In general, the higher a plugin's quality, the higher its search ranking (although this is by no means foolproof).

When you formulate your search, be as specific as possible. I'd recommend steering clear of the countless blog posts in the format of "25,000+ jQuery plugins." These are generally spammy lists designed to drum up traffic for sites, and the plugins they contain are rarely (if ever) well researched.

It may not be what you want to hear, but finding good quality jQuery plugins can be a struggle. That's because a significant number of them are fairly lousy.

What to Look for—A Ten-Point Inspection

The low barrier of entry into jQuery has led to its popularity both in site builds and in third-party plugins. This popularity is both a blessing and a curse. On the one hand, you can find a free plugin for just about any functionality you can think of. On the other hand, a good percentage of these plugins are poorly engineered or lacking in flexibility for your project's needs.

That said, you can analyze a number of factors in a plugin you're considering. Here is a checklist to consider when assessing a plugin's quality:

- **Would it be better to write it yourself?** If the functionality is very simple, it's probably best to just buckle down and write it yourself. After all, if you can write it in less than the time it takes you to read the rest of this list, why would you bother? Additionally, if the plugin is similar to something else you're using, it probably doesn't make sense to add another plugin and bloat your codebase. Rather, you should spend a little time extending the other plugin to accommodate both needs.

- **Is it well documented?** The plugin's documentation is almost as important as the plugin itself. The docs will be the first place you go when learning how to use the plugin, or when you run into a problem. Furthermore, spending the time to write good documentation is a sign that the developer cares about releasing a quality plugin, rather than just spinning off something they wrote for another project in an effort to get traffic on their blog.

- **Does it have a good support history?** Be sure to check how recently the plugin was updated. If it is consistently maintained, that's a good sign that the developer cares about a quality release, and also that he or she will help you if any problem you can't solve arises. If the plugin is released as a blog post, check and see the last comment the author responded to. Also check the last time the developer fixed a bug or added a feature. Of course, the plugin may be so completely developed that there's nothing more to add, but good support is a very good sign.

- **Does it use a standard argument signature pattern?** When looking at the documentation, you'll see how the plugin accepts arguments. And after using a number of plugins, you'll see some common trends to how plugin options are passed.

  There's no one right way to handle options, but any plugin that has a bizarre argument signature pattern is a big red flag. It's a sign that the developer is not overly familiar with plugin development or that the developer hasn't bothered to think about the plugin's architecture.

- **Does it have simple markup requirements?** If the plugin relies on any markup in the source, the format of this markup is important.

  This issue is two-fold. First, strange or rigid markup requirements make plugins harder to use, because you will have to adjust your markup to suit the plugin's specific needs. Second, markup that is semantically poor or requires seemingly unnecessary elements indicates a lack of skill in the plugin developer.

- **Does it use quality CSS?** If the plugin uses CSS, that CSS matters as well. Good CSS is an indication that the plugin developer is good with front-end work. Poor or excessive CSS is not necessarily a deal breaker, but it is certainly a red flag.

- **Is there a list of supported browsers?** If the developer has tested the plugin across different browsers, the developer will probably say which browsers those are. It's a really good sign if the developer lists exactly which browsers were tested, along with the version numbers. But at the very least, the developer should mention that it "works in all modern browsers" or something to indicate concern about cross-browser development.

- **Does it have a minified version?** This point is a bit nitpicky, but you should check whether the plugin's web page provides a minified version. A minified version is a sign that the developer cares about performance and filesize. It's not absolutely essential, because the developer may be assuming you will include it in your site JS and minify that. But it's certainly a good sign if it includes a minified version, or the developer talks about filesize, gzipping, and so on.

- **Do other people use it?** One of the last things to check is how many other people use it. If it's on a site with user ratings, a high rating is certainly a good sign. Otherwise, do a Google search and see how many people are talking about the plugin, and how many "8000 jQuery Plugins" lists it has been included on. Of course, if the plugin is really new, you'll have to cut it some slack here.

- **Does it work?** Finally, the best way to check a plugin is to plug it into your code and see for yourself. This is the most time-consuming step, so do this only when you're confident that it deals sufficiently with the other issues discussed in this list. Once it's in your code, make sure that it accomplishes what you want and has decent performance. Finally, be sure to test the plugin in all the browsers you support before integrating it too deeply into your code. Alternatively, if the plugin author provides unit tests, you can simply run those in the environments you want to support. Unit tests are also an excellent indicator of quality, since it means the developer has taken time to test the plugin thoroughly.

Summary

In this chapter, you found out how to use a foundation of other scripts to jumpstart your app.

You read about the JavaScript libraries jQuery and Zepto, and the advantages of avoiding libraries altogether to write your own vanilla JavaScript. Then you learned about larger frameworks such as Bootstrap and jQuery UI, and the pros and cons of using a framework.

Next, you read about smaller utility scripts: Modernizr and HTML5 Shiv. You then were exposed to HTML5 Boilerplate, which combines libraries, utility scripts, and base styling to create a template. This template is less heavy-handed than some frameworks but still provides many of the same advantages.

Finally, you discovered jQuery plugins: where to find them and how to determine whether a given plugin is worth using. Now, you're ready to roll up your sleeves, and start coding in the next chapter.

Additional Resources

For a list of JavaScript Libraries go to `http://en.wikipedia.org/wiki/List_of_JavaScript_libraries`.

Library Documentation

jQuery: `http://api.jquery.com/`

Zepto: `http://zeptojs.com/`

Closure: `https://developers.google.com/closure/library/docs/overviewhttps://developers.google.com/closure/library/docs/overview`

MooTools: `http://mootools.net/docs/core`

Library Feature Comparison: `http://en.wikipedia.org/wiki/Comparison_of_JavaScript_frameworks`

Other Library Resources

jQuery Fundamentals: `http://jqfundamentals.com/http://jqfundamentals.com/`

jQuery Tutorials: `http://docs.jquery.com/Tutorials`

The Essentials of Zepto.js: `http://net.tutsplus.com/tutorials/javascript-ajax/the-essentials-of-zepto-js/`

Framework Documentation

Bootstrap: `http://twitter.github.com/bootstrap/`

jQueryUI: `http://api.jqueryui.com/`

jQuery Mobile: `http://view.jquerymobile.com/`

Sencha Touch: `http://docs.sencha.com/touch/http://docs.sencha.com/touch/`

Miscellaneous Scripts

Modernizr: `http://modernizr.com/docs/`

html5shiv: `https://code.google.com/p/html5shiv/`

HTML5 Boilerplate: `http://html5boilerplate.com/`

jQuery Plugins

jQuery Plugins Registry: `http://plugins.jquery.com/`

Signs of a Poorly Written jQuery Plugin: `http://remysharp.com/2010/06/03/signs-of-a-poorly-written-jquery-plugin`

Building Your Own jQuery Plugins: `http://docs.jquery.com/`

Essential jQuery Plugin Patterns: `http://coding.smashingmagazine.com/2011/10/11/essential-jquery-plugin-patterns/`

Books

Learning jQuery, Third Edition by Jonathon Cather and Karl Swedberg; Packt Publishing (September 2011): ISBN 978-1849516549 `http://amzn.to/XHo8Ebhttp://amzn.to/XHo8Eb`

jQuery Cookbook by Cody Lindley; O'Reilly Media (November 2009): ISBN 978-0-596-15977-1 `http://shop.oreilly.com/product/9780596159788.do`

Bootstrap by Jake Spearlock; O'Reilly Media (April 2013): ISBN 978-1-4493-4391-0 `http://shop.oreilly.com/product/0636920027867.do`

jQuery UI by Eric Sarrion O'Reilly Media (March 2012): ISBN 978-1-4493-1698-3 `http://shop.oreilly.com/product/0636920023159.do`

Part II

Building the Front End

Chapter 3
Backbone.js

Backbone gives your app structure. It provides a sensible framework that stores your app's data, relaying that data to the user as onscreen content. It can also manage syncing that data with the database or local storage. In this chapter, you find out how to store your app's data using Backbone models and collections. You then learn how to tie that data to the content that gets displayed to the user. Any changes in the content will be automatically updated on the screen. Additionally, you discover how to sync Backbone data with a database server, allowing you to save and fetch the data and create a state that is persistent across different sessions.

This chapter also covers how to tie different URLs to different states of your app, enabling you to build navigation and bookmarking support for your app. Finally, you find out how to set up custom handlers for any changes in your data, and also how to manipulate and sort collections.

Getting Started with Backbone

Although Backbone isn't necessarily easy to learn, it's certainly worth the effort, and if you already have experience with a back-end Model-view-controller (MVC), getting started with Backbone will be a lot easier. That's because the concepts of Backbone are harder to grasp than the actual implementation and usage.

What Is Backbone?

Backbone is a JavaScript MVC framework, which brings all the concepts of an MVC pattern commonly found on server side frameworks, to the front end. Basically, it allows you to decouple your app's data from the view and user interface that is displayed to the viewer.

Backbone provides methods for saving your data in models. You can then sync these models to the view. That means that whenever the data changes, those changes are automatically reflected in the content on the screen. Additionally, these models can be synced with the server using Ajax requests. Again, any changes can be automatically synced in both directions, ensuring that the data in your app stays persistent across different pages and sessions.

> Some people have argued that Backbone isn't truly an MVC, that it's more of an MVP (Model-View-Presenter). Although the argument isn't completely semantic, it's a bit inane, similar to the classic nerd argument of whether you prefer Star Wars or Star Trek. The point is that the way you use Backbone is similar to the classic patterns in an MVC. It is designed to separate concerns and decouple the presentational layer from the data.

Why Should You Use Backbone?

Everything that Backbone does, you could build in yourself. In fact you've probably already built a lot of it. But Backbone takes all of those disparate scripts, and unifies them in a single framework that is written well and thoroughly tested. In short, Backbone makes handling data a piece of cake. It avoids the spaghetti-code that is typically written when associating JavaScript data with onscreen content, and syncing that data via Ajax.

When you use Backbone, the data in your app remains completely isolated from the content that is displayed to the user. It also maintains a separation between the data and the processes for syncing it with the server.

Backbone streamlines the development process, allowing you to develop the different components of your app independently with interchangeable parts.

Backbone Basics

Backbone has four basic components:

- Models represent individual objects of data.
- Collections are groups of those models.
- Views represent the parts of the user interface and can display the data in models and collections to the user.
- Routers handle the relationship of the views with the URL in the browser, so when the user navigates to a certain URL, it displays a specific state of your application.

The relationship between these components is illustrated in Figure 3-1.

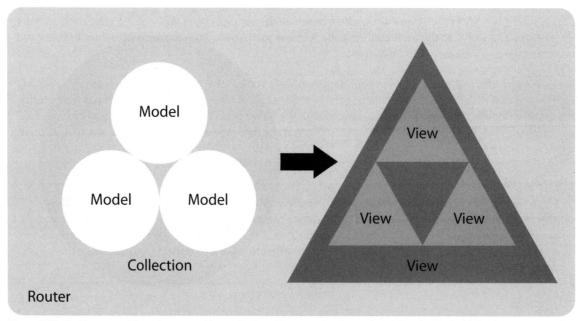

Figure 3-1 In Backbone, models can be grouped into collections. These can then be used to define views, which often have parent and subviews. All of this is driven by routers (optionally).

But Backbone is so much more than these basic building blocks. It has change events that update the view whenever a model changes. It has validation to ensure that all the data is properly formed. And it can be set up to automatically sync the data with an external server or local storage to ensure persistent models.

When to Use Backbone

Once you start using Backbone, you'll wonder how you built certain projects without it. However, you'll also find out that Backbone isn't for everything. In fact, for a lot of projects, Backbone is overkill.

Backbone is best suited for apps that need to handle a lot of data, especially if that data is intimately tied to the content on the screen. It's also ideal for apps that have a lot of data going back and forth from the server. However, it's not really a good idea to use Backbone for less interactive sites. Even if the site uses a lot of JavaScript, you have to ask yourself whether the site handles a lot of *data*. You can always build in JavaScript using stand-alone libraries and plugins, and even use JavaScript template engines without touching any Backbone.

This isn't a filesize issue, since Backbone is pretty lightweight. Rather it's a development issue—programming with Backbone requires a lot of extra set up. On data-driven sites and apps, that extra set up will actually save you time in the long run, but on more static sites, it's just not worth the extra time and effort.

Setting Up Backbone

To use Backbone, first download the core from `http://backbonejs.org`. You'll also need to download Backbone's only dependency, Underscore.js, from `http://underscorejs.org/`.

Then include both scripts on the page, with Underscore first:

```
<script src="js/underscore.min.js"></script>
<script src="js/backbone.min.js"></script>
```

Even when combined, these files are extremely lightweight, adding up to less than 10K when gzipped.

Backbone doesn't need to work with jQuery or any other library, but it does play nicely with any jQuery-type library. Most of the examples in this chapter use jQuery, so make sure to include it before the Backbone script above. Now, you're ready to dig into Backbone and start building apps with structure.

> Even though Backbone doesn't explicitly require jQuery or Zepto for its basic functionality, you'll need one of those libraries if you want to do any DOM manipulation inside of views and for RESTful persistence in models.

Models in Backbone

Models in Backbone are the basic building blocks of your app's data layer. For instance, you might have an object of data to represent a user in your app:

```
user: {
  username: 'jonraasch',
  displayName: 'Jon Raasch',
  bio: 'Some nerd who writes web books',
  avatar: 'j134jks.png'
}
```

In Backbone, this data is saved as a model. But Backbone's models do so much more than store this data. They contain smart defaults, change events, validation, and more.

A good Backbone setup starts by defining these models for your app's data schema. This won't necessarily have a one-to-one relationship with your back-end data schema, but it will probably be close. Next, you set up event listeners to track any changes to the model. But most importantly, you also create a set of validation rules that will run against your model's properties before the save action executes. That way, you can create unit tests for the business logic of your app and weed out potential data issues before they arise. Having this clear separation between your models and the views that represent them can make writing tests for your business logic a whole lot easier. You can focus solely on what each specific piece of functionality aims to achieve without worrying about visual elements that may or may not be on the page.

Creating a Model

To create a new model, use Backbone's `Model.extend()` method:

```
// create the model
var Fruit = Backbone.Model.extend({});

// create a new instance of the model
var apple = new Fruit({
  type: 'apple',
  color: 'red',
  condition: 'shiny'
});
```

Now, you can access any attribute of the model using the `get()` method:

```
console.log( apple.get('color') );
```

You can also set any attribute value using the `set()` method:

```
apple.set('condition', 'bruised');
apple.set({ type: 'banana', color: 'yellow' });
```

As you can see, you can either set a key-value pair or set a group of attributes using an object.

Creating Computed Attributes

You can also create custom computed attributes, for example:

```
var Fruit = Backbone.Model.extend({
  description: function() {
```

```
      return this.get('color') + ', ' + this.get('condition') + ' ' + this.
get('type');
    }
});

var apple = new Fruit({
  type: 'apple',
  color: 'red',
  condition: 'shiny'
});

console.log( apple.description() );
```

This example returns the string `red, shiny apple`. Notice how you're using the `get()` method with interpolated strings.

Setting Defaults

You can also set up smart defaults for your model. That way, you can create a new item without setting all the attributes:

```
var Fruit = Backbone.Model.extend({
  defaults: {
    condition: 'perfect'
  }
});

var apple = new Fruit({
  type: 'apple',
  color: 'red'
});

console.log( apple.get('condition') );
```

Here you set up a default for the condition of the fruit. This snippet outputs the condition as "perfect," even though you haven't set it.

Defaults can save you a lot of time in cases where an attribute is most often one way or another. But don't get too heavy handed with them; there are still some attributes that you should set every time you create an object. For instance, you don't want to set a default type of fruit here, because each one needs to be different.

Using the Initialize Function

The initialize function is a constructor that gets called when the model instantiates. To use it, you simply assign a function to that object property when passing in the configuration object:

```
var Fruit = Backbone.Model.extend({
  initialize: function() {
    console.log('Fruit model initialized');
  }
});
```

This callback fires whenever you create a new instance of this model.

Using Backbone Events

Backbone's models also contain a number of events, which allow you to track whenever a model is added, removed, modified, and so on.

Binding Events to Your Model

You can bind any of these events using the `on()` method within the `initialize()` function. For instance, to trigger an event whenever a new item is added with your model, you write

```
var Fruit = Backbone.Model.extend({
  initialize: function() {
    this.on('add', function() {
      console.log('Fruit added - ' + this.get('type'));
    });
  }
});
```

Notice how I use `this.get()` to access one of the attributes of this model, the context of each event handler is bound the model instance itself.

Tracking Model Changes

Probably the most widely used event in Backbone is the change event because it allows you to bind changes in your model with visual changes in the view. I talk about the view in greater detail later this chapter, so for now I'll keep it simple and ignore actually changing the DOM.

To track any change to your model, you write

```
var Fruit = Backbone.Model.extend({
  initialize: function() {
    this.on('change', function() {
      console.log('Values for this model have changed');
    });
  }
});
```

This callback fires whenever an attribute changes in your model.

Additionally, you can track changes to an individual attribute of your model using `change:[attribute]`:

```
var Fruit = Backbone.Model.extend({
  initialize: function() {
    // track changes in the condition attribute
    this.on('change:condition', function() {
      console.log('The condition of this fruit has changed.
  Might be getting moldy.');
    });
  }
});
```

This callback fires only when the `condition` attribute of a model changes, as in this example:

```
apple.set('condition', 'moldy');
```

> When attaching change events for multiple attributes, beware of execution order issues. It's difficult to determine which attribute listener will fire first, so either make sure the callbacks are completely independent or bind a single change event and check for changes on each attribute manually.

Validating Your Model

Probably the most important part of setting up your model is creating validation. That way, you can do a sanity check and prevent malformed data from ever being saved. For example, you can set up validation to make sure a certain property is numeric:

```
var Fruit = Backbone.Model.extend({
  // validate the model whenever it changes
  validate: function( options ) {
    if ( options.quantity && !_.isNumber( options.quantity ) ) {
      return 'Quantity must be a number';
    }
  }
});

// create a new instance of the model
var apple = new Fruit({
  name: 'apple'
});

// add an error event handler - this fires if it fails validation
apple.on( 'error', function( model, error ) {
  console.log( error );
});

// set a malformed quantity to trigger a validation error
apple.set( 'quantity', 'a bunch' );
```

Here's what's going on in this snippet:

1. I'm creating a validation function to check for malformed data in the fruit model.

2. If quantity is set, Underscore's `isNumber()` method checks that it's a number. Underscore is a prerequisite for Backbone, so there's no additional weight for using its methods.

3. An error event fires if the model fails validation.

The result is that if someone tries to set the quantity property to a non-numeric value, it triggers the error handler and passes the validation error message `Quantity must be a number`. More importantly, this data will never be saved to the model, ensuring that the model's data remains properly formed.

> Since model validation is so important, it's a good idea to set up unit tests on your models to check that they always match your app's business logic.

Working with Collections in Backbone

In Backbone, a collection is a group of models. If models are objects, you can think of a collection as an array of these objects. Although collections in Backbone don't do much more than group these models, they're still important to understand. After all, you'll probably end up using a lot of them.

Creating a Collection

This code creates a collection of items using the fruit model:

```
// create a model
var Fruit = Backbone.Model.extend({});

// create a collection with this model
var Fruits = Backbone.Collection.extend({
  model: Fruit
});
```

Here, the collection is based on the model. Now you can add a new item to this collection schema:

```
var Fruit = Backbone.Model.extend({});

var Fruits = Backbone.Collection.extend({
  model: Fruit
});

// create a new instance of the collection
var fruitbowl = new Fruits({ type: 'apple', color: 'red' });

// add another model to the collection
fruitbowl.add({ type: 'banana', color: 'yellow' });
```

Here you can see two ways of adding items to the collection. First, you can add an item when the collection is created; then you can add others using add().

> Alternatively, you can add multiple items when you create the collection by passing an array of objects.

Creating Collection Events

As with models, you can attach event handlers to your collections. All the same events are available: add, remove, change, and so on. However, with collections, you'll probably find yourself using a few new patterns:

Namely, the `add` and `remove` events become much more important because you'll want to track whenever new items are added or removed from the collection array. For example, this script fires events whenever an item is added or removed from a collection:

```
var Fruit = Backbone.Model.extend({});

var Fruits = Backbone.Collection.extend({
  model: Fruit,
  initialize: function() {
    this.on('add', function() {
      console.log('New fruit added');
    });

    this.on('remove', function() {
      console.log('Fruit removed');
    });
  }
});
```

Note that this won't trigger the `add` event handler callback when instantiating a new collection with objects.

You can also attach these events to the model for the same result.

Understading Backbone Views

In Backbone, views represent the user interface elements of your application that can often represent your data models. Although they're intimately related to the markup on the page, don't think of views as the markup for your app; rather, they are the logic for rendering markup.

Although you could use Backbone without views, the view is where the framework really starts to shine, because you can bind events for any changes that happen in your models and collections to the view, thereby tying any changes in your app's data to visual changes in the DOM. If you haven't tried this out before, you'll be amazed at what it does to your workflow. In my opinion, binding the data to views is the primary reason to use Backbone, because it eliminates the large amount of spaghetti code you'd use otherwise.

Creating a View

Creating a view is similar to creating a model or collection:

```
var FruitView = Backbone.View.extend({
  el: '#my-element',

  render: function() {
    this.$el.html('Markup here');

    return this;
  }
```

```
    });

    var appleView = new FruitView({
      model: apple
    });
```

Several things are going on in this snippet:

1. The `el` refers to the element that the view is inserted into. In this case, Backbone finds the element in the DOM that matches the CSS selector `#my-element`. This is one of a few different ways to create view elements.

2. The `render` function is called to render the view. This is an optional function that is not called automatically. In this case, jQuery's `html()` is used to render the content.

3. When a new instance of this view is created, an instance of the model that's to be tied to the view is passed in. This approach is optional; it's just a good practice for any view that is bound to a particular model. That way, you can access the model at any point in the view using `this.model`.

Using Render Functions

Render functions are completely optional. In fact, they're a common convention rather than part of Backbone itself. It's up to you to create them and call them when necessary, for instance whenever a particular model changes.

Calling the Render Function

Most times, you'll want to call the render function when the view initializes; otherwise, your view won't get displayed on the page. For example, you render the following view when it's created:

```
    var MyView = Backbone.View.extend({
      el: '#my-element',

      initialize: function() {
        this.render();
      },

      render: function() {
        this.$el.html('Hello World!');

        return this;
      }
    });

    var myView = new MyView ();
```

Here, when the view is initialized, it finds the DOM element with the ID `my-element`, and replaces the inner HTML of the element with `'Hello World!'`.

The render function returns `this`. That's a pretty common pattern, because it allows the render function to remain chainable like the other parts of the Backbone API.

Often, you will want to bind the render function to changes in a particular model. You'll soon find out how to do that using a callback from a change event.

Rendering a Model

In most cases, Backbone views are tied to a model, which means that you probably need to access attributes of that model in the render function. For example, you may want to render data about a particular user. First, start with the model:

```
// create the model for the user
var User = Backbone.Model.extend({});

var user = new User({
  username: 'jonraasch',
  displayName: 'Jon Raasch',
  bio: 'Some nerd'
});
```

Next, create a view that is tied to this model:

```
// create the view
var UserView = Backbone.View.extend({
  el: '#user-card',

  initialize: function() {
    this.render();
  },

  render: function() {
    // create a link to the user's profile as a wrapper
    var $card = $('<a href="/users/' + this.model.get('username') +
      '">');

    // add the user's name
    var $name = $('<h1>' + this.model.get('displayName') +
      '</h1>').appendTo($card);

    // add the user's bio
    var $bio = $('<p>' + this.model.get('bio') +
      '</p>').appendTo($card);

    // append this element to the DOM
    this.$el.html ($card);

    return this;
  }
});

// create a new instance of the view, tying it to the user model
```

```
var userView = new UserView({
  model: user
});
```

This code demonstrates a couple of new patterns. For one, jQuery is being used to build various bits of markup for the view. To drive the content of this markup, you leverage values from the model by using `this.model.get()`. These refer to whichever model is set when you create a new instance of the view. Finally, the element that was created is appended to the DOM.

~~Best~~ Worst Practices

You may have noticed that the code for this render function is pretty sloppy. It mixes a lot of markup in the JavaScript and is the epitome of the spaghetti code that coders try to avoid. For now, I will mix jQuery and markup to make the examples easier to follow. However, this is actually a bad practice. In the next chapter, I show you how to use templates to separate your markup from your JavaScript, an approach you should use 99 percent of the time. But in the meantime, just bear with me.

Using the View Element in Backbone

Whenever you create a view in Backbone, the view is necessarily tied to an element. That's the point in the DOM where the content will be rendered. Depending on the situation, you can either reference an existing element in the DOM or create a new view element on the fly.

Accessing the View Element

Because the view element is so important in Backbone, you can use a couple of different methods to expose it. First, you can access it along the view object you create:

```
var myView = new MyView();

// log the DOM reference of the view's element
console.log( myView.el );
```

As you can see, you can access the view element at any time using `el`.

Additionally, Backbone provides a jQuery/Zepto reference to the view element. You can access this reference using `$el`:

```
var myView = new MyView();

// hide the view element using jQuery
myView.$el.hide();
```

However, this works only if you're using jQuery, Zepto, or a similar library. Like I said earlier, Backbone plays well with these libraries, but it doesn't necessarily *need* to be used with them.

$el **is an example of how Backbone has been evolving with the community. Prior to version 0.9, it had become a common pattern to define this yourself in the view's initialize function with** this.$el = $(this.el).

Referencing an Existing Element

In many cases, it makes sense to reference an element that already exists in your markup. To reference an existing element, simply pass a CSS selector to el when you create your view:

```
var MyView = Backbone.View.extend({
  el: '#my-element',

  render: function() {
    this.$el.html('Markup here');

    return this;
  }
});
```

Here, Backbone finds the element with the ID my-element and uses it for the view. You can pass any CSS selector you want. However, make sure you pass a CSS selector string as opposed to a DOM reference. For example, you can't pass a jQuery reference such as $('#my-element').

When referencing an existing element, make sure that your CSS selector references a unique element, unless you want the view to modify all the elements you reference.

Referencing an existing element is a good idea if you have a fairly static piece of your page that needs to be altered based on the data in Backbone. Say that you have a welcome message in your header (for example, Welcome Kate) that needs to be changed if the user modifies her display name. Take a look at some code, starting with the markup:

```
<header>
  <div class="welcome-message">Welcome</div>
</header>
```

Next, create a model for the user that contains her display name:

```
// create a model for the user
var User = Backbone.Model.extend({});

var user = new User({
  displayName: 'Kate'
});
```

Once you have your model, you can set up the view:

```
// create the view for the welcome message
var WelcomeMessageView = Backbone.View.extend({
  // tie it to the element that exists on the page
  el: 'header .welcome-message',

  initialize: function() {
    // bind any changes in this view's model to its render function - in
    // this case you only need to track changes in the displayName
    // attribute
    this.model.on( 'change:displayName', this.render, this );

    // also call the render function when the view initializes
    this.render();
  },

  // the render function displays data the model data on the page
  render: function() {
    var displayName = this.model.get('displayName');

    this.$el.html('Welcome ' + displayName);

    return this;
  }
});

// create a new instance of the welcome message view
var welcomeMessageView = new WelcomeMessageView({
  model: user
});
```

There's a lot going on here, so allow me to walk you through it:

1. The view is created and associated with the `<div class="welcome-message"></div>` in the markup.

2. The initialize function is created and calls the render function whenever there is a change in the display name of your user. It also calls the render function when a new instance is created for the view so that it renders a solid base state.

3. In the render function, the value of the user model's `displayName` property is used to display the welcome message.

4. Finally, a new instance of the view is created. It passes in the user model created earlier.

Now, any changes in the model are bound to visual changes in the browser. To test it, try changing the model in your JavaScript console:

```
user.set('displayName', 'Katherine');
```

You should see the change occur in the welcome message on the page.

Creating a New View Element

You've already learned how to reference an existing DOM element for your view, but sometimes you'll want to create a new element for a view in Backbone. To do so, simply set the `tagName` when you create your view:

```
var MyView = Backbone.View.extend({
  tagName: 'li'
});

var myView = new MyView;
```

You can also set a class name and/or ID for your element:

```
var MyView = Backbone.View.extend({
  tagName: 'li',

  className: 'container', // you can use multiple class names here,
    // e.g. 'container list-item'

  id: 'my-view-wrapper'
});

var myView = new MyView;
```

This creates a `<li class="container" id="my-view-wrapper"></li>`.

Although these settings are all useful for creating exactly the right markup element, they are all in fact optional. If you don't set anything (and don't set an `el`), Backbone simply uses a `<div></div>` without any class or ID.

If you're creating a view element on the fly, be sure *not* to set the `el`.

This approach makes the most sense when you're injecting new content into the DOM. For example, say that you want to create a list of elements for each item in a collection. Although the list may live in an existing DOM element, you'll want to create a new view element for each item. I walk through a practical example of this approach in the next section.

Using Nested Views in Backbone

When you build your app in Backbone, you'll use a lot of nested views. Although they can get a bit hairy, nested views are a necessary evil. Fortunately, a number of best practices can help you keep nested views more organized.

To make this happen, you're going to have to roll up your sleeves. Take a look at some code, starting with the markup:

```
<ul id="band-wrapper"></ul>
```

Because you're populating this list with Backbone, the markup is straightforward. Next, you create the collection:

```
var Band = {};

// create the model
Band.Member = Backbone.Model.extend({});

// create the collection
Band.Members = Backbone.Collection.extend({
  model: Band.Member
});

// populate the collection
var band = new Band.Members([
  { name: 'John' },
  { name: 'Paul' },
  { name: 'George' },
  { name: 'Ringo' }
]);
```

As you can see here, you're creating a collection of four band members.

Creating a View for Each List Item

Now, you create a view for each band member:

```
Band.Member.View = Backbone.View.extend({
  tagName: 'li',

  render: function() {
    // add the name to the list item
    this.$el.text(this.model.get('name'));

    return this;
  }
});
```

The code here is straightforward: a `<li>` is created for each band member, and then it is populated with the member's name. But how are you going to get these elements on the page and render the complete list of band members? Well, to do that, you need a parent view.

Creating a Parent View for the List

The `Band.Member.View` already builds markup for each band member on the fly. Now, it's time to reference the element on the page and fill it with the individual band member views. To accomplish this, you create a second view for the overall list, which acts as your parent view:

```
// create a view for the band
var Band.Members.View = Backbone.View.extend({
  el: '#band-wrapper',

  initialize: function() {
```

```
      this.render();
   },

   render: function() {
     // loop through all of the items in the collection, creating a
     // view for each
     this.collection.each(function(bandMember) {
       var bandMemberView = new Band.Member.View({
         model: bandMember
       });
     });

     return this;
   }
});

// create a new instance of the band view
var bandView = new Band.Members.View({
   collection: band
});
```

Again, a lot is going on here:

1. A new view is created for the list that is linked to the `<ul>` markup from the beginning of this example.

2. When this view is initialized, it is rendered. That render function loops through the collection of band members, creating a new view for each using the band member view set up earlier.

3. A new instance of the overall list view is created. It passes in the collection of band members. You can pass in `collection` similarly to the way `model` was passed in previous examples.

Linking the Parent and Child Views

But you're not done yet. You still have to actually render the individual items in the list. To do that, you link the two views together. First, you need to make some changes to the parent view's render function:

```
// create a view for the band
var Band.Members.View = Backbone.View.extend({
   el: '#band-wrapper',

   initialize: function() {
     this.render();
   },

   render: function() {
     // empty out the view element
     this.$el.empty();

     // cache this before entering the loop
     var thisView = this;

     // loop through all of the items in the collection, creating a
     // view for each
```

```
    this.collection.each(function(bandMember) {
      var bandMemberView = new Band.Member.View({
        model: bandMember
      });

      // save a reference to this view within the child view
      bandMemberView.parentView = thisView;

      // render it
      bandMemberView.render();
    });

    return this;
  }
});
```

The first change is to empty out the view element, which is necessary because you'll be filling it up with the new list items in the child view. But don't worry about that now. You come back to it later. Next, the value of `this` is cached as `thisView`. Later, you'll need that value in the collection loop, which will overwrite the `this` context.

Now, for the important part: Within the collection loop, you're defining a reference to the parent view that you'll be able to access within the child. Because it allows you to make sense of how the views are related to each other, this is a crucial practice when dealing with nested views.

Next, you call the child view's render function. Previous examples called the render function from the view's initialize function. But that doesn't work here because you need the `parentView` reference, which isn't defined when the child view initializes.

Last but not least, you have to modify the child view's render function to connect with the parent view:

```
// create a view for each band member
var Band.Member.View = Backbone.View.extend({
  tagName: 'li',

  render: function() {
    // add the name to the list item
    this.$el.text(this.model.get('name'));

    // append the new list item to the list in the parent view
    this.parentView.$el.append( this.$el );

    return this;
  }
});
```

Here, the only change is that you are referencing `this.parentView.$el` to grab the view element from the parent view, which you're then using to append the list item. With the parent and child views connected, the band member list renders as shown in Figure 3-2.

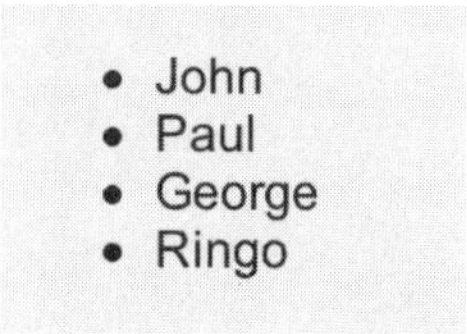

- John
- Paul
- George
- Ringo

Figure 3-2 The band list is rendering properly now.

Tracking Changes in the Collection

Finally, you want to track any changes that are made to the collection. To do so, you can set up listeners in the parent view's initialize function:

```
// create a view for the band
var Band.Members.View = Backbone.View.extend({
  el: '#band-wrapper',

  initialize: function() {
    // share the "this" context with the render function
    _.bindAll( this, 'render' );

    // add various events for the collection
    this.collection.on('change', this.render);
    this.collection.on('add', this.render);
    this.collection.on('remove', this.render);

    // render the initial state
    this.render();
  },

  render: function() {
    ...
  }
});
```

Fortunately, this part is a little easier to follow:

1. The use of _.bindAll() ensures that the this context is shared with the render function.

2. A number of different events are set up for the collection. First, there's a change event in case any collection item changes its values. Then add and remove events track the overall number of items in the collection.

To test that your event listeners are working, add a new band member in your JavaScript console:

```
band.add({name: 'Yoko'});
```

As you can see in Figure 3-3, the view updates in the browser.

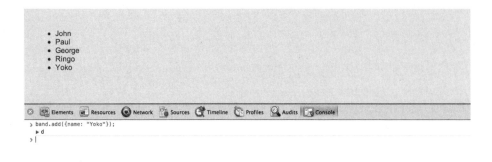

Figure 3-3 Any changes to the collection are being rendered on the page.

Here, the entire list is re-rendered even if one name changes. It's a lot easier to code this way, but the performance is slightly worse than if you only re-rendered an individual list item. However, chances are that the performance loss will be completely unnoticeable, and not worth the extra effort. Remember to avoid premature optimization until you see a performance issue.

Putting It All Together

Just to wrap up, here's the entire example of nested views:

```
var Band = {};

// create the model
Band.Member = Backbone.Model.extend({});

// create the collection
Band.Members = Backbone.Collection.extend({
  model: Band.Member
});

// populate the collection
var band = new Band.Members([
  { name: 'John' },
  { name: 'Paul' },
  { name: 'George' },
  { name: 'Ringo' }
]);

// create a view for each band member
Band.Member.View = Backbone.View.extend({
  tagName: 'li',

  render: function() {
```

```
      // add the name to the list item
      this.$el.text(this.model.get('name'));

      // append the new list item to the list in the parent view
      this.parentView.$el.append( this.$el );

      return this;
    }
});

// create a view for the band
Band.Members.View = Backbone.View.extend({
  el: '#band-wrapper',

  initialize: function() {
    // share the "this" context with the render function
    _.bindAll( this, 'render' );

    // add various events for the collection
    this.collection.on('change', this.render);
    this.collection.on('add', this.render);
    this.collection.on('remove', this.render);

    // render the initial state
    this.render();
  },

  render: function() {
    // empty out the view element
    this.$el.empty();

    // cache this before entering the loop
    var thisView = this;

    // loop through all of the items in the collection, creating a
    // view for each
    this.collection.each(function(bandMember) {
      var bandMemberView = new Band.Member.View({
        model: bandMember
      });

      // save a reference to this view within the child view
      bandMemberView.parentView = thisView;

      // render it
      bandMemberView.render();
    });

    return this;
  }
});

// create a new instance of the band view
```

```
var bandView = new Band.Members.View({
  collection: band
});
```

Just to recap what's going on here:

1. The model and collection of band members is created.

2. Then a view for each individual band member is created. This creates a `<li>` on the fly and inserts it into the view element for the parent view.

3. A parent view for the overall list of band members is created and tied to the `<ul>` in the markup.

4. The initialize function for the parent view renders the view and also binds the render function to various changes in the collection.

5. The render function for the parent view empties out the view element; then loops through each item in the collection. For each of these items, it creates a new instance of the child view and passes a reference to itself so the child view can access the parent.

6. The collection loop finally renders the band member view, which appends each `<li>` to the page, thereby rendering the entire content.

Saving and Fetching Data

Backbone is all about data, and that data won't do much good unless it is able to persist somewhere. Chances are, you'll want to save the data either on the server or in the user's local storage.

Although it doesn't do everything for you, Backbone makes it easy to automatically sync data changes with a persistence layer. Much like views and other parts of Backbone, the framework doesn't do all the work; Backbone just provides structure you can use to make syncing easier.

Syncing a Model on the Server

Saving a model on the server is actually pretty easy in Backbone. In this example, I only cover how to handle this on the front-end; it's up to you to program the backend REST API. Backbone can also be set up to work with local storage. If you'd like to avoid setting up a back-end API, skip ahead to the "Using the LocalStorage API with Backbone" section; then come back and follow these examples.

> In Chapter 6, you find out how to build back ends in Node.js, but for now, just use whatever you're comfortable with: PHP, Rails, and so on.

Saving the Model

First, start with a simple model of user data:

```
// create the model
var User = Backbone.Model.extend({});
```

```
// create a new user
var user = new User({
  displayName: 'Jon Raasch',
  username: 'jonraasch'
});
```

Now, to save this model on the server, you only have to make a couple of changes:

```
// create the model
var User = Backbone.Model.extend({
  // url of the REST API
  url: './path-to-api/'
});

// create a new user
var user = new User({
  displayName: 'Jon Raasch',
  username: 'jonraasch',
  bio: 'Some nerd.'
});

// save it
user.save();
```

As you can see, you made only two changes to save this model on the server:

1. A URL points to your REST API. This URL is added to the model declaration by passing the option `url`.

2. It is saved using `myModel.save()`.

When you save this model, an HTTP POST is made to the model's URL with the following JSON as payload data:

```
{
  "displayName":"Jon Raasch",
  "username":"jonraasch",
  "bio":"Some nerd."
}
```

Fetching from the Server

If you're saving data on the server, you'll probably also need to fetch it. That way, any data you save on the server can be loaded the next time the user visits the page. To fetch a model from the server, simply set up a sync URL and call `myModel.fetch()`:

```
// create the model
var User = Backbone.Model.extend({
  // url of the REST API
  url: './path-to-api/'
});

// create a new user
var user = new User;

// fetch the data from the server
user.fetch();
```

Here, this snippet makes an HTTP GET request to `./path-to-api/` and fills the model with the JSON that is returned.

Fetching from the server is also useful when you want to make sure that changes in the data of your models stay synced with the server. For instance, if multiple users can change the models on the back end, you'll need to set up an interval to check and make sure that no one has changed anything:

```
// check for changes every 5 seconds
setInterval(function() {
  myModel.fetch();
}, 5000);
```

This snippet polls the server for changes every five seconds. In Chapter 9, you read more about polling techniques and building real-time apps with Backbone and Node.js.

Providing Success and Error Callbacks

Backbone's sync functions also provide success and error callbacks should you need them. For instance, you can use these callbacks when you save your user model:

```
// save it
user.save({}, {
  // success callback
  success: function() {
    console.log('User saved successfully');
  },

  // error callback
  error: function() {
    console.log('There was a problem saving the user');
  }
});
```

As you can see here, you first pass an empty object to your `save` function and then an `options` object with the success and error callbacks.

You can also pull information about the error from the error callback's second argument:

```
// save it
user.save({}, {
  // success callback
  success: function() {
    console.log('User saved successfully');
  },

  // error callback
  error: function(data, err) {
    // pull the status code and text of the error
    console.log('Error: ' + err.status + ' - ' + err.statusText);
  }
});
```

Here, you're logging the response code and error message to the console. For example, if the page can't be found, this callback will return `Error: 404 — Not Found`.

> It's important to note that the error callback also fires if the model fails Backbone validation—for example, if you set up a `validate()` function on your model.

You can also set up success and error callbacks when you fetch. The only difference is that the `options` object is passed as the first argument in `fetch()`:

```
// fetch the model from the server
user.fetch({
  success: function() {
    console.log( 'User data fetched from server' );
  },

  error: function() {
    console.log( 'Unable to fetch user data' );
  }
});
```

Request Types

Backbone uses a number of different HTTP request methods to fulfill its sync API: POST, GET, PUT and DELETE. These are important for the REST API because they provide relevant context about the request to the server. In fact, one of the best parts about syncing with Backbone is that it handles these different request types automatically. The different requests are used as follows:

- **POST:** When you save a new model
- **GET:** When you fetch
- **PUT:** When you save changes to a model
- **DELETE:** When you destroy a model

> Internally, Backbone actually uses CRUD, which stands for create, read, update, and delete. But when it converts these to jQuery or Zepto's Ajax API, it maps them to POST, GET, PUT, and DELETE, respectively.

Emulating HTTP and JSON

If you're having problems syncing in Backbone, there may be a conflict between your server and the way Backbone posts to it. Fortunately, Backbone provides some easy workarounds that will get it working on just about any server.

First, if your server can't handle PUT and DELETE requests, you'll want to set it to emulate HTTP:

```
// fix problems with certain REST request types
Backbone.emulateHTTP = true;
```

Adding this snippet will cue Backbone to use POST for what would normally be update or delete operations. Additionally, if your server can't handle requests that are encoded as JSON, set it to emulate JSON:

```
// fix problems with JSON encoding
Backbone.emulateJSON = true;
```

This snippet serializes the JSON and posts it under a single parameter, `model`, for example:

```
[model] => {
  "displayName":"Jon Raasch",
  "username":"jonraasch",
  "bio":"Some nerd."
}
```

In general, it's a good idea to set up your server to handle the types of requests that Backbone creates, for a variety of performance reasons. But if that's too difficult, feel free to use these quick fixes.

> I have to emulate JSON when I'm developing locally in the `Sites` directory of my Mac. That's because Mac's built-in server can't handle requests encoded as `application/json` by default. Configuring Backbone to use `emulateJSON` ensures that the data is passed as if from a standard web form, using `application/x-www-form-urlencoded`.

Using the LocalStorage API with Backbone

By default, Backbone syncs to the server using REST APIs, but you can also set it up to use the `localStorage` API. It's actually really easy. First, download the local storage adapter here: `https://github.com/jeromegn/Backbone.localStorage`. Then include this script after the Backbone core.

The script does most of the work for you, overwriting the `Backbone.sync` API (which you learn about later in this section). The only thing you have to do is configure it to use `localStorage` on each model or collection you want to save.

For example, to save the user model you built earlier in local storage, you write

```
// create the model
var User = Backbone.Model.extend({
  // define the local store with a unique name
  localStorage: new Backbone.LocalStorage('user-store')
});
```

The only difference is that instead of defining the URL of a server-side API for your model, you're defining a `localStorage` store. Now, you can use all the same methods to sync: `save()`, `fetch()`, and so on.

> Be sure to define the local storage with a name that's unique across your entire domain, or it will overwrite other locally stored data.

Likewise, you can save collections in local storage:

```
// create the collection
var Users = Backbone.Collection.extend({
  // define the local store with a unique name
  localStorage: new Backbone.LocalStorage('collection-store')
});
```

Best of all, the local storage adapter doesn't completely overwrite `Backbone.sync`, which means that you can still save models and collections on the server. Simply set the `url` for any model you want to save on the server and `localStorage` for any model you want to save in local storage.

Although local storage is very useful, keep in mind that some older browsers do not support it. You can find a compatibility table here: `http://www.html5rocks.com/en/features/storage`.

> You can also connect Backbone to WebSockets. Chapter 9 explains how to use WebSockets with Node, JS, and Backbone to create real-time apps.

Saving a Collection on the Server

As you may have guessed, you can also sync collections. However, syncing collections can get a bit more complicated.

Fetching a Collection

First, you pull an entire collection down from the server using `myCollection.fetch()`:

```
// create the model
var User = Backbone.Model.extend({});

// create the collection
var Users = Backbone.Collection.extend({
  model: User,
  url: './path-to-api/'
});

// create a new collection
var users = new Users;

// fetch the collection from the API
users.fetch();
```

This snippet fills the collection with all the objects that are returned from the API. It expects a JSON array of objects, , for example:

```
[
    { "username":"user1",  "displayName":"User 1" },
    { "username":"user2",  "displayName":"User 2" },
    { "username":"user3",  "displayName":"User 3" }
]
```

Saving a Collection

Although fetching a collection is pretty straightforward, it's a lot more complicated to save it back to the server, because although you can fetch a collection all at once, you need to save the individual models separately. But that doesn't mean you should be iterating through all the models and saving them at once. Rather, you should create listeners on each of the models to save changes whenever they occur.

This is also a great opportunity to talk about some best practices for how to set up syncing in a practical example. To make things easier, I'm going to use local storage for this example. To follow along, download the local storage adapter covered earlier in the Using the LocalStorage API with Backbone section.

> If you'd prefer to work with a server-side API, you can set one up for this example as well. But be sure to switch all the `localStorage` declarations for `url` locations of the API.

Setting Up the Collection

First, you set up your model and collection:

```
// create the model
var User = Backbone.Model.extend({});

// create the collection
var Users = Backbone.Collection.extend({
  model: User,
    // set up the local storage handler
    localStorage: new Backbone.LocalStorage('users')
});

// create a new instance of the collection
var users = new Users;
```

Here, you've created a collection of users that sync with local storage.

Fetching the Existing Data

Next, fetch any existing data from local storage by adding a `fetch()` after you create the collection:

```
// create the model
var User = Backbone.Model.extend({});
```

```
// create the collection
var Users = Backbone.Collection.extend({
  model: User,
  // set up the local storage handler
  localStorage: new Backbone.LocalStorage('users')
});

// create a new instance of the collection
var users = new Users;

// fetch the collection from local storage
users.fetch();

// log the collection
console.log( users.toJSON() );
```

After you fetch the collection, you use `toJSON()` on the collection to log the collection to the console. However, at this point, there's no saved data to fetch, so the collection remains empty.

Adding Models to the Collection

Next, you add a model to the collection. But first create a handler on the model that will save any added models for later:

```
// create the model
var User = Backbone.Model.extend({
  initialize: function() {
    // add handler to save any added model
    this.on('add', this.addHandler);
  },

  addHandler: function() {
    // save the model when it's created
    this.save();
  }
});

// create the collection
var Users = Backbone.Collection.extend({
  model: User,
  // set up the local storage handler
  localStorage: new Backbone.LocalStorage('users')
});

// create a new instance of the collection
var users = new Users;

// fetch the collection from local storage
users.fetch();

// log the collection
console.log( users.toJSON() );
```

As you can see here, you use `this.on()` to track any added model events. This handler saves any model that's added.

Now, you can add a couple of models to make sure the script is working. In your JavaScript console write

```
users.add({username: 'user1'});
users.add({username: 'user2'});
```

Reload the page, and you should see your script console logging out the two new users, as shown in Figure 3-4.

Figure 3-4 The two users are added to the collection.

One thing you may notice is that an ID has been added to each user with a pretty long string of numbers. That's because Backbone needs a unique identifier for each item in a collection when it's saved in local storage. Don't worry; these are added automatically by the local storage adapter. You can also add them manually if you prefer; simply define an `id` attribute for your model.

Tracking Model Changes

Now that you're tracking added models, you need to also track any changes. To do so, attach another `this.on()` listener:

```
// create the model
var User = Backbone.Model.extend({
  initialize: function() {
    // add handlers to save any changes to the model
    this.on('add', this.addHandler);
    this.on('change', this.changeHandler);
  },

  addHandler: function() {
    // save the model when it's created
    this.save();
  },
```

```
    changeHandler: function() {
      // only save what has changed
      this.save(this.changed);
    }
  });
```

Here the `changeHandler` fires whenever a model has changed. But rather than save the entire model, it saves only the pieces that have changed, using Backbone's built-in `model.changed` value. That value is an object containing only those attributes that have changed.

It won't make a huge difference when dealing with local storage, but it's still an important practice to understand. When syncing to the server, this practice can make a big performance difference—it reduces the size of the request the server has to handle *and* also shrinks the HTTP request that the user has to upload.

Now, you can test that the `changeHandler` is working by changing some values in your JavaScript console:

```
users.first().set('username', 'newUserName');
```

This line pulls the first user off the collection and changes the username. When you refresh the new name is saved to local storage.

Tracking Deleted Models

You also need to set up tracking for whenever a model is deleted. For this, you need a new sync method, `destroy()` for example:

```
myModel.destroy();
```

As you may have guessed, this method deletes the model from the persistence layer. Now build this into another listener, to track remove events:

```
// create the model
var User = Backbone.Model.extend({
  initialize: function() {
    // add handlers to save any changes to the model
    this.on('add', this.addHandler);
    this.on('change', this.changeHandler);
    this.on('remove', this.removeHandler);
  },

  addHandler: function() {
    // save the model when it's created
    this.save();
  },

  changeHandler: function() {
    // only save what has changed
    this.save(this.changed);
```

```
    },

    removeHandler: function() {
      // destroy the model from the server
      this.destroy();
    }
  });
```

Now, you can test it in your JavaScript console:

```
users.remove( users.first() );
```

This line removes the first item from the collection. If you refresh the page, you'll see that the change has also been saved to local storage.

Putting It All Together

Now the collection syncing script is complete. You piece the code together as follows:

```
// create the model
var User = Backbone.Model.extend({
  initialize: function() {
    // add handlers to save any changes to the model
    this.on('add', this.addHandler);
    this.on('change', this.changeHandler);
    this.on('remove', this.removeHandler);
  },

  addHandler: function() {
    // save the model when it's created
    this.save();
  },

  changeHandler: function() {
    // only save what has changed
    this.save(this.changed);
  },

  removeHandler: function() {
    // destroy the model from the server
    this.destroy();
  }
});

// create the collection
var Users = Backbone.Collection.extend({
  model: User,
  // set up the local storage handler
  localStorage: new Backbone.LocalStorage('users')
});

// create a new instance of the collection
var users = new Users;
```

```
// fetch the collection from local storage
users.fetch();

// log the collection
console.log( users.toJSON() );
```

To recap what's going on here:

1. A model and collection are created and that collection is tied to local storage.

2. When the collection loads, the data from local storage is fetched so that saved data gets reflected in the collection anytime the user revisits the page.

3. In the model, you set up different event handlers to `save()` added or modified models, as well as `destroy()` removed ones.

> You can make this script more concise by removing the add and delete handlers, and simply passing `this.save` and `this.delete` to the `on()` event binder. I avoided that for consistency reasons, but feel free to make the change yourself.

Saving Collections in Bulk

Alternatively, you can build in a handler to avoid saving each model separately and, instead, save the entire collection as a single request.

Building a Custom Save Function

For instance, you can build your own `save()` function for the collection:

```
var Users = Backbone.Collection.extend({
  model: User,
  url: './path-to-api/',

  initialize: function() {
    _.bind( this.save, this );
  },

  // create a custom save function
  save: function() {
    // save this to the server using jQuery's AJAX API
    $.ajax({
      type: 'post',
      // pull in the URL from the collection
      url: this.url,
      // convert the collection data to JSON
      data: this.toJSON()
    });
  }
});
```

Here, you've built a custom `save()` function for your collection that does the following:

1. Calls jQuery's Ajax API to post the data.

2. Uses the API URL from the collection

3. Converts the collection data to JSON and sends it to the server as part of the payload request.

Now, you can call this function whenever you want by using `users.save()`.

> **Bulk saving collections alongside the local storage adapter is a little more complicated because of how it works internally. But it's not a major issue since local storage doesn't use requests.**

Drawbacks of Bulk Posting

Although this approach may seem easier, it's not necessarily the best one, especially when dealing with a server-side API. That's because you're posting the entire collection back to the server when only a small part of it may have changed. For instance, if you've changed only one attribute of one model, it doesn't really make sense to post the entire collection. Not only will the server have to process a much larger request but also the JSON will be larger, increasing the size of the HTTP request.

In general, it's much better for performance to post individual changes to the API, unless a whole lot has changed at once (in which case, you can avoid sending a ton of different requests and consolidate them).

Using Backbone.sync

If you are using jQuery or Zepto, you probably won't have to touch `Backbone.sync`. That's because Backbone automatically uses the `$.ajax()` API from these libraries to handle syncing. However, if you're using another library or your own vanilla JS, you'll have to overwrite `Backbone.sync` to utilize your own Ajax handler.

When creating your own `Backbone.sync` implementation, you need to create separate handlers for each request type:

```
Backbone.sync = function(method, model, options) {
  switch(method) {
    case 'create':
      // what to do for create requests
    break;

    case 'read':
      // what to do for read requests
    break;

    case 'update':
      // what to do for update requests
    break;

    case 'delete':
```

```
        // what to do for delete requests
      break;
    }
};
```

To be honest, I've never actually modified `Backbone.sync`. Chances are you won't have to either, but if you do, it will get a bit complicated because you have to handle all four request types and also all of the various options for syncing.

Working with Routers

Routers allow Backbone to bind a particular view state to a given URL. That means when a user requests a URL, it displays a related set of content in the view.

Routers are very important when you're building a single-page app (SPA). For example, have you ever used an app and then tried to use the back button or bookmark a page, only to find that it brings you back to the start page of the app? That's a perfect example of a poor user experience. Fortunately, routers make back button and bookmarking support a piece of cake.

> If you've been building SPAs without Backbone, you've probably already used something to provide back button support, such as Ben Alman's excellent BBQ plugin for jQuery (`http://benalman.com/projects/jquery-bbq-plugin/`).

How Routes Work

By default, Backbone routers set up routes that work with hashes. For example, if the path to your app is `www.mydomain.com/my-app`, some routes may look like this:

```
www.mydomain.com/my-app#step1

www.mydomain.com/my-app#step2
```

Now, if the user navigates from the app's landing page to `#step1` and then to `#step2`, these links work with his back button. When the user clicks the back button, he will first go to `#step1` and then back to the landing page of your app.

But the paths alone don't do anything; you have to set up the app to respond to each hash URL. For instance, JavaScript should display the step 1 content whenever the URL points to `#step1` and the step 2 content when it points to `#step2`. That way, new content will be displayed when the user clicks the back button, just as though routed to a new static URL. Likewise, the user can bookmark any of these hash links or share one of the links with a friend, and the freshly loaded page will still show the correct content.

> Later in this chapter, you find out how to create cleaner URLs with `pushState`.

Setting Up Routers

Assuming you built your app using the object-oriented, decoupled patterns I've been stressing, setting up routers should be pretty easy. The routers themselves are easy to implement. The only problem you might encounter is an app that isn't set up to easily display different routed pages.

Creating Routes

The basic router setup is as follows: Define a couple of routes; then define what your app does on those routes:

```
var Workspace = Backbone.Router.extend({
  routes: {
    'settings': 'settings', // #settings
    'help':     'help'      // #help
  },

  settings: function() {
    // whatever you need to init the settings page
    console.log('Settings init');
  },

  help: function() {
    // whatever you need to init the help page
    console.log('Help init');
  }
});
```

Here, set up routes are using an object of key-value pairs:

- The keys are the URL hash for the route—for example, "settings" is `#settings`.
- The values reference a function to be called when the browser encounters this hash. For example, if the browser goes to `#help`, it will call the `help()` function.

Setting Up the History API

Simply setting up your routes isn't enough to establish routing or implement back button support in your app. You still have to invoke the history API. To start up routing, add the following code:

```
Backbone.history.start();
```

Now, you see the appropriate message in your console if you change the URL to www.my-app.com/my-app-url#settings. Although this works just fine in most browsers, you may experience some issues in IE. To get around these compatibility problems, be sure to start the history API *after* the page loads. For instance, if you're using jQuery you would write

```
$(function() {
  Backbone.history.start();
});
```

That approach solves any IE issues.

> If the app has already rendered the current page and you don't want the route to fire again, you can pass `silent: true`, **e.g.** `Backbone.history.start({silent: true})`.

Navigating

Now, you can trigger different routes just by passing hash URLs to the browser—for example:

```
<a href="#settings">Settings</a>
```

Or you could even invoke these with JavaScript:

```
window.location.hash = 'settings';
```

Although both of these techniques will successfully route to the different pages of your app, later in the "PushState Versus Hashchange" section, you learn about a more robust approach that will work with hashes as well as the `pushState` API. The better approach is to trigger different routes using `Backbone.history.navigate()`:

```
Backbone.history.navigate('settings', {trigger: true});
```

Here, Backbone changes the browser's URL hash to `#settings`. The `trigger` option indicates that the API should also call the route function for that URL.

In rare cases, you may want to change the route but not register it in the browser's history (for example, not include it in the back button history). That way, the user can bookmark the page or share a link with a friend without having to pass through that page every time she clicks the back button. This approach makes sense if you're doing a lot of meaningless routing but still want to allow linking. To prevent the new route from registering as part of the browser history, pass `replace: true`:

```
Backbone.history.navigate('settings', {trigger: true, replace: true});
```

Setting Up Dynamic Routes

Backbone's routers are pretty comprehensive—you can even use them to set up dynamic routes. For instance, if your app has a search page, you could set up the following:

```
var Workspace = Backbone.Router.extend({
  routes: {
    'search/:query': 'search', // #search/monkeys
  },

  search: function(query) {
    ...
  }
});
```

This dynamic route passes in anything after the slash as the first argument of the `search()` function, which means that you can set up a link `#search/whatever-they-search-for` and pass the search query to the route handler. You can also set up multiple dynamic parameters:

```
var Workspace = Backbone.Router.extend({
  routes: {
    'search/:query':        'search', // #search/monkeys
    'search/:query/p:page': 'search'  // #search/monkeys/p7
  },

  search: function(query, page) {
    ...
  }
});
```

Here, you've set up pagination for your search page. Now, if the user is on `#search/monkeys/p7`, she's routed properly. Additionally, if she's on the first page of the search, the router still works without the page parameter. Furthermore, note the interplay between static and dynamic parameters: the static p coexists alongside the dynamic `:page`.

PushState Versus Hashchange

So far you've used Backbone's routers with the default URL hash implementation. A route using a hash might look like this:

```
www.my-app.com/path-to-app#route
```

However, these paths can start to look ugly, especially when dealing with dynamic parameters, such as this:

```
www.my-app.com/path-to-app#search/monkeys/p7
```

Fortunately, the HTML5 spec provides `pushState`, which allows you to route to normal-looking URLs without changing the page in the browser. For instance, those URLs would be changed to the following:

```
www.my-app.com/path-to-app/route
www.my-app.com/path-to-app/search/monkeys/p7
```

As you can see, the paths look a lot cleaner with `pushState`.

Using PushState

Implementing `pushState` in Backbone is a piece of cake. Simply define it as an option when you start the history API:

```
Backbone.history.start({pushState: true});
```

However, if your app doesn't live at the root of your domain, you will experience some problems here because `pushState` URLs look like normal URLs, which means there's no way for Backbone to discern what is part of `pushState` and what is part of the path to your app. To get around this, pass the `root` option:

```
Backbone.history.start({pushState: true, root: '/path/to/my-app'});
```

Enabling Backward Compatibility with Modernizr

Since `pushState` is part of the newer HTML5 spec, you may be wondering what happens in older browsers. Although Backbone won't handle fallbacks automatically, you can set one up easily using Modernizr. You just include Modernizr (which you can find at `http://modernizr.com`) and then pass the `pushState` option as follows:

```
Backbone.history.start({ pushState: Modernizr.history });
```

Now, supported browsers use `pushState`, and unsupported browsers revert to the standard hash implementation.

Best Practices for Using pushState

Besides making URLs look prettier, `pushState` has some important implications for your app's architecture. If you use `pushState` correctly, it will make your app much more robust across different environments and situations. However, if you use it incorrectly, it can make your app much worse.

The issue primarily comes up when JavaScript isn't working. That's not only a problem for people who have actively disabled JavaScript; it's also an issue when JavaScript breaks and while JavaScript is still loading.

Without JavaScript, hash URLs won't load at all. For example, if a user bookmarks a hashed URL and then revisits that page with JavaScript disabled, that user lands on the app's start page. Additionally, the start page also displays while the JavaScript is loading and then jumps to the correct content once it initializes. `pushState` gives you a way to fix this issue. Because the `pushState` paths are just the same as normal URLs, you can handle the page change on the server as well as in the JavaScript.

Thus, when the user revisits a `pushState` URL, you can generate the appropriate content statically via the back-end-generated markup. That way, the page will still work if the user has disabled JavaScript or the JavaScript is taking a while to load. The user can even navigate through the pages of your app without any JavaScript at all.

> Even though your app most likely depends on a lot of JavaScript, always provide as much content as you can without JavaScript, for those rare cases where JavaScript isn't working.

However, this golden opportunity is also a double-edged sword. If you don't provide any content from the server, the app might be completely broken with `pushState`. The problem won't crop up when the user stays on the page and uses the back button. But if the user bookmarks the page or shares the link with a friend, the page will load from that static URL.

If your app is set up on `www.my-app.com/path-to-app` and the `pushState` URL is `www.my-app.com/path-to-app/route`, make sure that the back end serves up your app on that URL as well. Otherwise, the page will `404`, and the app will be completely broken whether your user has JavaScript working or not.

So, even if you don't want to set up meaningful static content on that URL, at the very least include your basic app so that Backbone can kick in and serve the right content with JavaScript. The easiest way to do so is to rewrite all the pages under your app to route back to the homepage of the app. For example, on an Apache web server, you could do this in your `.htaccess` file using `mod_rewrite`:

```
# enable rewrites
RewriteEngine on

# rewrite all the pages under your app back to the app
RewriteRule ^my-app\/(.*)$ /my-app [QSA,L]
```

This quick-and-dirty fix ensures that your app loads properly for JavaScript users. But I strongly encourage you to consider providing some meaningful static content for all your routes.

More About Events

You already know how to attach events such as `add`, `remove`, and `change` to your models and collections using the `on()` method. In this section you'll learn more about event binding and unbinding in Backbone.

> In some of the Backbone literature, you may have noticed `bind()` being used in place of `on()`. That's just an older syntax that was deprecated in favor of jQuery's `on()` pattern.

Unbinding Events

In addition to binding events with `on()`, you can just as easily unbind events using the `off()` method:

```
Fruit.off('remove');
```

This snippet unbinds all `remove` listeners from the model. But if you've attached a number of different listeners, you can remove an individual listener by referencing it as separate function:

```
var removeCallback = function() {
  console.log('Fruit removed - ' + this.get('type'));
},

removeCallback2 = function() {
  console.log('Bummer');
};

var Fruit = Backbone.Model.extend({
  initialize: function() {
    this.on('remove', removeCallback);
    this.on('remove', removeCallback2);
  }
});

...

Fruit.off('remove', removeCallback2);
```

This script unbinds only the second callback.

Finally, you can unbind all events from an object by passing no argument:

```
Fruit.off();
```

Triggering Events Manually

Sometimes, you'll want to trigger an event manually. Sure, you could just fire the callback that is bound to the event, but it's often easier or more accurate to trigger the event itself. For instance, say that you have a couple of different callbacks assigned to different objects but still want to fire whatever callback is assigned. Triggering events is easy; just use the `trigger` method:

```
Fruit.trigger('add');
```

This will trigger the add event on this model, firing whichever callback has been assigned with `on()`.

Binding "this"

One of the biggest stumbling points when dealing with Backbone is the fact that the `this` context changes whenever you pass a function as a callback. This issue comes up primarily when dealing with events and the `on()` API, since that is where you see the most callbacks in Backbone.

You may have noticed that some of the examples use lines of code like the following:

```
_.bind( this.render, this );
```

This underscore function will bind the object in the first argument, to the value of 'this' of each specified function when it's called. Typically, that approach is used so that callback functions retain the context of the calling object when they're invoked, rather than an unintended context. In most cases, you can use this easy catch-all technique, but there may come a time when you need to pass an individual context to a certain function. In those cases, you can pass the context as the third argument manually when you assign the callback:

```
this.model.on('change', this.render, this);
```

This example is almost identical to other `on()` handlers you've already seen: It calls the view's render function whenever the model changes. The only difference is the third argument, which is where you can pass the `this` context.

In this case, the third argument ensures that `this` persists in the change handler. But you can also pass anything you want here. For example, when you set up nested views, you set up a `parentView` value in the child view. Sometimes, that value might be a more relevant value of `this`, in which case you can pass that value instead:

```
this.model.on('change', this.render, this.parentView);
```

Here, `this.parentView` will become the `this` context in the render function.

The All Event

You can use a variety of events in Backbone:

- add

- remove

- change

- change:[attribute]

- destroy

- sync

- error

- all

One particular event type to note is `all`, which is a catch-all listener you can use to track all these events at once. This can be really useful if you want to set up all your event handlers in a single place.

The type of event is passed as the first argument with this handler, which you can use to set up your own switch:

```
// create the model
var User = Backbone.Model.extend({
  initialize: function() {
    // set up a catch-all listener
    this.on('all', this.allHandler);
  },

  // Backbone passes the type of event as the first argument
  allHandler: function(eventType) {
    // switch based on the event type
    switch(eventType) {
      case 'add':
        // whatever you want to do on add
      break;

      case 'remove':
        // whatever you want to do on remove
      break;

      case 'change':
        // whatever you want to do on change
      break;
    }
  }
});
```

You may be wondering why you'd use this approach instead of separate handlers for each event type. Indeed, if your handlers are all completely independent, you have no need for this type of approach. But if you're depending on one event firing before another, it's best to set each one up manually in an `all` event, because it's difficult to determine which event fires first in Backbone. Using this approach, you avoid any race conditions.

Manipulating Collections

So far, you've used collections in a pretty basic way. You've used them to group related models and then loop through those items. However, you can do a lot more with collections, such as pull certain items, filter by different keys, and sort based on custom sort functions.

Pulling Collection Items

Once you've added a number of different items to your collection, you can pull them off in a couple different ways. But, first, create a collection so you have something to work with:

```
// create the model
var Fruit = Backbone.Model.extend({});

// create the collection
var Fruits = Backbone.Collection.extend({
  model: Fruit
});

var fruitbowl = new Fruits;

// add items to the collection
fruitbowl.add({ type: 'apple', color: 'red', quantity: 3 });
fruitbowl.add({ type: 'apple', color: 'yellow', quantity: 5 });
fruitbowl.add({ type: 'banana', color: 'yellow', quantity: 1 });
fruitbowl.add({ type: 'orange', color: 'orange', quantity: 3 });
```

Now, you can dig in and pull individual items off this collection.

Pulling Collection Items by Index

First, you can pull any collection item by passing its index to at():

```
var thirdFruit = fruitbowl.at(2);
```

This snippet pulls the third item in the collection (since the indexes start with 0), which in this case is a banana.

There are also special functions for pulling the first and last collection items:

```
// first item
var firstFruit = fruitbowl.first();

// last item
var lastFruit = fruitbowl.last();
```

Here, the first() and last() functions pull the red apple and the orange, respectively.

Later in the "Sorting a Collection" section I show you how to sort your collection. However, even if you haven't sorted your collection, you can still pull items based on the order they are inserted.

Matching Certain Collection Items

You can also pull items from your collection based on their attributes. To do so, pass in filter rules to `where()`:

```
var apples = fruitbowl.where({ type: 'apple' });
```

This snippet pulls any items with this type from your collection. This can be a single item or multiple items, depending on what is matched (or no items for that matter).

In this example, `where()` pulls both of the apples as a separate collection. You can then pull an individual apple off of this collection using the `index` methods used earlier (or a more specific filter).

Sorting a Collection

You can also sort your collection a couple different ways. Sorting is important when pulling collection items by index and also when looping through the collection items in order.

Using "Sort By" Functions

By default, collections stay in insertion order; the first item you add to the collection is first, the second item is second, and so on. But you can alter their default order by setting a comparator function:

```
fruitbowl.comparator = function(fruit) {
   // sort by quantity
   return fruit.get('quantity');
};
```

Here, the items will be sorted according to the value of their `quantity` attribute. When applied to the collection you created earlier, this comparator changes the order as follows:

```
[
  {"type":"banana","color":"yellow","quantity":1},
  {"type":"apple","color":"red","quantity":3},
  {"type":"orange","color":"orange","quantity":3},
  {"type":"apple","color":"yellow","quantity":5}
]
```

As you can see, the items are sorted by quantity. Where two items have the same quantity (the red apple and the orange), the order defaults to the original insertion order.

Creating Custom Sort Functions

So far, you've created a "sort by" comparator function, meaning that it sorts according to the values of a single metric. That's great when you want to sort something in ascending order based on a numeric value, or sort strings alphabetically. That simple type of comparison is used automatically if your comparator function accepts only one argument. But you can also create a custom sort function with a lot more control by passing two arguments to your comparator, as shown here:

```
fruitbowl.comparator = function( fruit1, fruit2 ) { ... }
```

However, custom sort functions are a bit more complicated. Whereas sort by comparisons simply return a value to compare, custom sort functions must do the sorting themselves. That means you should return the following:

- Return −1 if the first model should come before the second.
- Return 0 if they are of the same rank.
- Return 1 if the second model should come before the first.

For instance, you can sort the fruit in reverse alphabetical order:

```
// create a custom comparator to sort in reverse alphabetical order
fruitbowl.comparator = function(fruit1, fruit2) {
  // get the names for each fruit
  var fruitName1 = fruit1.get('type'),
  fruitName2 = fruit2.get('type');

  // compare the strings
  if ( fruitName1 < fruitName2 ) return 1;
  if ( fruitName1 > fruitName2 ) return -1;
  return 0;
};
```

Here, if the second fruit has a higher alphabetical value, you return 1 (because you want the higher alphabetical values to come first). Conversely, if the first fruit has a higher alphabetical value, you return −1. Finally, you return 0 if they are the same. As you can see, the custom comparator places the fruits in reverse alphabetical order:

```
[
  {"type":"orange","color":"orange","quantity":3},
  {"type":"banana","color":"yellow","quantity":1},
  {"type":"apple","color":"red","quantity":3},
  {"type":"apple","color":"yellow","quantity":5}
]
```

I kept this example simple, but if you want to get a bit fancier, you can also use the native JavaScript string comparison localeCompare():

```
// create a custom comparator to sort in reverse alphabetical order
fruitbowl.comparator = function(fruit1, fruit2) {
  // get the type names for each fruit
  var fruitName1 = fruit1.get('type'),
  fruitName2 = fruit2.get('type');

  // compare the strings with localeCompare
  return fruitName2.localeCompare( fruitName1 );
};
```

localeCompare() is particularly handy for this type of sorting because it returns the appropriate 1, 0 or −1 value. Normally, you use firstString.localeCompare(secondString), but they are reversed here for reverse alphabetical order.

Manually Triggering Sorting

Comparator functions keep the collection in order automatically. For example, you can add additional items to the collection:

```
// add items to the collection
fruitbowl.add({ type: 'apple', color: 'red', quantity: 5 });
fruitbowl.add({ type: 'orange', color: 'orange', quantity: 3 });

// create a comparator
fruitbowl.comparator = function(fruit) {
  // sort by quantity
  return fruit.get('quantity');
};

// add additional items
fruitbowl.add({ type: 'peach', color: 'pink', quantity: 2 });
fruitbowl.add({ type: 'plum', color: 'purple', quantity: 4 });
```

Even though some items are added to this collection after the comparator function is defined, the collection is still kept in order. In fact, the collection won't be sorted at all until the additional items are added. That's because adding a comparator doesn't trigger a sort—sorting is only triggered by adding new elements. Thus, in some cases, you will need to resort your collection. For example, if you add a new comparator function without adding any new items or if you change the value of a certain attribute, you will need to resort your collection manually. Fortunately, you can accomplish this easily using `sort()`:

```
// set the quantity of oranges to zero
// this won't automatically change the sort order
fruitbowl.where({ type: 'orange' }).set( 'quantity', 0 );

// trigger a resorting
fruitbowl.sort();
```

Here, someone ate all the oranges, so you have to manually resort your collection.

Summary

In this chapter, you found out how to use Backbone to bring structure to your app. You started by learning why you should use Backbone, and when to avoid it. Then you discovered the basics of setting up your data in Backbone models and collections.

Next, you learned how to tie the data in models to visual changes on the screen through Backbone views. You also found out how to sync that data to a persistence layer. Then you learned how to use routers to map certain URLs to different JavaScript–generated pages of your app, building in back button and bookmarking support. Finally, you read about how to use Backbone's event handlers to track a variety of events, and how to manipulate collections.

In the coming chapters, you discover how to use a variety of other JavaScript techniques. However, the book will keep coming back to Backbone, because it's the foundation upon which the rest of the code is built.

Additional Resources

Backbone Documentation: `http://backbonejs.org/`

Underscore Documentation: `http://underscorejs.org/`

Best Practices in Backbone:

Backbone Boilerplate: `https://github.com/tbranyen/backbone-boilerplate`

Backbone Patterns: `http://ricostacruz.com/backbone-patterns/`

Backbone Books:

Developing Backbone.js Applications (free e-book, highly recommended): `http://addyosmani.github.com/backbone-fundamentals/`

Backbone.js on Rails: `https://learn.thoughtbot.com/products/1-backbone-js-on-rails`

Backbone Tutorials:

Getting Started With Backbone.js: `http://net.tutsplus.com/tutorials/javascript-ajax/getting-started-with-backbone-js/`

Build a Contacts Manager Using Backbone.js: `http://net.tutsplus.com/tutorials/javascript-ajax/build-a-contacts-manager-using-backbone-js-part-1/`

Anatomy of Backbone.js: `http://www.codeschool.com/courses/anatomy-of-backbonejs`

Chapter 4

Using JavaScript Templates

Templates are the best way to generate long strings of markup in JavaScript. Instead of creating markup piece by piece by appending individual elements to the DOM, you build a template that generates an entire chunk of markup at once. Templates eliminate the need to mix markup into your JavaScript, and make generating DOM content much more intuitive, because they provide a dedicated place for markup, which will compile according to the variables you pass into it. That means your JavaScript can still drive the content of the template, without having to mix with it.

In this chapter, you learn why you should be using templates and about some different libraries you can use for templating. Then you discover the basics of using Underscore templates: how to mix markup strings with variables, and how to include basic bits of JavaScript such as loops. You also find some best practices on how and where to include your templates. Finally, I'll tie in what you learned in Chapter 3 and teach you how to incorporate templates into Backbone using them to render views.

Introduction to Templates

JavaScript templates will revolutionize the way you inject markup into the DOM. They make it easy to generate long strings of markup that are driven by JavaScript variables, yet remain separate from the domain logic of your application.

Why Use Templates?

When it comes to code organization, JavaScript templates are one of the most important techniques you can use. Templates allow you to separate messy markup from your JavaScript. Nothing looks quite as ugly as JavaScript that is riddled with strings of markup—it's the epitome of spaghetti code.

Separation of Concerns

When you insert markup inline in your JavaScript, you're coupling the JavaScript very tightly to the DOM. Then, if you ever need to make a markup change for styling or content reasons, you have to modify your script. It's much better to keep the markup in a separate location—a template that you can modify independently from the rest of your JavaScript. That way you decouple the app's presentation layer from its domain logic.

Performance

Templates also tend to outperform other alternatives because the markup is compiled independently as a string, rather than inserted bit by bit into the DOM. That means you have to manipulate the DOM only once to render its initial state: at the point you finally insert the compiled template.

Altering the DOM remains one of the biggest performance sinkholes in front-end development. Every time you make changes to the visible page, the browser has to re-render it, which can trigger reflows. Reflows occur whenever the browser has to adjust the other content on the page to accommodate a geometry change in the DOM. For instance, if you increase the width of a floated element, it can push other floated elements down to the next line, and therefore push all the following content down as well.

Often, triggering reflow is unavoidable—after all, you've got to modify the page sometimes. But it's best to batch these changes so as to trigger a single reflow, rather than repeatedly appending new elements to the DOM. And that's exactly how most template engines handle it.

> **To get an idea of how reflow works, take a look at this visualization in a Gecko-based browser:** `http://youtu.be/ZTnIxIA5KGw`.

Understanding the Different Template Libraries

Template libraries fall into two main categories: those with embedded JavaScript and those that are logic-less. The former group allows you to use JavaScript logic within the template, whereas the latter allows you only to pass in variables and use a few predefined functions.

The argument for logic-less templates is that they adhere to the general purpose of templates: separation of concerns. Advocates of this approach want their templates as "dumb" as possible, with all of the logic in the actual JavaScript. However in practice, logic-less template frameworks can actually reduce the separation of concerns because working with them often requires you to prepare the data in a way that is tightly coupled to the presentational layer. For instance, if you need JavaScript to reformat date strings, would you rather include that in your domain logic or in the template itself? Ultimately, the choice depends on your development style.

Underscore.js

Underscore is a utility belt library that provides a range of functions that solve common JavaScript tasks. It also has a basic JavaScript template engine that helps separate rendered markup from your core JavaScript files.

Although Underscore's templates aren't as fully featured as those in other template libraries, you're unlikely to need a richer functionality. And because Underscore is a prerequisite of Backbone, it's a very attractive option for any project that uses Backbone.

I use Backbone on just about every project that requires templates, so Underscore is my template library of choice. It doesn't add any extra weight to the app and allows you to embed JavaScript for any functionality it lacks.

To learn more about Underscore, visit `http://underscorejs.org/`.

> **The examples in this chapter all use Underscore, but the concepts can be extended to any library you prefer.**

Handlebars.js

Handlebars.js is a very popular template solution that's basically an extension of Mustache.js —another "logic-less" template library.

Handlebars provides a few conveniences you won't find in Underscore:

- You can set up a context for variables to make it easier to step through large objects.
- There are a couple built-in loops you can use instead of JavaScript loops.
- You can use a special comment syntax in your template.
- You can define simple helper functions, for instance to combine two variables.

A lot of the features in Handlebars are pretty useful, but other than the comments, they are all things you can do in Underscore by mixing in a little JavaScript.

The question is more one of approach:

- Since templates are meant to separate markup from JavaScript, do you really want to be mixing a lot of JavaScript into your templates?
- On the other hand, you'd still be using Handlebars to do scripting tasks. So why would you want to learn new methods when you're already comfortable writing JavaScript? And do you really need that extra bloat?

To learn more about Handlebars, visit `http://handlebarsjs.com`.

> **Handlebars.js can precompile templates, which is often better for performance.**

Transparency

Transparency is an interesting template solution that works a bit differently from the others. Transparency ties the data in your app in the form of JSON objects to actual DOM elements. Then rather than compiling a long markup string and inserting it, Transparency uses the cached DOM references to replace miniature strings one by one.

It's lauded by some for its substantial benefits in performance when compared to all the other options. However, the way Transparency binds data to the DOM defeats the purpose of using templates. Rather than decoupling your markup and JavaScript, it creates the tightest coupling possible between your app's data and presentation layer. That makes it difficult to implement and an even larger pain to maintain.

You can find out more about Transparency at `http://leonidas.github.com/transparency`.

Micro Templating

A while ago, John Resig posted a micro template solution on his blog that is extremely lightweight, weighing in at around 1K. Micro templating is by far the smallest template option, and it's also the most minimalist. But if you don't need anything extra, it can be a very attractive option. To learn more about micro templating, visit `http://ejohn.org/blog/javascript-micro-templating`.

The template engine in Underscore is actually based on the micro templating solution proposed by Resig.

Making the Right Choice

With all the templating solutions out there, it can be hard to choose the right one. Here are four things you need to consider:

- **Functionality:** Does the solution provide everything you need? On the other hand, does it provide too much, and thereby bloat your codebase?

- **Performance:** How fast do the templates compile? Can you precompile them? There's a pretty handy JSPerf comparing different options here: `http://jsperf.com/dom-vs-innerhtml-based-templating/365`.

- **Flexibility:** How easy is it to use? Transparency tops out all the competitors in performance, but it strictly binds the template to the DOM, thereby defeating the purpose of templates.

- **Maturity:** As tempting as it may be, using a templating engine that is still in its infancy is not often the smartest choice. For business critical applications, you may make a smarter choice by selecting a library that is tried and tested.

If you're still having trouble deciding which template library is right for you, head over to `http://garann.github.com/template-chooser` where you can get help in narrowing down your choices by the features you need.

Using Underscore Templates

This chapter uses Underscore templates, because they're easy to use and you're already including Underscore as a prerequisite for Backbone.

Underscore Template Basics

Using Underscore templates is actually pretty easy. Simply define the template, pass in your variables, and insert it into the DOM.

Using Templates

The first step is defining the template:

```
var myTemplate = _.template('Welcome, <%= name %>');
```

This example uses Underscore's `template` method to define a new template. The text in the template works as follows:

- There's some static text that will be output as is (`"Welcome, "`).

- There's also a variable "name", enclosed in `<%= ... %>`. The value of the variable is passed in when you compile the template.

In Underscore, code is interpolated using `<% ... %>`. Here the added equals sign (`<%=`) indicates that the template should output this code when it compiles.

The next step is compiling the template. To do this, you call the function you defined for the template and pass in an object whose properties map to the variable names you defined in the template string.

```
var compiled = myTemplate({name: 'Jon'});
```

When the template compiles, it passes in the variable you defined here. Now use `console.log(compiled)` to see the completed string:

```
Welcome, Jon
```

And that's all there is to it. Although this chapter goes through a lot of additional actions you can perform with templates, fundamentally none are much more complicated than passing in basic variables and rendering that text.

Interspersing Markup

You can also combine markup in your templates. After all, building simple strings isn't really the best use of templates. You can do that in your JavaScript. The main reason to use templates is to avoid putting markup in your JS. For instance, you can create a template for a small section of web content:

```
var myTemplate = _.template('<article>\
<hgroup>\
  <h1><%= title %></h1>\
  <h2><%= subtitle %></h2>\
</hgroup>\
<p><%= description %></p>\
</article>');
```

Here a variety of markup elements are mixed with variables. Each line ends with a backslash, which allows you to build a multiline string in your JavaScript.

> Working with backslashes can be pretty annoying, so later in this chapter in the "Reviewing Template Best Practices section," I'll show you a better way.

Now you can compile this template with some variables:

```
var compiled = myTemplate({
  title: 'JavaScript Templates',
  subtitle: 'Are pretty awesome',
  description: 'They take the markup out of your JavaScript'
});
```

You have the template compiled, but you still need to get it on the page. You can inject this content into the DOM in several ways:

- Select an element by ID and insert it.
- Replace an element.
- Append it to the body.

To keep things simple, here's an example that appends it to the body using jQuery:

```
$('body').append(compiled);
```

Figure 4-1 shows this content is rendering on the page.

JavaScript Templates
Are pretty awesome

They take the markup out of your JavaScript

Figure 4-1: The page has been rendered using templates.

Just to recap, here's the code all together:

```
// build the template
var myTemplate = _.template('<article>\
<hgroup>\
  <h1><%= title %></h1>\
  <h2><%= subtitle %></h2>\
</hgroup>\
<p><%= description %></p>\
</article>');

// compile the template with variables
var compiled = myTemplate({
  title: 'JavaScript Templates',
  subtitle: 'Are pretty awesome',
  description: 'They take the markup out of your JavaScript'
```

```
    });

    // append it to the DOM
    $('body').append(compiled);
```

Using Different Interpolation Strings

By default, Underscore uses ERB-style delimiters—variables are set off in `<% ... %>`. But you can also set up your own delimiters. For instance, to use Handlebars.js style `{{ ... }}` interpolation, define it in `_.templateSettings`:

```
    _.templateSettings = {
      interpolate : /\{\{(.+?)\}\}/g
    };
```

As you can see here, you set the `interpolate` setting with a regex. Now you can use the new delimiters in your templates:

```
    // build the template with the new delimeters
    var myTemplate = _.template('Welcome, {{ name }}');

    // compile the template with variables
    var compiled = myTemplate({name: 'Jon'});
```

Here, the template you defined earlier is being compiled with the new interpolation pattern.

Setting up a different interpolation setting isn't only about style. It is sometimes necessary, for example, when the default <% clashes with other tags reserved for other languages.

Reviewing Template Best Practices

The previous examples used backslashes to build multiline strings in JavaScript. Although that works, it can get pretty annoying. Additionally, I've been talking about how important it is to keep the markup out of your JavaScript. Sure the templates keep it all in one place, but so far it's still in the JS, which is a really bad practice. Fortunately, there's a much better way to handle templates.

Separating Your Templates

The best way to include JavaScript templates is to completely isolate them from the rest of your JavaScript. To do so, include the template in a separate `<script>` tag on the page, for example:

```
    <script type="text/template">

    <article>
      <hgroup>
        <h1><%= title %></h1>
        <h2><%= subtitle %></h2>
      </hgroup>
```

```
   <p><%= description %></p>
   </article>

   </script>
```

Notice here that you don't need the backslashes at the end of each line—that's because this isn't a string; it's a separate script.

Also, pay close attention to the `type` attribute of the script tag. Normally, a JavaScript script tag uses `type="text/javascript"` (or no `type` at all for HTML5). However, here `type="text/template"` is used to indicate that this is a template, not JavaScript. That's absolutely essential; otherwise, the browser will try to evaluate and run this as JavaScript (and undoubtedly throw errors).

Next you need to pull this into Underscore. To do so, first attach an ID to the script tag:

```
<script type="text/template" id="my-template">
...
</script>
```

Now you can pull in the text of this script using jQuery and use that to define the template:

```
var myTemplate = _.template( $('#my-template').text() );
```

And you're done—you can now use the template as normal, passing in variables to compile it.

> It's worth noting that documents not using the HTML5 doctype don't validate as correct markup when you use this approach. Additionally, if you're worried about very old browsers and use the XHTML doctype, make sure to enclose your template in `//<![CDATA[ ... //]]>`. However, you'll also need to account for this when you pull in the template text.

Using External Templates

Alternatively, you can use external templates. The approach is similar: First use a `<script>` tag; however, this time add an external `src`:

```
<script type="text/template" src="my-template.html"
id="my-template"></script>
```

Now it gets a little more content, because you have to request the template content using Ajax:

```
$.ajax({
   // get the template url from the script tag
   url: $('#my-template').attr('src'),

   // what to do once it loads
   success: function(data) {
      // after it loads, define your template
```

```
    var myTemplate = _.template(data);

    // compile it
    var compiled = myTemplate({
      title: 'JavaScript Templates',
      subtitle: 'Are pretty awesome',
      description: 'They take the markup out of your JavaScript'
    });

    // append it to the DOM
    $('body').append(compiled);
  },

  // in case something goes wrong
  error: function() {
    console.log('Problem loading template');
  }
});
```

As you can see, you're first using the `src` attribute from the script tag to define the URL for the Ajax request. Then you compile the template in the success callback, after Ajax returns the template text.

Considering that you'll probably be doing this for a number of templates, you should define a function to handle it for you:

```
// load an external template
var loadTemplate = function(src, callback) {
  $.ajax({
    url: src,

    // what to do once it loads
    success: function(data) {
      // after it loads, define your template
      var template = _.template(data);

      // call the callback, passing in the template
      callback(template);
    },

    // in case something goes wrong
    error: function() {
      console.log('Problem loading template: ' + src);
    }
  });
};
```

This function requests the template text using Ajax, creates the template function, and then passes that to a callback so you can compile it or do whatever else you need to do:

```
// example usage
loadTemplate( $('#my-template').attr('src'), function(template) {
  // compile it
```

```
var compiled = template({
  title: 'JavaScript Templates',
  subtitle: 'Are pretty awesome',
  description: 'They take the markup out of your JavaScript'
});

// append it to the DOM
$('body').append(compiled);
});
```

Here you call your template loading function, passing in two arguments:

- The template URL that you pull from the script tag
- A callback to handle the returned template

> If you're not using the HTML5 doctype, leveraging external templates will avoid the HTML validation issues.

External Versus Inline

Although external templates have their merits, it's a good idea to keep them on the page itself for a couple reasons:

- Including an external file means an extra HTTP request. If you often use multiple templates on a page, the performance implications can be substantial.
- Markup is already included on the page, and the templates are essentially more markup. In most cases, it makes sense to keep the template in the HTML, because that's where the rest of the markup lives.
- It's just a lot easier to manage; as you can see, the Ajax script for the external template means having to navigate different callbacks for each template.

Using JavaScript in Templates

In addition to text and variables, you can also use JavaScript within your templates.

Basic If-Then Conditionals

One useful technique is to include basic conditionals statements. For instance, you can determine whether a check box is checked in your template:

```
<input type="checkbox" <%= checked ? 'checked' : '' %> />
```

Now you can pass in a Boolean for the checked variable; if it's `true`, the check box is checked when the template compiles. Additionally, you can check to see whether a variable exists at all. For instance, your content might require a title, but not always a subtitle. You can handle that with a simple `if` statement:

```
<hgroup>
  <h1><%= title %></h1>
  <% if ( typeof subtitle !== 'undefined' ) { %>
  <h2><%= subtitle %></h2>
  <% } %>
</hgroup>
```

Here the `<h1>` prints no matter what, but the `<h2>` prints only if `subtitle` has been defined.

Notice how the `<% %>` delimiter around the `if` statement doesn't include the equals sign. That's because you want to evaluate some JavaScript and not print it. The following `<h2>` on the other hand is not contained in a delimiter so it will print (and so will the variable it contains because that uses `<%= %>`).

> It's important to check whether variables are undefined in Underscore templates. Unlike jQuery, Underscore throws errors when variables are undefined.

Loops

You can also use any of the loops available to you in JavaScript. Loops can be very useful in templates, for instance when you want to populate a list:

```
<h2><%= listTitle %></h2>

<ul>
  <% for ( var i = 0, len = listItems.length; i < len; i++ ) { %>
  <li><%= listItems[i] %></li>
  <% } %>
</ul>
```

Here a `for` loop is used to iterate over the items in the `listItems` array. Next, pass in this array when you compile the template:

```
var compiled = template({
  listTitle: 'Reasons I like templates',

  listItems: [
    'Keeping JavaScript clean',
    'Separating concerns',
    'Faster DOM insertion'
  ]
});
```

As you can see in Figure 4-2, the items in the list render properly.

Reasons I like templates

- Keeping JavaScript clean
- Separating concerns
- Faster DOM insertion

Figure 4-2 This list has been populated using a `for` loop in the template.

And it doesn't stop with `for` loops; you can use `while`, `switch`, or any other JavaScript you want.

Each Loop

In addition to the standard JavaScript loops you already know, you can use an Underscore-specific loop: `_.each()`.

You already know how to use a `for` loop to iterate across an array of list items in your template. Well, you can accomplish the same thing a little more easily using Underscore's `each()` function:

```
<ul>
  <% _.each( listItems, function(item) { %>
  <li><%= item %></li>
  <% }); %>
</ul>
```

This code accomplishes exactly the same thing as the `for` loop demonstrated earlier. However, Underscore's `each` loop works a little differently, because it's a function. In this example, you passed in two arguments:

- An array or object to iterate through

- A callback function that defines a variable for each new item

Pay attention to the closing parentheses after the `each` loop finishes. It's there because the `<li>` is output in the callback function, not in a proper `for` loop.

Realistically, the `each` loop doesn't make a big difference when you're handling something like this because you can accomplish the same thing with a simple `for` loop. However, it really starts to shine when you want to iterate over all the items in an object (which is harder to handle natively). For instance, you can print all the key-value pairs in an object:

```
<ul>
  <% _.each( myObject, function(value, key) { %>
  <li><%= key %> : <%= value %></li>
  <% }); %>
</ul>
```

The only difference here is that the callback is accepting two arguments: the value and then the associated key.

Now you can pass an object when compiling this template:

```
var compiled = template({
  myObject: {
    boolean1: true,
    boolean2: false,
    string1: 'Hello',
    string2: 'World'
  }
});
```

When this renders, all of these variables are printed out, as shown in Figure 4-3.

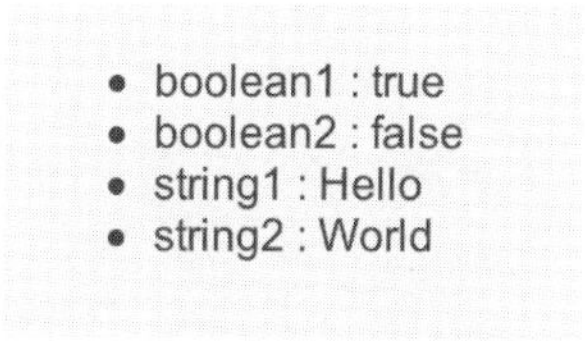

- boolean1 : true
- boolean2 : false
- string1 : Hello
- string2 : World

Figure 4-3 All of the key-value pairs in this object have been printed out with an `_.each()` loop.

Using Templates in Backbone

JavaScript templates and Backbone go hand in hand, because there's no better way to render the content in a Backbone view than with a JavaScript template. And since Backbone already depends on Underscore, there's no additional weight when using Underscore templates in your Backbone projects.

Setting Up the Model and View Without Templates

Before you get started, you need a model and view to work with. The basic idea is that you're going to set up a model and then pass the data in the model into a template to render the content in the view. Start by setting up the model. For this, I use a model from an example in Chapter 3:

```
// create the model for the user
var User = Backbone.Model.extend({});

var user = new User({
  username: 'jonraasch',
  displayName: 'Jon Raasch',
  bio: 'Some nerd'
});
```

Now, you take this content and render it on the page as a view. But before doing that with templates, review how this was handled in the previous chapter:

```
// create the view
var UserView = Backbone.View.extend({
  el: '#user-card',

  initialize: function() {
```

```
      this.render();
    },

    render: function() {
      // create a link to the user's profile as a wrapper
      var $card = $('<a href="/users/' + this.model.get('username') +
        '"/>');

      // add the user's name
      var $name = $('<h1>' + this.model.get('displayName') +
        '</h1>').appendTo($card);

      // add the user's bio
      var $bio = $('<p>' + this.model.get('bio') +
      '</p>').appendTo($card);

      // append this element to the DOM
      this.$el.empty().append($card);

      return this;
    }
});

// create a new instance of the view, tying it to the user model
var userView = new UserView({
  model: user
});
```

This code starts by associating the view with the DOM element `#user-card`. Then a `render` function uses various attributes from the model and adds them to the DOM using jQuery and inline markup.

You're probably noticing how sloppy all of this code is. There's a lot of ugly markup interspersed with separate calls to grab each individual bit of data from the model. Fortunately, you can clean this up a great deal by using templates.

Rendering a View with Templates

Converting this view to render with templates isn't too complicated. The first step is to convert the inline jQuery and markup into a template:

```
<script type="text/template" id="user-template">

<a href="/users/<%= username %>">
  <h1><%= displayName %></h1>

  <p><%= bio %></p>
</a>

</script>
```

The code already looks a lot cleaner, with simple markup interpolated with basic variables.

The next step is to define the template along the view:

```
// create the view
var UserView = Backbone.View.extend({
  el: '#user-card',

  template: _.template( $('#user-template').text() )
});
```

Here you define the template using the text from the script tag built for the template. You then assign that value along the view so that you can access it at any time with `this.template()`.

Now set up the `render` function as before, except this time, render the content with the template:

```
// create the view
var UserView = Backbone.View.extend({
  el: '#user-card',

  template: _.template( $('#user-template').text() ),

  initialize: function() {
    this.render();
  },

  render: function() {
    // compile the template with the model
    var compiled = this.template( this.model.toJSON() );

    // append the compiled markup to the DOM
    this.$el.html( compiled );

    return this;
  }
});
```

The first thing that happens in this code is that it compiles the template. To make it compile, you convert the model to an object and then pass that object into the template function. Since the keys of the model line up with the template created earlier, there's no need to alter this data (or fetch each attribute individually). Then you append the compiled code into the DOM element that's tied to the view.

Finally, for good measure add a change function to re-render this view if the model changes:

```
// create the view
var UserView = Backbone.View.extend({
  el: '#user-card',

  template: _.template( $('#user-template').text() ),

  initialize: function() {
    // re-render the view if the model changes
    this.model.on('change', this.render, this)
```

```
    this.render();
  },

  render: function() {
    // compile the template with the model
    var compiled = this.template( this.model.toJSON() );

    // append the compiled markup to the DOM
    this.$el.html( compiled );

    return this;
  }
});
```

Now the view will update whenever the model changes.

Because the text of the template is cached on the view, the JavaScript engine doesn't have to redo that lookup every time the model changes, which speeds up performance. But it can't compile until you actually render the view, because you have to take into account the changed model. To wrap up, here's the completed code:

```html
<script type="text/template" id="user-template">

<a href="/users/<%= username %>">
  <h1><%= displayName %></h1>

  <p><%= bio %></p>
</a>

</script>

<script type="text/javascript">
// create the model for the user
var User = Backbone.Model.extend({});

var user = new User({
  username: 'jonraasch',
  displayName: 'Jon Raasch',
  bio: 'Some nerd'
});

// create the view
var UserView = Backbone.View.extend({
  el: '#user-card',

  template: _.template( $('#user-template').text() ),

  initialize: function() {
    // re-render the view if the model changes
    this.model.on('change', this.render, this);

    this.render();
  },
```

```
  render: function() {
    // compile the template with the model
    var compiled = this.template( this.model.toJSON() );

    // append the compiled markup to the DOM
    this.$el.html( compiled );

    return this;
  }
});

// create a new instance of the view, tying it to the user model
var userView = new UserView({
  model: user
});
</script>
```

As you can see, the code is much cleaner and better organized than it was without the template.

Summary

Templates eliminate spaghetti code and allow you to build long strings of markup without having to intersperse HTML in your JavaScript. They make your codebase cleaner, and streamline the development process.

In this chapter, you learned how to use Underscore templates to generate markup that is compiled according to variables from your JavaScript. That way your markup can still be driven by JavaScript, without actually having to live alongside the JavaScript.

Finally, you found out how to use loops in your templates and also how to use them to render views in Backbone.

In the coming chapters, you extend your use of templates, combining them with a variety of other JavaScript techniques. Now that you understand Backbone and templates, you have the two pillars that make up the foundation of the rest of your app. It's time to dig in, and have some fun!

Additional Resources

Template Libraries

Underscore: http://underscorejs.org

Handlebars: http://handlebarsjs.com

Transparency: http://leonidas.github.com/transparency

Micro-Templating: http://ejohn.org/blog/javascript-micro-templating

Choosing a Template Library

Template Chooser: `http://garann.github.com/template-chooser`

Template Performance Comparison: `http://jsperf.com/dom-vs-innerhtml-based-templating/365`

Pros and Cons of Logic-Less Templates

Client-Side Templating Throwdown: `http://engineering.linkedin.com/frontend/client-side-templating-throwdown-mustache-handlebars-dustjs-and-more`

The Case Against Logic-Less Templates: `http://www.ebaytechblog.com/2012/10/01/the-case-against-logic-less-templates/`

Templates in Backbone

Backbone View Patterns: `http://ricostacruz.com/backbone-patterns/#view_patterns`

Backbone.js Lessons Learned and Improved Sample App: `http://coenraets.org/blog/2012/01/backbone-js-lessons-learned-and-improved-sample-app/`

Chapter 5
Creating Forms

Forms are an integral part of most apps and websites. In recent years, forms have progressed to a point in HTML5 where you can provide very rich functionality without any JavaScript at all. Of course, not all browsers support these advanced features, so you'll often need to provide JavaScript fallbacks. Fortunately, a lot of third-party polyfills are available that you can use to back up HTML5 form features automatically.

In this chapter, you learn how to use a progressive enhancement approach in your forms. You start with a solid-base state that works across all browsers, and then you add JavaScript features on top. You then discover a variety of HTML5 form features, such as special input types, widgets, and validation. Next, you learn how to use polyfills to support these features in older, non-supportive browsers. You also read about some techniques for posting your forms via Ajax. Finally, you find out how to connect your forms with Backbone, automatically generating the view and posting the form data with Backbone's syncing.

Understanding Progressive Enhancement

This chapter's general approach is one of *progressive enhancement,* which is widely accepted as the best practice for handling forms with JavaScript (and pretty much everything else you might augment with JS). This approach starts with a more limited foundation that works across all browsers, and then *progressively enhances* that base state with additional features wherever they can be supported. That's ideal because it provides a wide range of compatibility across different browsers and environments while also providing richer features wherever possible.

The Progressive Enhancement Approach

The basic progressive enhancement approach for forms is as follows:

1. Use standard HTML5 form markup to achieve a solid foundation for your form.

2. With JavaScript, leverage HTML5 attributes from the markup to determine what you want to do to each form element.

3. Add a scripting layer on top of these elements, widgetizing the form with date pickers and other widgets, as well as providing enhancements such as placeholder text, Ajax submission, and so forth.

Why Progressive Enhancement?

The logic of progressive enhancement is that it first provides an adequate base state that is universal across all the browsers you support. This notion is particularly important when it comes to forms, because these components are crucial to the overall goals of a site. For instance, you may find it acceptable that an intro video or animation on the homepage doesn't load, but would it be acceptable if the user can't submit an order form?

Or can't even log in? For that reason, it's absolutely essential that your forms work, in some capacity, across all the browsers and environments you want to support. Additionally, they'll need to remain accessible to assisted devices for vision impaired users and people with other disabilities.

Moreover, it's important to provide the best experience possible for your users. With all the advancements in web development, users have come to expect a streamlined experience, and JavaScript form enhancements are a big part of that.

Progressive enhancement provides the best of both worlds: basic support for all users and richer features wherever they're supported.

Deciding Which Environments to Support

You've probably already realized that your forms need to work in older versions of IE and other browsers that don't support HTML5. But they also need to work even if the user has turned off JavaScript. Yes, your site should work (at least a little bit) without any JavaScript at all.

Even if you aren't worried about users who have turned off their JavaScript, keep in mind that when JavaScript breaks, it often stops all other scripting on the page. A site that depends entirely on JavaScript can therefore be quite brittle. It's much better to provide yourself some outs so that a small bug can't disable other functionality on the page.

Additionally, if your JavaScript is loading slowly, the user won't have to wait for it. They can begin entering form data while the JavaScript loads. As Jake Archibald said, "Everyone has JavaScript disabled while they're downloading your JavaScript."

This chapter demonstrates how to use HTML5 form elements, but these all default back to basic form elements in unsupported browsers. Then I show you how to add a JavaScript layer on top of your forms in a way that enables your users to be able to use the forms without JavaScript. Even though you end up posting the form with Ajax, the user will still be able to submit the form the old fashioned way.

There are many conflicting views on how many users have turned off their JavaScript (or have a device that doesn't support it). Some numbers are as high as 5 percent, but that seems like an exaggeration. The truth is that this stat is pretty hard to determine. Most analytics, such as Google Analytics, run in JavaScript, so there's no way to discover how many users have it turned off. Some enterprise-level analytics like Omniture have worked around this, but I'm skeptical about the quality of their data.

You can't figure out JavaScript support from the server side or the user agent. So the only way to calculate this stat is a combination of front and back end analytics. But what happens if the user leaves the page before the JavaScript instantiates? Or before it's able to relay its first bit of data via Ajax? These uncertainties can inflate numbers and cause alarming stats like *5 percent of users don't have JavaScript*.

Letting HTML5 Do the Work for You

The foundation of your form will be built on HTML5, which offers elements that provide a surprisingly rich level of interactivity, without any JavaScript whatsoever. In fact, the HTML5 elements provide a better experience than you could deliver with JavaScript. They are fast, bug-free, and easy to implement. They'll still work even if scripting breaks elsewhere on the page. All things considered, you should use native browser functionality whenever possible. It just doesn't make sense to reinvent the wheel.

However, keep in mind that these elements will work only in contemporary browsers. You'll need to use JavaScript to provide fallbacks if you want this richer functionality across the board. That said, most HTML5 form features still work at a basic level in any browser. Older browsers can't understand the HTML5 elements and attributes, so they default to basic text inputs without any bells and whistles. That means that no matter what, your users will still be able to use your forms, even if they're on an older browser and JavaScript doesn't load.

HTML5 Input Types

Prior to HTML5, the input types were pretty basic:

- `text` inputs for plain text
- `password` inputs to hide typing
- `checkbox` and `radio` inputs for certain types of data
- `file` inputs for uploading files to the server
- And a handful of others like `hidden` and `submit`

Although these are certainly useful, they pale in comparison to the functionality introduced by HTML5. HTML5 input types include an assortment of useful widgets such as sliders, date pickers, and color pickers. Additionally, on mobile devices, many HTML5 input types provide special keyboards that make entering data easier.

Widgets

Although the HTML5 specification outlines a number of different form widgets, browser support is still a bit spotty. However, wherever a form widget is unsupported, it will simply revert to a standard text input.

> At the time of this writing, Firefox and IE both have pretty bad HTML5 form widget support.

Range Slider

The range slider is one of the most widely supported form widgets, working in the latest versions of all major browsers. To call a slider, use the following markup:

```
<input type="range">
```

This markup creates a slider widget, which you can use to control a number value, as shown in Figure 5-1.

Figure 5-1 The slider widget provides an intuitive control for numbers. This is how it appears in Chrome.

> **You can also change the slider's styling in WebKit browsers. To learn more, see** `http://css-tricks.com/value-bubbles-for-range-inputs/`.

You can also control some aspects of your slider:

```
<input type="range" min="0" max="100" step="5" value="30">
```

These attributes are as follows:

- `min` is the minimum value of the slider (the left side).
- `max` is the maximum value (the right side).
- `step` controls how much each tic of the slider should adjust the number (defaults to 1).
- `value` is the default starting place for the slider (defaults to halfway between the `min` and `max`).

At the very least, you need to set the `min` and `max` for your slider to provide reasonable boundaries for the number value.

Although the range slider is useful, it doesn't relay much information to the user. That's fine if you're using it for a "feeler" type value—for example, "How strongly do you feel about this question." But if you want to relay the actual number to the user, you need to tap into it with JavaScript. First, set up some basic markup:

```
<input type="range">
<span class="range-value"></span>
```

Next, you can hook into any changes in the range value using jQuery's `change()` handler:

```
$('input[type="range"]').change(function(e) {
  var $this = $(this);
  $this.siblings('.range-value').text($this.val());
});
```

Here an attribute selector first finds all range inputs. Then, whenever these inputs change, the sibling `.range-value` span is located and the text of that span is set to match the value of the range input. As Figure 5-2 demonstrates, this snippet displays the number value next to the slider.

Favorite Number ▭▭▭○▭▭ 64

Figure 5-2 The value of this range slider is displayed with JavaScript.

This script is working pretty well, but you also need to show the initial value of the range when the page loads. To do so, extract it into a function and call it in both cases:

```
$.fn.displaySliderVal = function() {
   this.siblings('.range-value').text( this.val() );
   return this;
};

$('input[type="range"]').change(function(e) {
   $(this).displaySliderVal();
}).displaySliderVal();
```

Here, a few changes have been made:

1. The script defines `displaySliderVal()`, a method on jQuery's prototype that allows chaining by returning the jQuery object.

2. `displaySliderVal()` is called on `$(this)` in the change handler.

3. `displaySliderVal()` is also called on the initial reference to `$('input[type="range"]')`, so it shows the default value.

> You can also use the number picker for numbers with `<input type="number">`.

Date Picker

Another useful widget is the date picker, which you can call with the following markup:

```
<input type="date">
```

This creates a date picker in some browsers, as shown in Figure 5-3.

Figure 5-3 The date picker in Chrome.

A History of Date Input Problems

Although it's probably the most widely used form widget, the date picker has had a pretty sordid past. For a couple years, both Safari and Chrome half-supported the date picker in a terrible way. Instead of a handy calendar-based widget, they used a basic select box with every possible date.

Because the user had to scroll through a seemingly endless dates to find the one he or she wanted, a bad user experience was created. It was especially bad with `datetime`, which comically had the user scrolling through every single minute of every single day.

The main problem wasn't just the shoddy user experience. It also was hard to overwrite with a JavaScript widget because the browser supported the date input, even though this could hardly be called adequate support. As a result, JavaScript couldn't use feature detection to replace these widgets and, instead, had to rely on browser sniffing (a notoriously bad practice). Fortunately, this is no longer the case. Chrome uses a calendar date picker, and Safari reverts to a basic text input (which should have been how all WebKit browsers handled this in the first place).

However, keep in mind that a calendar date picker doesn't always provide the best user experience. It's really useful for dates that are close to the current date (or an arbitrary start point). But because it's hard to switch years, a calendar date picker isn't a good idea for birthdates. You can see the issue in Figure 5-4.

Figure 5-4 Switching years in the date picker is a hassle. The user can still enter any date manually but will probably be thrown off by the usability issues in the widget.

Therefore, with birthdates and other dates that are more than a year or two old, it's a much better idea to use a combination of `<input type="date">`, `<input type="month ">`, and `<input type="year">`. Or use a JavaScript widget that handles the issue more gracefully.

Color Picker

Although most forms won't use the color picker, it can come in handy in the right situation. You can call it with the following markup:

```
<input type="color">
```

Browser support for the color picker is poor, but the current versions of Chrome and Opera both support it, as you can see in Figure 5-5.

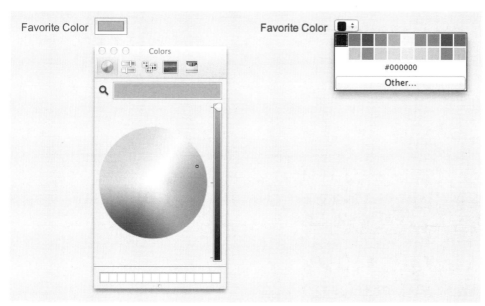

Figure 5-5 The color picker in Chrome (left) and Opera (right). They are different visually. The Chrome version is better for fine-grained control, whereas the Opera version is easier to use in most cases.

The color picker returns a hex value—for example, `#ff7f24`. You access this value with the same attribute selector used for the range input:

```
$('input[type="color"]').val();
```

> In addition to the widgets described here, there's also a search input. Its functionality isn't overly interesting, but it's useful at times.

Contextual Keyboards

Some HTML5 input types also have a special connotation on mobile devices such as phones and tablets. They display specialized keyboards that make it easier for the user to enter specific data.

These days most smartphones and tablets use a software keyboard, meaning a keyboard that displays on the touch screen whenever it's needed, as shown in Figure 5-6.

Figure 5-6 The standard keyboard on iPhone.

However, using these keyboards can be a bit cumbersome, especially on phones.

Fortunately, certain HTML5 input types trigger a special keyboard that makes entering data much easier. For example, the following markup displays a telephone number pad like the one shown in Figure 5-7.

```
<input type="tel">
```

Figure 5-7 This numeric keypad displays in iOS for `<input type="tel">`.

Other input types add special keys that help in the particular situations—for example, `<input type="email">` and `<input type="url">`—which are shown in Figure 5-8.

Figure 5-8 The email input (left) and URL input (right) on iPhone.

Another useful input type is `<input type="number">`, the result of which you can see in Figure 5-9.

These input types also have important connotations for semantics and form validation. You learn more about these in the next section.

Figure 5-9 The number input type calls up the number keyboard in iOS, so the user doesn't have to switch to it.

Interactive Features

In addition to the new input types, HTML 5 introduces several interactive features such as placeholder text and validation. That means native support for a variety of functionalities that previously could be supported only with JavaScript.

Placeholder Text

Placeholder text is displayed in a form element before the user enters a value. It's commonly used to provide a short hint about what should be entered in the field—for example, the particular format for a date input.

With HTML5, you can display placeholder text in your form fields using the `placeholder` attribute:

```
<input type="email" placeholder="john@example.com">
```

In the browser, this placeholder displays as lighter text that is replaced by whatever value the user enters. See Figure 5-10.

Figure 5-10 This placeholder text provides a visual cue that enhances user experience.

Placeholder text is a great way to provide a quick visual cue and speed up form entry. Remember, the faster users can enter data in your form, the more likely they will "convert" to another sale or signup. As you can see from this data, higher clarity of form requirements leads to better conversion rates: `http://www.lukew.com/ff/entry.asp?1416`.

You can also style the placeholder text with the following snippet for various browsers:

```
input::-webkit-input-placeholder {color:green;}
input::-moz-placeholder {color:green;}
input:-ms-placeholder {color: green;}
```

Note that you cannot combine these selectors—you must separate experimental selectors or browsers will ignore the entire block.

Autofocus

Autofocus is another way to speed up form entry. It brings the cursor into a specific field when the page loads so that the user can simply start typing instead of clicking or tabbing into the form. To use autofocus in your HTML5 forms, simply add the `autofocus` attribute to any element:

```
<input type="text" autofocus>
```

This attribute brings the cursor into this field when the page loads.

Besides not needing any extra code, native HTML5 autofocus works a lot better than the JavaScript alternatives, because JavaScript `focus()` scripts sometimes take a while to load. During that delay, the user may start typing into another field. However, once the `focus()` function executes, it hijacks the user's cursor into the autofocused field—and that results in a very bad user experience.

Validation

Native form validation is probably my favorite new feature of HTML5 forms. It allows you to skip the whole rat's nest of JavaScript form validation and have the browser do the work for you.

Basic Form Validation

Best of all, if you're using HTML5 input types, you're already 90 percent of the way there, because HTML5 forms validate against the input type. For example, if you have `<input type="email">`, HTML5 ensures that it's a properly formatted email address when the user submits the form, as you can see in Figure 5-11.

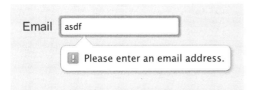

Figure 5-11 HTML5 displays an error message if the email address is formatted incorrectly.

It also takes into account any ranges you may have set—for example:

```
<input type="number" min="0" max="500">
```

This form throws an error if the number is outside of the bounds set in the markup (or if it isn't a number).

Additionally, you can make any field required by adding the required attribute:

```
<input type="text" required>
```

This field throws an error if the user fails to fill it out, as you can see in Figure 5-12.

Figure 5-12 This error message is thrown if the user fails to fill out a required field.

> Always validate on the server side for security reasons. Hackers can use older browsers and disable JavaScript to get around any front-end validation measures you may have enacted (or just post directly into your form handler).

Custom Validation Rules

You can also create your own validation rules for any fields that aren't covered. To do so, simply add a regex to the `pattern` attribute:

```
<input type="text" pattern="[a-zA-Z]+">
```

In this example, whatever the user enters will be checked against the regular expression `[a-zA-Z]+`, which only accepts letter values (no numbers, spaces, or special characters).

The only downside with creating your own custom rules is that the browser displays the generic error message shown in Figure 5-13.

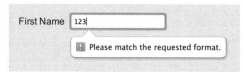

Figure 5-13 This generic validation error displays if the user enters data that doesn't match the pattern attribute.

Fortunately, you can add your own custom validation message using JavaScript. Simply add it to an `oninvalid` listener:

```
<input type="text" pattern="[a-zA-Z]+"
oninvalid="setCustomValidity('You may only enter letters.');" >
```

Here, the native `setCustomValidity()` method is used to display the custom message, as shown in Figure 5-14. You might be scoffing at the fact that I included this script inline in the markup. I did that mainly for simplicity's sake, but it's also not a bad idea here because the script is fundamentally tied to the markup for this element.

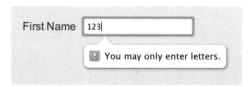

Figure 5-14 This custom validation message is displayed via JavaScript.

Although this custom validation message is more useful than the generic message, here are some caveats to consider:

▨ Native validation messages are localized for the user's language, and you're probably not planning on translating your message into hundreds of different languages.

▨ This validation message will display no matter the reason for the error. For instance, it will also display if the user enters more text than the `maxlength` or fails to fill out a `required` field.

For these reasons, it's best to avoid overwriting the default messages for `email`, `url`, and `number` unless you're very unhappy with the default text. Also, if you have multiple validation rules on a field, build in a check to determine exactly what triggered the error.

You may not care about localizing error messages if your site is provided only in English. But keep in mind that if you use custom messages for some fields and defaults for others, there may be validation error messages in multiple languages.

Using Polyfills for Older Browsers

Although HTML5 forms are fairly well supported in modern browsers, the sad reality is that a lot of your users probably haven't upgraded yet. Even if they have, support is spotty for certain features depending on which browser they use. So, you need to build backups for these components with JavaScript.

Finding Third-Party Polyfills

Fortunately, you're not the only person to have this problem, and there are a number of very comprehensive options out there. Best of all, these open-source offerings provide most of this functionality pretty much out of the box.

Polyfills are shims that provide backups for newer features that aren't available in older browsers. In general, polyfills use JavaScript to re-create native functionality wherever it is lacking. But they don't necessarily have to use JavaScript—for instance, polyfills for HTML5 video use Flash.

The Modernizr team maintains a great list of various polyfills at `https://github.com/Modernizr/Modernizr/wiki/HTML5-Cross-Browser-Polyfills`.

All the polyfills on that list are decent, and you should be able to find one for any HTML5 form functionality you need. Of course, if you can't find the perfect polyfill, you can always write your own.

Writing Your Own Polyfills

While you can download a polyfill for just about any form feature you need to support, I want to walk through some quick examples of how to build them yourself. As a result, you'll understand what's going on in whatever you download, and you'll be able to customize an existing polyfill or write your own if you're unhappy with the third-party options.

When building polyfills, remember to test in a browser that doesn't support the feature you're trying to implement. Otherwise, you'll think you're coding everything perfectly even if your script has bugs.

General Approach

In general, the best way to provide backups for HTML5 is to leverage the markup you've already written. That means you should hook into the different form elements and create functionality based on their attributes, exactly like HTML5 does in supportive browsers.

For example, you might have this `range` input:

```
<input type="range" min="0" max="100" value="30">
```

The best approach is to first leverage an attribute selector to determine when to display a JavaScript slider widget:

```
$('input[type="range"]');
```

Then use the various attributes to set the options for your JavaScript slider, setting the upper and lower bounds with the `min` and `max` and the initial value with the `value`.

Because it provides the loosest coupling, taking this sort of approach is always best for polyfills. The alternative of hardcoding specific values in your JavaScript means that you enter this data in two places, which is more complicated to develop and, more importantly, harder to maintain. The worst part is that you have to remember to make these changes, even though you won't see any issues in your A-list HTML5 browser.

Writing an Autofocus Polyfill

Autofocus is one of the easiest polyfills to write, because there isn't much more to do than find the element with the `autofocus` attribute and set `focus()` on it. For example, you can accomplish this in jQuery:

```
$('[autofocus]').focus();
```

This script uses an attribute selector to find any element with the `autofocus` attribute set, such as `<input type="text" autofocus>`. Then it uses the `focus()` method to call cursor focus into that element.

Implementing the Polyfill

Now, you need to determine when to use the polyfill. Note that because your polyfills will never be as good as native support, avoid implementing them whenever the functionality is supported natively.

In this example, the JavaScript fallback might cause usability problems—for example, if the user starts typing into a different form field before the JavaScript finishes loading. Once the polyfill kicks in, it hijacks the user's input cursor and places it into a different field, a problem that does not exist in the native implementation of `autofocus`.

Therefore, implement the polyfill only when autofocus isn't supported. But don't go looking up which browsers support `autofocus` and which don't. Browser-sniffing is a terrible practice that you should avoid unless absolutely necessary. Instead, use feature-checking and determine whether `autofocus` is supported using JavaScript. To do so, you can use Modernizr, which is available at `http://modernizr.com`.

After including Modernizr, you can build in a check for autofocus:

```
if ( ! Modernizr.input.autofocus ) {
  $('[autofocus]').focus();
}
```

This script uses the Modernizr API to determine whether autofocus is supported. It then calls supportive browsers.

> If the polyfill script is really large, consider loading it externally within this feature check. As a result, modern browsers don't get weighed down by a lot of code they won't use. Consider using a JavaScript loader like require.js to load scripts in this type of situation.

Improving Your Polyfill

Although that works on the basic level, pay careful attention when creating polyfills, because you want the polyfill to match native functionality, regardless of the situation. Taking the careful approach ensures that your polyfill won't give you any surprises. Remember that you primarily work in a browser that supports HTML5, so you won't necessarily see potential problems in your polyfill right away.

The steps for writing a robust polyfill are as follows:

1. Determine an edge-case behavior that might cause problems.

2. See how that situation is handled in browsers that natively support the functionality.

3. Mirror the native behavior in your polyfill.

4. Create unit tests to ensure the polyfill handles all situations appropriately.

For instance, you probably shouldn't have more than one element with autofocus on a page, but what happens if you do? Set up a test page in Chrome or another modern browser, and you will see that the cursor focus will be brought into the last element on the page with autofocus.

That's not necessarily a problem in the autofocus polyfill you wrote because jQuery loops through all the matching elements, bringing focus into each. Because it changes the focus with each new element in the loop, the focus ends up on the last element with autofocus. Sure, the approach is slightly worse for performance, but it's probably not worth optimizing such an edge case. However, what happens if you also have a focus event listener on each element? That handler will then fire twice rather than once. Fortunately, you can fix it easily using the :last pseudo-class:

```
$('[autofocus]').filter(':last').focus();
```

Here, the jQuery's filter() method is used to find the last element with autofocus. You could also attach :last in the main selector, but filter() is better for performance (in all situations, not just edge cases).

But wait a minute. Why don't you test focus events in a browser that natively supports autofocus? You'll see that they actually don't fire at all.

Is your head spinning? I'm not trying to torture you here; I'm just trying to show you how difficult it can be to write a truly robust polyfill, even for a simple feature like autofocus. I hope this exercise gives you more respect for the third-party polyfills you download, and if you ever have a problem with one of them, you can use these steps to patch it.

And I can keep going: How do elements with `tabindex` affect the order?

Writing a Placeholder Polyfill

Writing a polyfill for placeholder text is a little more complicated than writing one for autofocus, but it's still one of the easier HTML5 form features that you can implement.

Detecting Support

The first step to this polyfill is determining whether you actually need it. For this, you can turn again to Modernizr:

```
if ( ! Modernizr.input.placeholder ) {
    jsPlaceholder();
}
```

This snippet uses `Modernizr.input.placeholder` to detect placeholder support. If it's unsupported, a `jsPlaceholder()` function is called.

Determining the Goals

Before you dig in and start building this polyfill, think about what it should do:

1. The polyfill should take the text from the `placeholder` attribute and place it in the input field.
2. When users click into the field, the polyfill should remove the text so that they can add their own.
3. Then if users click out of the field without adding text, the polyfill should add the placeholder text again.
4. The polyfill shouldn't do any of this if users added text. You don't want the placeholder text to overwrite fields that have already been populated. Also, you don't want it to empty out the text of a field if users modified it—users should be able to revisit fields they've already changed without the fields emptying.
5. The polyfill should attach a placeholder classname whenever the placeholder is active. That way, the placeholder text can be styled differently than normal text.

Building the Basic Polyfill

Now that you've established the goals, you can get started with the polyfill. First, pull in any form field with the `placeholder` attribute; then attach blur and focus events to add and remove the placeholder text:

```
var jsPlaceholder = function() {
  // when the field gains focus
  $('[placeholder]').focus(function() {
    var $input = $(this);

    //  determine if the field is showing the placeholder text
```

```
    if ($input.val() === $input.attr('placeholder')) {
      // empty out the field and remove the placeholder class
      $input.val('');
      if ( $input.hasClass('placeholder') ) {
        $input.removeClass('placeholder');
      }
    }

  // when the field loses focus
  }).blur(function(){
    var $input = $(this);

    // replace the placeholder if they haven't entered any text
    if ($input.val() === '' || $input.val() === $input.
attr('placeholder')) {
      // add the placeholder text and class
      $input.val($input.attr('placeholder'));
      $input.addClass('placeholder');
    }
  // trigger the blur so the placeholder text is added on page load
  }).trigger('blur');
};
```

Now, walk through it step by step:

1. The polyfill begins by selecting any form field with a `placeholder` attribute.

2. It sets up a `focus()` event for when the user clicks into the field. If the text in the field matches the placeholder, it's removed along with the placeholder classname.

3. It sets up a `blur()` event for when the user clicks out of the field. Here, if the user hasn't entered text, it adds the placeholder text as well as the classname.

4. It triggers the `blur()` event, which adds the placeholder text when the page loads (but only if the field isn't populated).

Probably the most confusing part of this script is Step 4. Rather than explicitly adding the placeholder text when the page loads, you trigger the blur event the polyfill already handles. Thus, you don't have to repeat those lines.

> It's worth noting that this example doesn't exactly follow the W3C spec for placeholder implementation. In native implementations, the content of the input isn't removed on focus, rather it's removed once the user begins typing into the field. As an exercise, modify the script to follow the spec more accurately.

Submitting the Form

Now, you can see the placeholder text being added and removed from your form fields just like in supportive browsers. However, there are still some things you need to consider. Mainly, the polyfill replaces the values of the form elements with the placeholder text, which can cause problems when the form is submitted because these values will be passed as though the user entered them. To get around this issue, patch into the submit event of all the forms on your page:

```
// must remove placeholders when the form submits so they don't post
$('form').submit(function() {
  $(this).find('[placeholder]').each(function() {
    var $input = $(this);

    // empty the field if it is displaying the placeholder
    if ($input.val() === $input.attr('placeholder')) {
      $input.val('');
    }
  })
});
```

This example empties out the value of any field that is displaying the placeholder. Because it isn't preventing the default action of the `submit` event, it still posts as normal after this change is made. Be sure to bind this event handler somewhere within your `jsPlaceholder` function.

Handling Password Inputs

Now the script is working pretty much like you need it to. The only problem occurs if you have password inputs. Password inputs obfuscate their values, displaying text as *******. Although that's good for passwords, it's no good for placeholder text.

Unfortunately, this is a pretty tricky one to get around. You have to create a new text input for the placeholder text and switch it out for the password input. To make sure the user's password doesn't get displayed on the screen, you also have to switch back to the password input when the placeholder is inactive.

To implement this change, you modify your blur handler:

```
...

// when the field loses focus
}).blur(function() {
  var $input = $(this);

  // replace the placeholder if they haven't entered any text
  if ($input.val() === '' || $input.val() ===
    $input.attr('placeholder')) {
    // if password input, you have to clone it as a text input and
    // then remove this later (otherwise it will show up as ******)
    if ( $input.attr('type') == 'password' ) {
```

```
      var $newInput = $input.clone();
      $newInput.attr('type', 'text');
      $newInput.val($input.attr('placeholder'));
      $newInput.addClass('placeholder clone');
      $newInput.insertAfter($input);

      $input.hide();

      // add focus state to remove this input and show / focus the
      // original
      $newInput.focus(function() {
        $(this).remove();
        $input.show().focus();
      });
    }
    else {
      // add the placeholder text and class
      $input.val($input.attr('placeholder'));
      $input.addClass('placeholder');
    }
  }
  // trigger the blur so the placeholder text is added on page load
}).trigger('blur');
```

This blur handler first detects whether the field is a password input. Then the polyfill clones the input—as a result, the input retains all the classnames, styling, and so on, that have been applied to the original. You must then change the cloned input to a normal text input and add the placeholder text and classname, along with a clone classname to tap into later. Once that is complete, you can add the new field to the DOM and hide the old. Finally, add a focus handler to the cloned field. Consequently, when the user clicks into it, the polyfill removes this field, shows the password input, and moves the cursor into it.

But the blur handler is still not complete. You must modify the submit handler to remove any cloned fields so that they don't get posted with the form:

```
// must remove placeholders when the form submits so they don't post
$('form').submit(function() {
  $(this).find('[placeholder]').each(function() {
    var $input = $(this);

    // remove any cloned password inputs
    if ( $input.hasClass('clone') ) {
      $input.remove();
      return;
    }

    // empty the field if it is displaying the placeholder
    if ($input.val() === $input.attr('placeholder')) {
```

```
      $input.val('');
    }
  })
});
```

Putting It All Together

Now, the polyfill is working almost like native functionality. When all the code is pieced together, it looks like this:

```
var jsPlaceholder = function() {
  // when the field gains focus
  $('[placeholder]').focus(function() {
    var $input = $(this);

    //  determine if the field is showing the placeholder text
    if ($input.val() === $input.attr('placeholder')) {
      // empty out the field and remove the placeholder class
      $input.val('');
      if ( $input.hasClass('placeholder') ) {
        $input.removeClass('placeholder');
      }
    }

  // when the field loses focus
  }).blur(function() {
    var $input = $(this);

    // replace the placeholder if they haven't entered any text
    if ($input.val() === '' || $input.val() ===
      $input.attr('placeholder')) {
      // if password input, you have to clone it as a text input
      // and then remove this later
      // (otherwise it will show up as ******)
      if ( $input.attr('type') == 'password' ) {
        var $newInput = $input.clone();
        $newInput.attr('type', 'text');
        $newInput.val($input.attr('placeholder'));
        $newInput.addClass('placeholder clone');
        $newInput.insertAfter($input);

        $input.hide();

        // add focus state to remove this input and show / focus
        // the original
        $newInput.focus(function() {
          $(this).remove();
          $input.show().focus();
        });
      }
```

```
        else {
          // add the placeholder text and class
          $input.val($input.attr('placeholder'));
          $input.addClass('placeholder');
        }
      }
    // trigger the blur so the placeholder text is added on page load
    }).trigger('blur');

    // must remove placeholders when the form submits so they don't post
    $('form').submit(function() {
      $(this).find('[placeholder]').each(function() {
        var $input = $(this);

        // remove any cloned password inputs
        if ( $input.hasClass('clone') ) {
          $input.remove();
          return;
        }

        // empty the field if it is displaying the placeholder
        if ($input.val() === $input.attr('placeholder')) {
          $input.val('');
        }
      })
    });
  };

  // add placeholder polyfill if it's unsupported
  if ( ! Modernizr.input.placeholder ) {
    jsPlaceholder();
  }
```

Although this implementation handles placeholder text almost exactly like it's handled in supportive browsers, there is still one issue. Unfortunately, the user won't be able to enter the same text as the placeholder into any field because the script will think it's the placeholder text and remove it.

But that's a pretty extreme edge case, and one you just have to live with. If you can see a way around that, patch this script and message me on Twitter @jonraasch.

Combining Polyfills and Widgets

Finally, just because you're writing your own polyfill doesn't mean you have to start completely from scratch. You can modify an existing polyfill or use a third-party widget within your polyfill.

For example, jQuery UI provides a lot of form widgets that are similar to those in HTML5. You can easily leverage these widgets in a polyfill. Simply pull in information about the widget from the form markup and then pass that to the jQuery UI widget.

Connecting to a REST API

Now you need to think about how your form will be posted to the server. You can always post it the old-fashioned way using a submit button, but you're building a JavaScript app here. Using Ajax is a better idea. With Ajax, you can provide a more streamlined experience for your users. Instead of a hard page refresh, you can provide a nice JavaScript animation to indicate the form has been posted. Of course, the form should also be able to post the old-fashioned way in case JavaScript isn't working for some reason.

Before you can post the form, you need some markup:

```
<form method="post" action="my-api.php">
  <fieldset>
    <label for="name">Name:</label>
    <input type="text" name="name" id="name">
  </fieldset>

  <fieldset>
    <label for="email">Email</label>
    <input type="email" name="email" id="email">
  </fieldset>

  <fieldset>
    <label for="username">Username:</label>
    <input type="text" name="username" id="username">
  </fieldset>

  <fieldset>
    <label for="password">Password:</label>
    <input type="password" name="password" id="password">
  </fieldset>

  <fieldset>
    <input type="submit">
  </fieldset>
</form>
```

This is a pretty basic signup form that posts to `my-api.php`. This section covers only the front end of the REST API. Building the back end is up to you.

Later in the Forms in Backbone section, I show you how to connect this form to Backbone and sync automatically with the back end. But for now, I show you how to do it manually.

Posting the Form

Now, post the form using jQuery's Ajax API. First, hijack the form's submit event, then get the post method and URL from the form element:

```
// hijack the form's submit event
$('form').submit(function(e) {
  // prevent it from posting the old fashioned way
  e.preventDefault();

  // pull the post method and URL
  var $form = $(this),
  postMethod = $form.attr('method') || 'GET',
  postURL = $form.attr('action');

  // log it
  console.log('Form submitted to ' + postURL + ' via ' + postMethod);
});
```

The preceding code gets the `method` and `action` attributes off the form element. Notice how there's a failsafe if `method` is undefined—in that case, forms default to the `GET` method.

Next, use these variables to set up an Ajax request, pulling the various values off the form to create the post data:

```
// hijack the form's submit event
$('form').submit(function(e) {
  // prevent it from posting the old fashioned way
  e.preventDefault();

  // pull the post method and URL
  var $form = $(this),
  postMethod = $form.attr('method') || 'GET',
  postURL = $form.attr('action');

  // set up an AJAX request
  $.ajax({
    url: postURL,
    type: postMethod,
    data: {
      // pull the values off the form
      name: $form.find('input[name="name"]').val(),
      email: $form.find('input[name="email"]').val(),
      username: $form.find('input[name="username"]').val(),
      password: $form.find('input[name="password"]').val()
    },
    // on post success
    success: function(data) {
      // log the response
      console.log(data);
    },
    // on post error
    error: function(e) {
      // log error info
      console.log('Error submitting form - ' + e.status + ': ' + e.statusText);
    }
  });
});
```

Here, the post URL and method pulled off the form element are used to create an Ajax request. To build the post data, you pull the various elements off the form and fetch their values.

Setting Up a Universal Function

Pulling each value off the form manually is a pretty crude approach. It's annoying to implement, especially if you have to set it up for more than one form. But more importantly, it couples the JavaScript tightly to the DOM.

It's much better to set up a universal function you can use to post any form via Ajax. You've already seen how the form markup can drive this functionality after you pull the post method and URL off the form element. To take this to the next level, pull all the data you need from the form.

First, make sure the names of the fields in your form match up with the keys of the JSON you want to pass to the server. Once they match up, all you have to do is serialize the form data and post it:

```
// hijack the form's submit event
$('form').submit(function(e) {
  // prevent it from posting the old fashioned way
  e.preventDefault();

  // pull the post method and URL
  var $form = $(this),
  postMethod = $form.attr('method') || 'GET',
  postURL = $form.attr('action');

  // serialize the form data
  var postData = $form.serialize();

  // set up an AJAX request
  $.ajax({
    url: postURL,
    type: postMethod,
    data: postData,
    // on post success
    success: function(data) {
      // log the response
      console.log(data);
    },
    // on post error
    error: function(e) {
      // log error info
      console.log('Error submitting form - ' + e.status + ': ' +
  e.statusText);
    }
  });
});
```

This example takes advantage of jQuery's `serialize()` API, which converts all the data in a form into an object. `serialize()` is handy—without it you have to loop through all the elements in the form and pull the value from each.

Following this procedure ensures that every form in your app posts via Ajax.

> If you don't want to post every form via Ajax, you can set up a classname such as `post-via-ajax` to hook into when you set up the `submit()` **handler.**

Forms in Backbone

If you're using Backbone, you can set up your form to sync automatically with a REST API. Setting this up in Backbone is more complicated than simply setting up an Ajax script.

But Backbone provides a lot of other niceties you can use to enhance the experience of your form. In this example, you create a form that displays inline error messages as the user enters invalid data.

Setting Up the Form Model

The first step to creating a form in Backbone is defining the model. The idea is to do so before you write any markup. That's because Backbone is all about the data. In general, that's how you will work: creating an app that is driven by the data, not the other way around. So start by defining a model to store the various values you want when a user signs up. Notice that this process has nothing to do with forms; it's all about the business logic your app needs.

```
var User = Backbone.Model.extend({
  defaults: {
    name: '',
    email: '',
    username: '',
    password: '',
    passwordConf: ''
  }
});

var user = new User;
```

Here, you set up some defaults for the form fields. In order to sign up, users must provide their name, email, username, and password. They'll also have to confirm their password. For now, you set these to blank values, because the fields in the form will start out blank.

Normally, you'd build validation into your model using `validate()` in order to check the valid email, confirmed password, and so on. However, this form is a special case, and Backbone's native model validation will cause problems.

> For the sign-up process, the user's password needs to be part of this model. But after the user signs up, be sure not to relay it back to the front end. Use a session variable or some other means to keep the user logged in, without having to expose his or her password—this is absolutely essential for security.

Setting Up the Form View

Now that you have the model, it's time to set up the view and template, but first, start with the on-page markup:

```
<div id="signup-form-wrapper"></div>
```

This element is just a wrapper that you'll use to insert the form content into the DOM. In order to make the form accessible without JavaScript, you should also fill this wrapper with a static version of the form. However, I'm skipping that to make the example shorter. Now, define the view for the sign-up form:

```
var SignupView = Backbone.View.extend({
  el: '#signup-form-wrapper',
  template: _.template( $('#form-template').text() ),

  initialize: function() {
    // render the form
    this.render();
  },

  render: function() {
    // convert the model to an object
    var modelData = this.model.toJSON();

    // insert it into the DOM
    this.$el.html( this.template( modelData ) );
  }
});

// create a new instance of the view
var signupView = new SignupView({
  model: user
});
```

So far the view is pretty straightforward. First, you tie it to the wrapper element you already put on the page. Then you use an Underscore template. Finally, you render the view when it loads using the template and the data from the model. Now, you need to create the template. For this, you use similar markup to the sign-up form you built earlier this chapter:

```
<script type="text/template" id="form-template">
<form method="post" action="my-api.php">
  <fieldset>
    <label for="name">Name:</label>
    <input type="text" name="name" id="name" value="<%= name %>">
  </fieldset>

  <fieldset>
    <label for="email">Email:</label>
    <input type="email" name="email" id="email" value="<%= email %>">
  </fieldset>

  <fieldset>
    <label for="username">Username:</label>
```

```
      <input type="text" name="username" id="username"
value="<%= username %>">
    </fieldset>

    <fieldset>
      <label for="password">Password:</label>
      <input type="password" name="password" id="password" value="<%=
password
%>">
    </fieldset>

    <fieldset>
      <label for="password-conf">Confirm Password:</label>
      <input type="password" name="passwordConf" id="password-conf"
value="<%=
passwordConf %>">
    </fieldset>

    <fieldset>
      <input type="submit">
    </fieldset>
  </form>
</script>
```

Here, you create the form that posts to whichever location you need it to. Pay careful attention to the ID of the template's `<script>` element. The ID needs to match the selector you use in your view.

As you can see in Figure 5-15, the form is now rendering on the page.

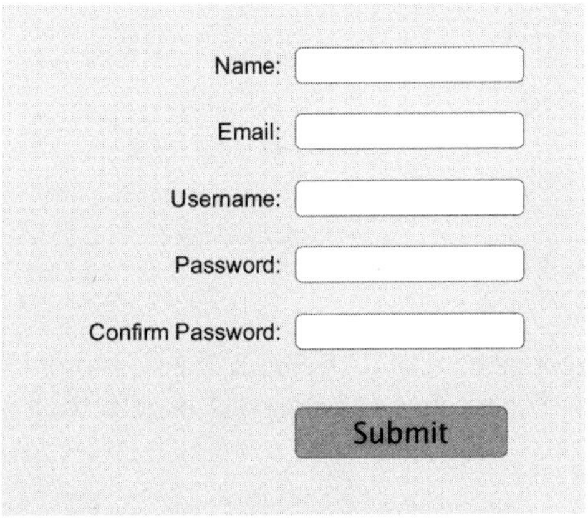

Figure 5-15 The sign-up form is being rendered from the model using an Underscore template.

Saving Form Fields to the Model

Now that you've built your view, you need to figure out a way to relay the data the user enters in the form back to the model. To do that, you need a new concept: Backbone view events.

You've already used internal Backbone events to track changes to models, collections, and so on. But now you'll use view events to bind different handlers to elements in the view. For instance, you can bind a handler for change events on any of the form fields:

```
var SignupView = Backbone.View.extend({
  el: '#signup-form-wrapper',
  template: _.template( $('#form-template').text() ),

  events: {
    'change input': 'inputChange'
  },

  initialize: function() {
    // bind the this context
    _.bindAll( this, 'inputChange' );

    // render the form
    this.render();
  },

  render: function() {
    // convert the model to an object
    var modelData = this.model.toJSON();

    // insert it into the DOM
    this.$el.html( this.template( modelData ) );
  },

  // whenever a form field changes
  inputChange: function(e) {
    var $input = $(e.target);

    // get the name of the key in the model
    var inputName = $input.attr('name');

    // set the new value in the model
    this.model.set(inputName, $input.val());
  }
});
```

Here, the `events` property of the view object is used to bind the change handler to the input. The syntax for that object is as follows: `'eventType selector': callback`. For example, to bind a click handler to all `<a>` elements, you write

```
myView.events = {
  'click a': clickHandler
}
```

The handler for the change event is pretty straightforward: You use the name and value off the input and use those to set the corresponding value in the user model.

It's important to bind the view events through Backbone. Doing so ensures that they are applied every time the view renders.

Adding Validation

Now, you need to set up validation for the fields in your form. Sure you could rely on HTML5 validation, but you're going to get a bit fancier here. I'm going to show you how to render inline validation messages through your view.

Normally, you set up validation on the model, but in this case, that's a bit too fussy. Because you're saving the data to the model at each step along the way, the script might throw errors while users are still entering data. For instance, when they enter the first password, it by definition doesn't match the password confirmation and throws an error every time. Worst of all, the script doesn't even save the password confirmation to the model, so there's no way to complete the form successfully.

The first step is to add a new model to store any errors:

```
// model for invalid fields
var Invalid = Backbone.Model.extend({});

var User = Backbone.Model.extend({
  defaults: {
    name: '',
    email: '',
    username: '',
    password: '',
    passwordConf: ''
  },

  initialize: function() {
    // tie in a sub-model to house invalid fields
    this.set('invalid', new Invalid);
  }
});


var user = new User;
```

This creates a new model for invalid fields and then ties that in as a sub-model of the original user model. It's important to define it in the user model's `initialize` function—if you set it as part of the defaults, all new instances of this model will be bound to the same instance of the `Invalid` model.

Now, you can add a custom validation function to your view, adding any errors to the `invalid` model:

```
var SignupView = Backbone.View.extend({
  el: '#signup-form-wrapper',
```

```
  template: _.template( $('#form-template').text() ),

  events: {
    'change input': 'inputChange'
  },

  initialize: function() {
    // bind the this context
    _.bindAll( this, 'validateForm', 'inputChange' );

    // render the form
    this.render();
  },

  render: function() {
    // convert the model and sub-model to an object
    var modelData = this.model.toJSON();
    modelData.invalid = modelData.invalid.toJSON();

    // insert it into the DOM
    this.$el.html( this.template( modelData ) );
  },

  validateForm: function() {
    // convert the model data to an object
    var data = this.model.toJSON();
    data.invalid = data.invalid.toJSON();

    // check for valid email
    var emailRegex = /[a-z0-9!#$%&'*+/=?^_`{|}~-]+(?:\.[a-z0-
9!#$%&'*+/=?^_`{|}~-]+)*@(?:[a-z0-9](?:[a-z0-9-]*[a-z0-9])?\.)+[a-z0-
9](?:[a-z0-9-]*[a-z0-9])?/;

    if ( data.email.length && ! data.email.match(emailRegex) ) {
      // add it to the invalid model
      this.model.get('invalid').set('email', 'Must provide a valid
email');
    }
    else {
      // otherwise remove it
      this.model.get('invalid').unset('email');
    }

    // check that passwords match
    if ( data.password.length && data.passwordConf.length && data.password
!=
  data.passwordConf ) {
      // add it to the invalid model
      this.model.get('invalid').set('password', "Passwords don't match");
      this.model.get('invalid').set('passwordConf', "Passwords don't
match");
    }
    else {
```

```
      // otherwise remove it
      this.model.get('invalid').unset('password');
      this.model.get('invalid').unset('passwordConf');
    }

    // if any invalid fields, return false, otherwise return true
    if ( _.size( this.model.get('invalid').toJSON() ) ) {
      return false;
    }
    else {
      return true;
    }
  },

  // whenever a form field changes
  inputChange: function(e) {
    var $input = $(e.target);

    // get the name of the key in the model
    var inputName = $input.attr('name');

    // set the new value in the model
    this.model.set(inputName, $input.val());

    // check if the form is valid, if not re-render it to display
    // error
    if ( ! this.validateForm() ) this.render();
  }
});
```

Here's a break down of this view:

1. If the user has filled out the email input, you check it against an email regex. If the email doesn't match, you're adding an error message to the `Invalid` sub-model.

2. However, if the email is valid, you remove any message from the `Invalid` sub-model. Consequently, if the user entered incorrect data previously, the script will remove the message once the data is sufficient.

3. If the user has filled out both password fields, you check to make sure they match. If not, you set both errors in the `Invalid` sub-model.

4. At the end of the validation function, you check the length of the `Invalid` sub-model using Underscore's `_.size()` method. That way, you can return `true` or `false`, depending on whether the form is valid.

5. At the end of the `inputChange()` function, you call the `validateForm()` function. If it returns false, you re-render the form to display any errors.

Because the validation function is called every time an input changes, the form renders errors as they occur; hence, the user can see potential problems before submitting the form. Additionally, take a look at the render function. It's mostly the same, except that you add the invalid object to the data that you're passing to the template—because you need that information to render the errors in the form.

Now, you need to add error messages to the template. You add a class to any field with an error, along with a
`<span>` to hold the error message:

```
<script type="text/template" id="form-template">
<form method="post" action="my-api.php">
  <fieldset>
    <label for="name">Name:</label>
    <input type="text" name="name" id="name" value="<%= name %>" <%=
    invalid.name ? 'class="error"' : "" %>>
    <% if ( invalid.name ) { %>
      <span class="error-message"><%= invalid.name %></span>
    <% } %>
  </fieldset>

  <fieldset>
    <label for="email">Email:</label>
    <input type="email" name="email" id="email" value="<%= email %>" <%=
invalid.email ? 'class="error"' : "" %>>
    <% if ( invalid.email ) { %>
      <span class="error-message"><%= invalid.email %></span>
    <% } %>
  </fieldset>

  <fieldset>
    <label for="username">Username:</label>
    <input type="text" name="username" id="username" value="<%= username
%>"
  <%= invalid.username ? 'class="error"' : "" %>>
    <% if ( invalid.username ) { %>
      <span class="error-message"><%= invalid.username %></span>
    <% } %>
  </fieldset>

  <fieldset>
    <label for="password">Password:</label>
    <input type="password" name="password" id="password" value="<%=
password
  %>" <%= invalid.password ? 'class="error"' : "" %>>
    <% if ( invalid.password ) { %>
      <span class="error-message"><%= invalid.password %></span>
    <% } %>
  </fieldset>

  <fieldset>
    <label for="password-conf">Confirm Password:</label>
    <input type="password" name="passwordConf" id="password-conf"
value="<%=
  passwordConf %>" <%= invalid.passwordConf ? 'class="error"' : "" %>>
    <% if ( invalid.passwordConf ) { %>
      <span class="error-message"><%= invalid.passwordConf %></span>
    <% } %>
  </fieldset>

  <fieldset>
```

```
      <input type="submit">
    </fieldset>
  </form>
</script>
```

As you can see here, you added the appropriate error messages. Now, you can hook into the error classname on the fields and add a red border with CSS. You should also display the error-message spans in red, as shown in Figure 5-16.

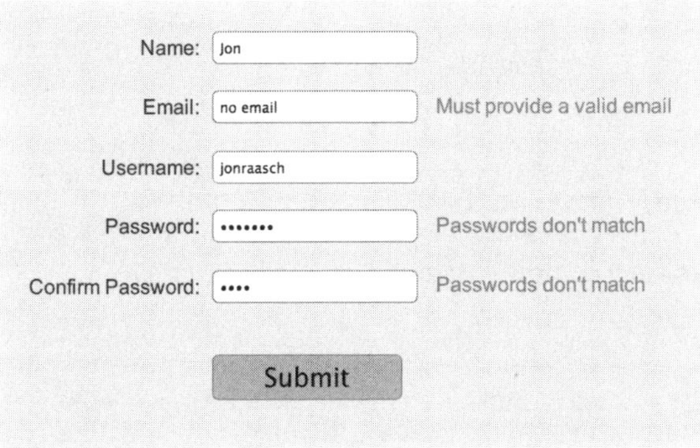

Figure 5-16 The form is displaying error messages properly.

Re-rendering the form to display errors removes the cursor focus from whichever field the user is editing. For an extra credit assignment, figure out a way to pull in what it currently focused before rendering and then reapply the focus afterward.

Cleaning Up the Template

After adding the validation messages to the form template, you may have noticed that it's getting a bit long and unwieldy. So now you should clean it up a bit. You can go about this a couple of ways. You could loop through the fields and generate the form. However, then you'd have to add some more code to your models, which would only concern how the form displays, so that's not such a good idea. The better approach is to create a helper function you can leverage within the template:

```
<script type="text/template" id="form-template">
<%
var displayField = function(fieldKey, fieldValue, displayName, inputType)
{
  if ( typeof( inputType ) === 'undefined' ) inputType = 'text'
  %>
  <fieldset>
    <label for="<%= fieldKey %>"><%= displayName %>:</label>
    <input type="<%= inputType %>" name="<%= fieldKey %>" id="<%= fieldKey
  %>" value="<%= fieldValue %>" <%= invalid[fieldKey] ? 'class="error"' :
  " "
```

```
    %>>
      <% if ( invalid[fieldKey] ) { %>
        <span class="error-message"><%= invalid[fieldKey] %></span>
      <% } %>
    </fieldset>
    <%
  }
  %>

  <form method="post" action="my-api.php">
    <% displayField('name', name, 'Name'); %>

    <% displayField('email', email, 'Email', 'email'); %>

    <% displayField('username', username, 'Username'); %>

    <% displayField('password', password, 'Password', 'password'); %>

    <% displayField('passwordConf', passwordConf, 'Confirm Password',
    'password'); %>

    <fieldset>
      <input type="submit">
    </fieldset>
  </form>
  </script>
```

Here, you create the helper function, `displayField()`, which accepts a few arguments:

1. The key of the field

2. The value of what has been entered into that field

3. The display name you want to show in the `<label>`

4. An optional input type that defaults to text inputs

Once you input the correct data, the helper outputs the correct markup. As you can see, the template is looking a lot more manageable.

> You could have included this helper in your JavaScript core—after all, your template can leverage any of the JavaScript in your app. But because this functionality is specific to the template, it's a better idea to just include the helper right there.

Required Fields

Now, your sign-up form looks pretty complete, but before you can submit the form, you need to make sure the user has filled out all the fields. To do so, modify the `validateForm()` function you built earlier:

```
validateForm: function(checkRequired) {
    // convert the model data to JSON
```

```
  var data = this.model.toJSON();
  data.invalid = data.invalid.toJSON();

  // save a message for required field - this will be reused a lot
  var requiredMsg = 'Required field';

  // check for valid email
  var emailRegex = /[a-z0-9!#$%&'*+/=?^_`{|}~-]+(?:\.[a-z0-
9!#$%&'*+/=?^_`{|}~-]+)*@(?:[a-z0-9](?:[a-z0-9-]*[a-z0-9])?\.)+[a-z0-
9](?:[a-z0-9-]*[a-z0-9])?/;

  if ( data.email.length && ! data.email.match(emailRegex) ) {
    // add it to the invalid model
    this.model.get('invalid').set('email', 'Must provide a valid email');
  }
  else {
    // otherwise remove it if it's not a required field
    if ( data.invalid.email != requiredMsg ) {
      this.model.get('invalid').unset('email');
    }
  }


  // check that passwords match
  if ( data.password.length && data.passwordConf.length && data.password
!= data.passwordConf ) {
    // add it to the invalid model
    this.model.get('invalid').set('password', "Passwords don't match");
    this.model.get('invalid').set('passwordConf', "Passwords don't
match");
  }
  else {
    // otherwise remove it if it's not a required field
    if ( data.invalid.password != requiredMsg ) {
      this.model.get('invalid').unset('password');
    }

    if ( data.invalid.passwordConf != requiredMsg ) {
      this.model.get('invalid').unset('passwordConf');
    }
  }

  // check required fields
  if ( checkRequired ) {
    // make sure that all the fields are filled out
    _.each(data, function(value, key) {
      // check everything except the invalid model
      if ( key == 'invalid' ) return false;

      // if empty field
      if ( ! value.length ) {
        // add it to the invalid model
        this.model.get('invalid').set(key, requiredMsg);
      }
      else {
```

```
        // otherwise remove the invalid flag - but only if it's
        // a required field flag
        if ( data.invalid[key] == requiredMsg ) {
          this.model.get('invalid').unset(key);
        }
      }
    }, this);
  }

  // if any invalid fields, return false, otherwise return true
  if ( _.size( this.model.get('invalid').toJSON() ) ) {
    return false;
  }

  return true;

},
```

Note that you first build in a `checkRequired` argument for the function to determine whether you're checking the required fields. It'd be pretty annoying to users if you constantly checked the required fields as they entered data into the form. So, you check them only when the form is actually submitted.

If the `checkRequired` argument is set, you use Underscore's `_.each()` method to loop through the fields in the model (skipping the `invalid` sub-model). If the field is empty, you pass the `requiredMsg` you set earlier in the function to the `invalid` sub-model; if the field isn't empty, you remove any invalid flag that was set previously. However, you need to check that you remove only required field errors from the invalid list; otherwise, you might remove an error message for an invalid email or mismatched password. So you compare the value in the `invalid` sub-model against the `requiredMsg` string. Finally, you must add the same failsafe to the email and password checks to ensure that you're not removing required field errors.

As shown in Figure 5-17, the empty fields throw errors if you call `signupView.validateForm(true)`.

Figure 5-17 When the form is submitted, you check that all the fields are filled.

To make this example simpler, I just assume all the fields are required. But you could set up a separate list of required fields in a new sub-model and only loop through the ones that are required.

Submitting the Form

Finally, you need to create a way to submit this form to the REST API. Fortunately, all of the user's input is already being stored in the model. You just have to set up a method to sync it. To do so, set up a submit handler in the view's `events` object:

```
var SignupView = Backbone.View.extend({
  el: '#signup-form-wrapper',
  template: _.template( $('#form-template').text() ),

  events: {
    'change input': 'inputChange',
    'submit form': 'saveForm'
  },


...


  // when the form submits
  saveForm: function(e) {
    // prevent it from saving the form the old fashioned way
    e.preventDefault();

    // validate the form
    if ( this.validateForm(true) ) {
      // if valid, save the model
      this.model.save();
    }
    else {
      // otherwise render the errors
      this.render();
    }
  }
});
```

Here, a submit handler is set up on the form that triggers your `saveForm()` callback. In this callback, the default behavior of the form is prevented to make sure it doesn't post the old-fashioned way. Then you call the `validateForm()` function, passing the `checkRequired` argument to make sure it checks required fields. If the form passes validation, it is saved so that Backbone automatically syncs the model via Ajax. Otherwise, it is re-rendered to display any errors. However, Backbone doesn't know where to post this form, so you still need to get the URL from the form's `action` attribute:

```
  // when the form submits
  saveForm: function(e) {
    // prevent it from saving the form the old fashioned way
    e.preventDefault();

    // validate the form
    if ( this.validateForm(true) ) {
      // set the API location using the URL from the form
      this.model.url = this.$el.find('form').attr('action');
```

```
      // if valid, save the model
      this.model.save();
    }
  else {
      // otherwise render the errors
      this.render();
    }
}
```

> **Alternatively, you could simply declare the url when you create the model, but let's keep the form markup driven.**

Now, Backbone will post the form data to the same URL the form posts to, but you still have a little work to do. Some superfluous information in the model should not be sent to the server. For instance, the `invalid` sub-model and the password confirmation are not really necessary data to send to the API. To reduce the size of this request, remove them when you call the `save()` method. Simply clean up an object of data you want to save and pass that in:

```
// when the form submits
saveForm: function(e) {
    // prevent it from saving the form the old fashioned way
    e.preventDefault();

    // validate the form
    if ( this.validateForm(true) ) {
        // set the API location using the URL from the form
        this.model.url = this.$el.find('form').attr('action');

        // clean up the data for the API
        var data = this.model.toJSON();
        delete data.invalid;
        delete data.passwordConf;

        // if valid, save the model
        this.model.save(data);
    }
    else {
        // otherwise render the errors
        this.render();
    }
}
```

This removes the unnecessary data from the model and passes that into the `save()` function. In that way, the script only passes relevant data to the API.

Putting It All Together

Now, your form is properly connected with Backbone. It is displaying inline errors as they occur in the form and then submitting the form data via Ajax. Piecing all the code together:

```
<div id="signup-form-wrapper"></div>

<script type="text/template" id="form-template">
<%
var displayField = function(fieldKey, fieldValue, displayName, inputType)
{
  if ( typeof( inputType ) === 'undefined' ) inputType = 'text'
  %>
  <fieldset>
    <label for="<%= fieldKey %>"><%= displayName %>:</label>
    <input type="<%= inputType %>" name="<%= fieldKey %>" id="<%= fieldKey
%>" value="<%= fieldValue %>" <%= invalid[fieldKey] ? 'class="error"' : ""
%>>
    <% if ( invalid[fieldKey] ) { %>
      <span class="error-message"><%= invalid[fieldKey] %></span>
    <% } %>
  </fieldset>
  <%
}
%>

<form method="post" action="my-api.php">
  <% displayField('name', name, 'Name'); %>

  <% displayField('email', email, 'Email', 'email'); %>

  <% displayField('username', username, 'Username'); %>

  <% displayField('password', password, 'Password', 'password'); %>

  <% displayField('passwordConf', passwordConf, 'Confirm Password',
'password'); %>

  <fieldset>
    <input type="submit">
  </fieldset>
</form>
</script>

<script type="text/javascript">
var User = Backbone.Model.extend({
  defaults: {
    name: '',
    email: '',
    username: '',
    password: '',
    passwordConf: ''
```

```
    },

    initialize: function() {
      // tie in a sub-model to house invalid fields
      this.set('invalid', new Invalid);
    }
});

// model for invalid fields
var Invalid = Backbone.Model.extend({});

var user = new User;

var SignupView = Backbone.View.extend({
  el: '#signup-form-wrapper',
  template: _.template( $('#form-template').text() ),

  events: {
    'change input': 'inputChange',
    'submit form': 'saveForm'
  },

  initialize: function() {
    // bind the this context
    _.bindAll( this, 'validateForm', 'inputChange', 'saveForm' );

    // render the form
    this.render();
  },

  render: function() {
    // convert the model and sub-model to an object
    var modelData = this.model.toJSON();
    modelData.invalid = modelData.invalid.toJSON();

    // insert it into the DOM
    this.$el.html( this.template( modelData ) );
  },

  validateForm: function(checkRequired) {
    // convert the model data to JSON
    var data = this.model.toJSON();
    data.invalid = data.invalid.toJSON();

    // save a message for required field - this will be reused a lot
    var requiredMsg = 'Required field';

    // check for valid email
    var emailRegex = /[a-z0-9!#$%&'*+/=?^_`{|}~-]+(?:\.[a-z0-
9!#$%&'*+/=?^_`{|}~-]+)*@(?:[a-z0-9](?:[a-z0-9-]*[a-z0-9])?\.)+[a-z0-
9](?:[a-z0-9-]*[a-z0-9])?/;

    if ( data.email.length && ! data.email.match(emailRegex) ) {
```

```
        // add it to the invalid model
        this.model.get('invalid').set('email', 'Must provide a valid
email');
    }
    else {
      // otherwise remove it if it's not a required field
      if ( data.invalid.email != requiredMsg ) {
        this.model.get('invalid').unset('email');
      }
    }

    // check that passwords match
    if ( data.password.length && data.passwordConf.length && data.password
!=
  data.passwordConf ) {
        // add it to the invalid model
        this.model.get('invalid').set('password', "Passwords don't match");
        this.model.get('invalid').set('passwordConf', "Passwords don't
match");
    }
    else {
      // otherwise remove it if it's not a required field
      if ( data.invalid.password != requiredMsg ) {
        this.model.get('invalid').unset('password');
      }

      if ( data.invalid.passwordConf != requiredMsg ) {
        this.model.get('invalid').unset('passwordConf');
      }
    }

    // check required fields
    if ( checkRequired ) {
      // make sure that all the fields are filled out
      _.each(data, function(value, key) {
        // check everything except the invalid model
        if ( key == 'invalid' ) return false;

        // if empty field
        if ( ! value.length ) {
          // add it to the invalid model
          this.model.get('invalid').set(key, requiredMsg);
        }
        else {
          // otherwise remove the invalid flag - but only if
          // it's a required field flag
          if ( data.invalid[key] == requiredMsg ) {
            this.model.get('invalid').unset(key);
          }
        }
      }, this);
    }

    // if any invalid fields, return false, otherwise return true
```

```
      if ( _.size( this.model.get('invalid').toJSON() ) ) {
        return false;
      }
      else {
        return true;
      }
    },

  // whenever a form field changes
  inputChange: function(e) {
    var $input = $(e.target);

    // get the name of the key in the model
    var inputName = $input.attr('name');

    // set the new value in the model
    this.model.set(inputName, $input.val());

    // check if the form is valid, if not re-render it to display
    // error
    if ( ! this.validateForm(false) ) this.render();
  },

  // when the form submits
  saveForm: function(e) {
    // prevent it from saving the form the old fashioned way
    e.preventDefault();

    // validate the form
    if ( this.validateForm(true) ) {
      // set the API location using the URL from the form
      this.model.url = this.$el.find('form').attr('action');

      // clean up the data for the API
      var data = this.model.toJSON();
      delete data.invalid;
      delete data.passwordConf;

      // if valid, save the model
      this.model.save(data);
    }
    else {
      // otherwise render the errors
      this.render();
    }
  }
});

// create a new instance of the view
var signupView = new SignupView({
  model: user
});

</script>
```

Just to recap what's going on here:

1. You create a template to display the form. It uses a helper function to display each form field along with any error message that may have occurred.

2. You create a model for the form data, along with a sub-model of invalid fields.

3. You build the view and attach events to track changes in the form fields, as well as the submission of the form.

4. When the view initializes, you render it with the template.

5. You validate the form fields every time one of them changes. You check the Email field against a regex and make sure the passwords match.

6. When the form submits, you also make sure that all the fields are filled.

7. Whenever a form input changes, you save the change in the model and validate the form, re-rendering it if there are error messages.

8. You hijack the form's submission event. If it's valid, you pull the post URL from the form and then sync a cleaned up version of the model with the server. However, if it's invalid, you re-render the form to show any error messages.

Summary

In this chapter, you took your app's forms to the next level. You learned about the progressive enhancement approach and how to use native HTML5 form features to enhance your forms without any JavaScript whatsoever.

Then you found out how to back up HTML5 features for older browsers using third-party polyfills, as well as how to write your own polyfill. Next, you discovered how to hijack the form's default submission behavior and, instead, post it to your API using Ajax. Finally, you learned how to integrate forms into Backbone, creating a data-driven form that displays inline error messages as they occur, and syncs with the server automatically.

Forms are an essential part of just about any app. A good form experience engages users and encourages them to complete signups, checkouts, and other critical actions related to your app's business logic. Consequently, many companies have discovered that the quality of their forms are directly linked to profits.

Additional Resources

HTML5 Form Basics

The Current State of HTML5 Forms: `http://www.wufoo.com/html5/`

Making Forms Fabulous with HTML5: `http://www.html5rocks.com/en/tutorials/forms/html5forms/`

A Form of Madness (Dive into HTML5): `http://diveintohtml5.info/forms.html`

HTML5 Form Tutorials

How to Build Cross-Browser HTML5 Forms: `http://net.tutsplus.com/tutorials/html-css-techniques/how-to-build-cross-browser-html5-forms/`

Constraint Validation: Native Client Side Validation for Web Forms: `http://www.html5rocks.com/en/tutorials/forms/constraintvalidation/`

Make Disaster-Proof HTML5 Forms: `http://www.netmagazine.com/tutorials/make-disaster-proof-html5-forms`

Usability

Web Form Design by Luke Wroblewski (highly recommended): `http://amzn.to/YFjZXq`

An Extensive Guide to Web Form Usability: `http://uxdesign.smashingmagazine.com/2011/11/08/extensive-guide-web-form-usability/`

Forward Thinking Form Validation: http://alistapart.com/article/forward-thinking-form-validation

Accessibility

W3C Recommendations for Form Accessibility: `http://www.w3.org/TR/WCAG10-HTML-TECHS/#forms`

Screen Reader Form Accessibility: `http://webaim.org/techniques/forms/screen_reader`

Accessible Forms: http://www.jimthatcher.com/webcourse8.htm

Polyfills: `https://github.com/Modernizr/Modernizr/wiki/HTML5-Cross-Browser-Polyfills`

Widgets

HTML5 Forms: `http://www.useragentman.com/blog/2010/07/27/creating-cross-browser-html5-forms-now-using-modernizr-webforms2-and-html5widgets-2/`

jQuery UI: `http://jqueryui.com/`

Part III

Working with Server-Side JavaScript

Chapter 6

Intro to Node.js

If you've read anything about web development in the past couple years, you've certainly heard a lot about Node.js. But why all the hype? It seems clear at this point that Node is more than a fad, so why are so many developers excited about Node?

In this chapter you learn what Node is good for, which is directly related to how it works internally. You also learn about the differences between Node and client-side JavaScript, as well as strategies for coming into Node from the frontend. Next you install Node and build your first Node app. You learn how to use the Node REPL, and about Node's module system and installing third party modules using NPM. Finally, you learn about some general patterns and best practices in Node, including:

- Global variables and scope across modules
- Asynchronous and synchronous functions
- Streams
- Custom events and event handlers
- Child processes

Why Node?

It's no accident that Node became so popular. So many people are talking about Node because it's an excellent solution for building many modern web apps. Node is a great fit for apps with heavy input / output (I/O) and light computation. That means you should use Node if your app relies on heavy communication between the server and client, but doesn't need to do anything too complex on the server-side.

Using Node with Real-Time Apps

You've probably heard about Node in relation to "real-time" apps, such as collaborative document editors. That's because these types of apps require a lot of I/O and also benefit from Node's asynchronous nature. For example, a document app for a single user might autosave the doc every minute or so. But with a collaborative app, you need to save it a lot more often to make sure any changes get relayed to each user in relative real-time. Additionally, you need to check frequently for any changes that may have been pushed from other users. All things considered, real-time collaborative apps make for a ton of I/O.

You learn how to build real-time apps in Chapter 9.

Don't get me wrong; just about any server can handle heavy I/O for a handful of users at a time. The question is how well your app is going to scale. Of course, having a ton of users is a good problem to have. But this is one issue you can't afford to wait to optimize. The conventional logic of avoiding premature optimization doesn't apply when you're talking about potentially overhauling the entire app. If your app is going to need to handle a heavy I/O load, you'll need to anticipate and build for scale from day one. You'll need to build it with Node or another I/O friendly server.

How Most Servers Work

Most server-side technologies process multiple requests on individual threads. For instance, if you build a PHP app on Apache, each request has to be handled with a separate child process. For that, the server ramps up additional threads as needed to accommodate the additional requests.

It all works reasonably well if there isn't too much load, but you will see considerable lag if you try to run more than a couple hundred threads in parallel. The lag occurs while the client waits for the server to get around to processing the additional threads. Managing load on a multi-threaded system is a matter of brute force—you typically need to buy more processing power, which doesn't come cheap.

Additionally, programming for multi-threaded servers is significantly more complicated, since the app has to be thread-safe.

Understanding How Node Works

The reason Node is able to handle large amounts of I/O gracefully, has to do with how it handles multiple concurrent connection requests.

As you might have guessed, the traditional multi-threaded approach doesn't scale well enough for many modern web apps. But Node handles things differently. In a nutshell, Node processes requests using a single non-blocking thread with an event loop. Multiple requests are queued up, and processed in turn using asynchronous callback functions.

Node isn't the only server to use a single thread; other high-speed servers such as Nginx take the same approach. But Node is particularly good at it, since it runs JavaScript. Over the years, web browsers have made substantial efforts to optimize their JavaScript engines. Since these engines run code as a single, non-blocking thread, with an asynchronous event loop, they have become very good at passing around asynchronous functions, both in timing events such as `setTimeout` and interface events such as `onclick`. Which brings me to the V8 Engine.

Using the V8 JavaScript Engine with Node

Node uses the lightning-fast V8 engine that Google programmed for Chrome. V8 compiles JavaScript to native machine code before executing it. This approach produces significantly faster code than other engines.

The compiled code is further optimized at runtime, dynamically caching portions of the code, and eliding expensive runtime properties. When all of this is put together, it produces the fastest JavaScript engine ever built. But don't trust me; see for yourself. Visit the V8 benchmarks at `http://v8.googlecode.com/svn/data/benchmarks/v7/run.html` and compare Chrome to another browser.

Coming to Node from the Front End

Although you will be more familiar with the syntax, working with Node is very different from working with JavaScript on the front end. Sure, you'll be able to use the core language you're already used to, but you will have to learn entirely new concepts. The problems you'll solve with Node are fundamentally different from those on the client-side.

That said, there are some aspects of Node development that make it easier to learn than other backend languages. Namely, event loops and the way that Node runs a single thread of asynchronous calls will be very familiar to anyone who has worked with JavaScript.

Just like in front-end JavaScript, Node executes code line-by-line, and allows you to set up callbacks to handle any events that need to be processed. These callbacks are then handled in order. However, the way these asynchronous callbacks are processed isn't entirely the same. Whereas on the client, you have one user triggering various callbacks, your Node app can have any number of users at once. That means there are even fewer guarantees of execution order—you need to be much more careful to avoid race conditions stemming from dependencies between one asynchronous function firing before another.

Installing Node

Before you can get started with Node, you need to install it. There are a few ways to do this:

- Clone the git repo and compile
- Download a tarball and install via the command line
- Download an automated package installer for your platform
- Use a package manager such as MacPorts

Unless you're already using a package manager, installing from the repo is the best option—it's really easy and allows you to update to different versions of Node quickly.

If you're not comfortable with the command line, Node development is going to be pretty difficult. So it's a good idea to get started with one of the command line installations rather than the automated package installer. Additionally, since Node is such a new technology, it's always best to use the latest stable build.

> **If you installed Weinre in Chapter 1, you already have Node installed.**

Mac/Linux Installation

Installing the Node core on Mac and Linux is pretty easy. You just have to download the Node source and compile it.

Getting and Compiling the Source

First, make sure you have git installed: `https://help.github.com/articles/set-up-git`. Then, clone the repo from the command line (in Terminal):

```
git clone https://github.com/joyent/node.git
cd node
git checkout
```

These commands clone the Node repo and then check out the latest version of the source code.

> If you'd like to avoid using git, you can also download the source from `http://nodejs.org/dist/latest/`.

Once you have the source, you can compile it:

```
./configure --prefix=/opt/node
make
sudo make install
```

These commands configure the installation, and then make and install. Node takes a few minutes to compile, so grab a cup of coffee or read on to the next section.

It's also a good idea to add the Node executables to your system path for ease of use. Add the following line to your `~/.profile`, `~/.bash_profile`, `~/.bashrc` or `~/.zshenv`:

```
export PATH=$PATH:/opt/node/bin
```

Using a Package Installer

Alternatively, you can use a package installer. Simply go to `http://nodejs.org/dist/latest/` and download the latest installer (the .pkg file). Just open up the file and follow the instructions in the wizard to install Node automatically.

Using a Package Manager

There are also a few package managers you can use to install Node quickly. For instance, on Mac you can install Node using MacPorts (`http://www.macports.org/`):

```
port install nodejs
```

Or with Homebrew (`http://mxcl.github.com/homebrew/`):

```
brew install node
```

For a list of other package managers that support Node, visit: `https://github.com/joyent/node/wiki/Installing-Node.js-via-package-manager`.

Compiling with Xcode 4.5

If you're using Mac, you can configure Node to work with Xcode. First, download and install Xcode, which is free from the App Store: `https://developer.apple.com/technologies/tools/`. Then, install the command line tools by going to Xcode: Preferences->Downloads->Install Command Line Tools. Finally, compile the source code with Xcode paths:

```
export CC=/Applications/Xcode.app/Contents/Developer/Toolchains/
XcodeDefault.xctoolchain/usr/bin/clang
export CXX=/Applications/Xcode.app/Contents/Developer/Toolchains/
XcodeDefault.xctoolchain/usr/bin/clang++
./configure
make
sudo make install
```

Windows Installation

Node is really geared to a Linux / UNIX type environment. But you can still install it on Windows if you're running a Windows machine and don't want to install Ubuntu. Just like on Mac / Linux there are two ways to go about this installation. You can either build an install if you want more control over the process, or install a precompiled version if you want to get up and running quickly.

Building a Windows Install

To start, make sure you have Python and Visual Studio installed. Then in `cmd.exe`, do the following:

```
C:\Users\ryan>tar -zxf node-v0.8.16.tar.gz
C:\Users\ryan>cd node-v0.8.16
C:\Users\ryan\node-v0.8.16>vcbuild.bat release
[Wait 20 minutes]
C:\Users\ryan\node-v0.8.16>Release\node.exe
> process.versions
{ node: '0.8.16',
  v8: '3.6.6.11',
  ares: '1.7.5-DEV',
  uv: '0.6',
  openssl: '0.9.8r' }
>
```

The executable will then be in `Release\node.exe`.

Installing Without Building

You can also install a pre-compiled version of Node on your Windows system. First, download it from `http://nodejs.org/dist/latest/node.exe`. Put `node.exe` in a clean directory, and add that directory to your PATH variable, so the node commands are available throughout `cmd.exe`.

Next, find a recent version of the NPM `.zip` archive from `http://nodejs.org/dist/npm/`. Unpack that to the same directory as the `node.exe` file, and you're done. You should now be able to run Node and NPM from anywhere you want.

Using a Package Installer

You can also use an automated package installer to install Node on Windows. Simply download the latest `.msi` package from `http://nodejs.org/dist/latest/` and run the install wizard.

Checking Your Install

After your Node install finishes on Mac, Linux or Windows, you can verify the install by typing the following into the command line:

```
node --version
```

If everything went smoothly, you should see it return a version number—for instance `0.8.16`. Now you're ready to dive in and build your first Node app.

> If you want to manage multiple Node versions on the same system, install NVM: `https://github.com/creationix/nvm`.

Getting Started with Node

Although Node might seem intimidating at first, getting started is actually pretty easy. No intro to Node would be complete without the ubiquitous "Hello World" example, and I'm just as excited as you are.

Creating the Server

The first step is to open up a text editor and include the `http` module, which you use to create the HTTP server:

```
// load http module
var http = require('http');
```

Here you use the `require()` method to include the module. The `http` module is one of the core Node modules. (Later this chapter you learn more about modules and how to include external modules in your app.) Next, use the `http` module to create the server:

```
// load http module
var http = require('http');

// create http server
var server = http.createServer( function(request, response) {});
```

Here the `createServer()` method accepts a callback, which passes objects for the `request` and `response`.

> You're going to see a lot of callbacks and closures when working with Node. They are the bread and butter of the asynchronous event loop.

Adding the Content

Next, use `response` to create your page content:

```
// create http server
var server = http.createServer( function(request, response) {
  // header
  response.writeHead(200, {
    'Content-type': 'text/plain'
  });

  // write content
  response.write('Hello World!');

  // send the response
  response.end();
});
```

There are a few things going on in this code block:

1. The `writeHead()` method defines the HTTP headers for the page. In this case, it uses a response code of 200 (for OK) and passes the plain-text content-type.

   Other response codes might be 404 (for file not found), and other headers might be `'cache-control': 'max-age=3600 , must-revalidate'` (to cache the page for an hour).

2. The `write()` method writes the actual 'Hello World' message to the page.

3. The `end()` method closes the response and sends the header and content to the client.

Wrapping Things Up

Now the Hello World script is creating the server and all the content for the page, but you're not done yet. You still need to create a path to access the script, which you can do using the `listen()` method:

```
// listen on port 8000
server.listen(8000);
```

Here the server you created earlier is set up on port 8000. The `listen()` method also accepts a second argument for the hostname, but you don't need that yet because you're just building this locally. Finally, it's a good idea to log what happened to the console:

```
// log it to the console
console.log('Server running on port 8000');
```

Here the script uses the same `console.log()` method you're already familiar with from client-side development. However, instead of outputting this message in the browser, it will be logged in the terminal.

Now the Hello World example is complete. Putting all the code together:

```
// load http module
var http = require('http');
```

```
// create http server
var server = http.createServer( function(request, response) {
  // header
  response.writeHead(200, {
    'Content-type': 'text/plain'
  });

  // write content
  response.write('Hello World!');

  // send the response
  response.end();
});

// listen on port 8000
server.listen(8000);

// log it to the console
console.log('Server running on port 8000');
```

Running the Script

The final step is actually running the script. To do so, save this file as `helloworld.js` and then type the following into the command line:

```
node helloworld.js
```

Now the server is running and you should see the message you logged to the console:

```
Server running on port 8000
```

Finally, navigate to `http://localhost:8000` and you should see your first Node app in action, as shown in Figure 6-1.

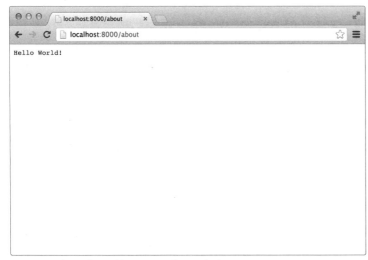

Figure 6-1 The Hello World script is working in the browser.

Simplifying the Script

The Hello World script is working exactly as it should, but there are a couple ways that you can make it simpler. First, you can pass any content you want to write to the page into the `response.end()` method. That means you can eliminate the `response.write()` call and shorten the script a bit:

```
// load http module
var http = require('http');

// create http server
var server = http.createServer( function(request, response) {
  // header
  response.writeHead(200, {
    'Content-type': 'text/plain'
  });

  // send the response with the content
  response.end('Hello World!');
});

// listen on port 8000
server.listen(8000);

// log it to the console
console.log('Server running on port 8000');
```

Additionally, most of the methods in Node are chainable, just like those in jQuery and Underscore. You can see this in action by chaining the `listen()` method to the `createServer()` method:

```
// load http module
var http = require('http');

// create http server on port 8000
http.createServer( function(request, response) {
  // header
  response.writeHead(200, {
    'Content-type': 'text/plain'
  });

  // send the response with the content
  response.end('Hello World!');
}).listen(8000);

// log it to the console
console.log('Server running on port 8000');
```

As demonstrated here, `listen()` is chained to the previous method, allowing you to shorten the script a bit further. Now close the previous Node session by hitting Ctrl+C in your terminal window, and then reopen it with `node helloworld.js`. `http://localhost:8000` shows the Hello World script working exactly as before.

Using the Node REPL

Before you dive deeper into Node, it's a good idea to get comfortable with the read-eval-print loop (REPL). Pronounced "repple," it allows you to run Node code directly in the terminal. To access the REPL, simply call Node from the command line, passing in no variables:

```
node
```

Now you should see a prompt (>), where you can enter Node commands to be executed on the fly, as shown in Figure 6-2.

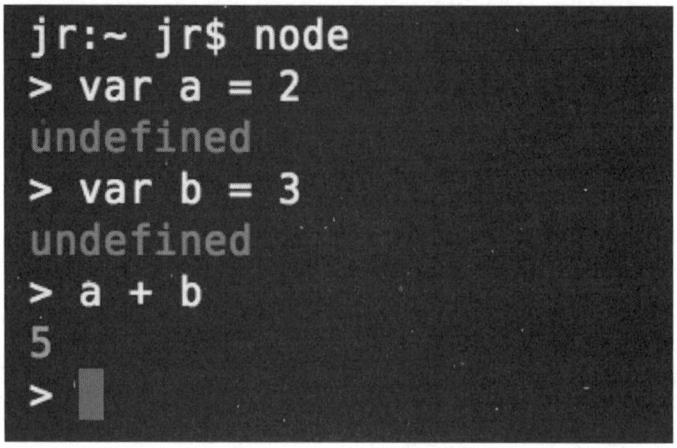

Figure 6-2 The REPL allows you to execute Node commands on the fly.

The REPL is useful for testing small bits of code. It's especially handy when you're first getting used to Node development, since you can quickly test code for the concepts you're learning.

REPL Features

The REPL functions largely like the normal command line: you can use the up arrow to access previous commands and the tab key to complete commands. Additionally, you can use the underscore (_) to pull the result of the last expression, which is shown in Figure 6-3.

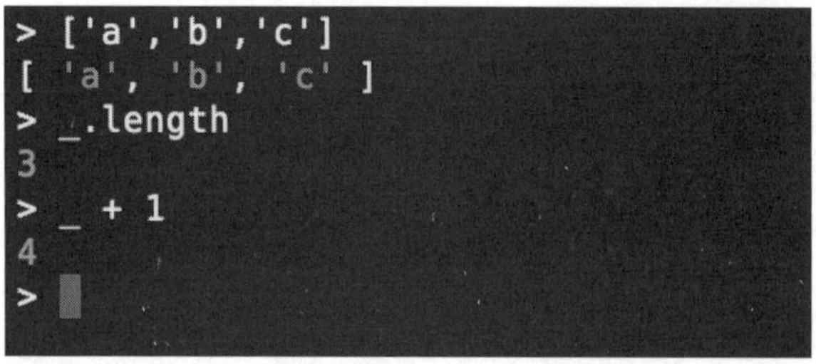

Figure 6-3: The _ pulls the result of the previous expression in REPL.

The REPL even handles multi-line expressions gracefully. Simply start entering a function, or another unclosed tag, and the REPL automatically extends to multiple lines, as shown in Figure 6-4.

```
jr:node jr$ node
> function myFunc() {
... return true;
... }
undefined
> myFunc()
true
```

Figure 6-4: The REPL handles multi-line expressions automatically.

Additional REPL Commands

There are a few extra commands you can use in REPL, which you can see if you type the following in your REPL prompt:

```
.help
```

As shown in Figure 6-5, this outputs a list of REPL commands.

```
jr:~ jr$ node
> .help
.break  Sometimes you get stuck, this gets you out
.clear  Alias for .break
.exit   Exit the repl
.help   Show repl options
.load   Load JS from a file into the REPL session
.save   Save all evaluated commands in this REPL session to a file
>
```

Figure 6-5: REPL also provides some additional handy commands.

Break

If you get lost in a multiline entry, you can start over again by typing:

```
.break
```

However, keep in mind that you lose everything you entered.

Save and Load

You can actually develop your entire application in the REPL. But be careful: if the terminal window crashes you'll lose everything. So when working in the REPL, remember to save early and save often. To save the current REPL session to a file, you can use the `.save` command—for instance:

```
.save ~/path-to/my-file.js
```

Likewise, you can load the contents of a file into the REPL session:

```
.load ~/path-to/my-file.js
```

Exit

Finally, to terminate your REPL session, use the exit command:

```
.exit
```

Alternatively, you can press Ctrl+D. But don't forget to save if there's anything you want to keep!

Node Modules

Rather than implement every possible feature into every build, the Node core is kept as lean and streamlined as possible using modules. Modules are just files that store encapsulated bits of JavaScript.

> Node's module system is modeled after CommonJS.

Including Modules

You've already seen modules in action. For example, the Hello World example used the `http` module:

```
var http = require('http');
```

As you can see here, including a module is as simple as using the `require()` method. You can also include a specific object from a module, rather than all objects:

```
var createServer = require('http').createServer;
```

> It's important to remember that `require` is a synchronous method. Unlike most of the methods you'll use in Node, `require` blocks the main thread. You'll learn more about synchronous and asynchronous methods in the Node Patterns section.

External Modules and NPM

In addition to the core modules, you can install a vast number of external modules to speed up your development process. Although you can import these modules manually, it's a lot easier to use the Node Package Manager (NPM). NPM makes it easy to download, install and update various modules, similar to Ruby gems. Assuming you're using Node version 0.4 or higher, NPM is already bundled with the Node core, so you won't need to install it. But it's still a good idea to update NPM. You can do this with NPM from the command line:

```
npm update -g npm
```

This updates to the latest NPM that's supported by the version of Node you're running.

Installing Modules with NPM

Now, you can install a given module using `npm install`, for instance you can use the following command to install Underscore:

```
npm install underscore
```

This installs Underscore into the `./node_modules` folder. But make sure to call this command from the root of whatever application is going to use the module. That way the module will install into that app's `node_modules` directory.

Now you can use Underscore in your app just like any other module:

```
var _ = require('underscore');

var myArray = [ 1, 5, 3, 8, 7, 1, 4 ];

_.without(myArray, 1);
```

Likewise, you can also uninstall a module at any point, using `npm uninstall`:

```
npm uninstall underscore
```

Installing Modules Globally

You can also install modules globally using NPM. To do so, simply add the `-g` flag. For instance, if you want to make sure Underscore is available for any app you build in Node, you can write:

```
npm install underscore -g
```

Instead of installing this to your app's `node_modules` folder, this command installs it to `~/lib/node_modules`, ensuring the module is available for any Node build.

Installing Dependencies

One of the best parts about using NPM is that it automatically installs any dependencies a module needs. To get a better idea of how dependencies are handled in Node, install the `express` module. Express is a very popular framework that you will learn more about in the next chapter. But before installing it, take a look at its dependencies using `npm view`:

```
npm view express dependencies
```

This command outputs a JSON object of dependencies:

```
npm http GET https://registry.npmjs.org/express
npm http 304 https://registry.npmjs.org/express

{ connect: '2.7.1',
  commander: '0.6.1',
  'range-parser': '0.0.4',
  mkdirp: '0.3.3',
  cookie: '0.0.5',
  'buffer-crc32': '0.1.1',
  fresh: '0.1.0',
  methods: '0.0.1',
  send: '0.1.0',
  'cookie-signature': '0.0.1',
  debug: '*' }
```

> It's a good idea to take a look at a module's dependencies before installing it, so that you know what you're getting into.

Next, install Express using `npm install`:

```
npm install express
```

You already know that NPM installs dependencies, but take a look in `node_modules` just to be sure:

```
ls node_modules
```

While you should see `express`, along with any other modules you've installed, you won't see any of the dependencies. But don't worry, they're still installed.

Rather than install the dependencies to the `node_modules` folder at the root of your application, NPM installs them in a `node_modules` subfolder of the `express` module. Check this subfolder:

```
ls node_modules/express/node_modules/
```

You should then see a listing of all the dependencies that have been installed.

Node handles dependencies this way to avoid any collisions. Different modules might depend on different versions of the same module. If these were all installed to the top level `node_modules` directory, it could create a major problem.

Finding Modules

Just like with jQuery plugins, searching for Node modules can be a challenge. First, where do you look? And more importantly, how do you know if a module is any good? To find modules use `npm search` or peruse module directories. If you already have a pretty good idea of what you're looking for, using `npm search` from the command line is a good option. For instance, you can search for any modules related to Grunt (which you learned about in Chapter 1):

```
npm search grunt
```

`npm search` typically returns a lot of different modules, so you have to do some digging to find the one you want. Use `npm view` to take a look at any of the various options. There are also a number of module directories out there. Here are some good places to look:

- The Node module wiki (`https://github.com/joyent/node/wiki/modules`)
- NPM registry (`https://npmjs.org/`)
- Nipster! (`http://eirikb.github.com/nipster/`)
- The Node Toolbox (`http://nodetoolbox.com/`)

Even though Node is a fairly new technology, it is quite popular, and as such it already has many third-party contributions. While it's great to be able to find an out-of-the-box solution for pretty much any Node problem you may have, the flip side is that a lot of these solutions are not of a high enough quality. So, when you find multiple options for a given module, how do you determine which one to use?

The easiest test is popularity: a Google search shows you which modules people are talking about. The Node Toolbox also organizes modules by popularity on GitHub, as well as lists the most depended on modules. Beyond that, take a look at the star rating on Nipster. Finally, check on GitHub to make sure the module is actively supported and up to date with the current version of Node.

> **One module you should definitely install is Supervisor. Supervisor monitors the files in your Node app, and restarts the server whenever a change is made to a `*.js` file. It makes development much easier. Learn more here:** `https://github.com/isaacs/node-supervisor`.

Node Patterns

The next three chapters discuss practical techniques for building apps in Node. For now I'll walk you through some general concepts, so that your app is built on a firm foundation of best practices.

Modules and Global Variables

You've already discovered a bit about including external modules from third parties. But did you know that you can create your own modules as well? Much like you might partition a portion of client-side JavaScript into your own library, it is a good idea to piece Node scripts into modules. Writing your own modules gives your app structure, and improves collaborative development efforts. It also makes it easier to reuse code across multiple projects.

Creating Your Own Modules

When creating your own modules, simply place them in the `node_modules` directory like any other module. To reference them later you use the `require()` method. For instance, if you have the module `my-module.js` in your `node_modules` directory, you can include it with the following statement:

```
var myModule = require('my-module');
```

But if you'd rather use a different structure, feel free to include modules anywhere else on your system. Simply point to the correct path:

```
var myModule = require('~/path-to/my-module.js');
```

> **If you think other developers can benefit from your module, please share it on GitHub or Bitbucket.**

Global Scope Among Modules

One important thing to remember when writing your own modules is that global variables work a bit differently than you might expect. For example, in client-side JavaScript, you can define a global variable by omitting the `var` keyword:

```
globalVar = true;
var localVar = false;
```

On the front-end, this approach ensures that the `globalVar` is available in all the functions of the app, no matter which file calls that variable. However, Node handles globals differently. In Node, any variable you define globally will be available only in that module. Since modules map directly to files, each variable is available only within a given file.

Creating Global Variables

You can get around this scope issue by writing the following:

```
GLOBAL.globalVar = true; // try to avoid this
```

This defines `globalVar` such that it can be accessed across all the modules in your app. However, you should never define a global variable in Node, unless you have a very, very good reason. Keep in mind that the global context of modules is set up that way for a reason: it avoids variable collisions across different modules. Globals in Node will be used across your entire application, meaning all the modules and scripts in your Node server. Therefore the potential collision problems are exponentially greater than those in a client-side app.

The Global Object

To take a look at what has been defined on the global scope, open a REPL session and type `global`. That command lists everything in the global namespace object, a portion of which you can see in Figure 6-6.

The `global` object stores all of this information, much like `window` in client-side JavaScript. However, since there's no browser window, Node stores it in `global`. As you can see, there are a lot of variables defined on the global namespace. But that doesn't mean you should add to it. Due to potential collision problems, defining your own globals is a risky business.

Using Exports

In general you should avoid defining global variables in Node. Instead, whenever you need to share variable scope, do so manually. To share scope, you have to explicitly declare whatever you want to share from a module using `exports`. For example, your module might contain the following function:

```
var sayHello = function() {
  console.log('Hello World!');
};
```

If you call `sayHello()` from the same module, it work just as you'd expect. However, if you require the module in your `app.js`, the function is no longer available:

```
var myModule = require('my-module');

sayHello(); // this won't work
```

```
> global
{ ArrayBuffer: [Function: ArrayBuffer],
  Int8Array: { [Function: Int8Array] BYTES_PER_ELEMENT: 1 },
  Uint8Array: { [Function: Uint8Array] BYTES_PER_ELEMENT: 1 },
  Uint8ClampedArray: { [Function: Uint8ClampedArray] BYTES_PER_ELEMENT: 1 },
  Int16Array: { [Function: Int16Array] BYTES_PER_ELEMENT: 2 },
  Uint16Array: { [Function: Uint16Array] BYTES_PER_ELEMENT: 2 },
  Int32Array: { [Function: Int32Array] BYTES_PER_ELEMENT: 4 },
  Uint32Array: { [Function: Uint32Array] BYTES_PER_ELEMENT: 4 },
  Float32Array: { [Function: Float32Array] BYTES_PER_ELEMENT: 4 },
  Float64Array: { [Function: Float64Array] BYTES_PER_ELEMENT: 8 },
  DataView: [Function: DataView],
  global: [Circular],
  process:
   { title: 'node',
     version: 'v0.8.4',
     moduleLoadList:
      [ 'Binding evals',
        'Binding natives',
        'NativeModule events',
        'NativeModule buffer',
        'Binding buffer',
        'NativeModule assert',
        'NativeModule util',
        'NativeModule module',
        'NativeModule path',
        'NativeModule tty',
        'NativeModule net',
        'NativeModule stream',
        'NativeModule timers',
        'Binding timer_wrap',
        'NativeModule _linklist',
        'Binding tty_wrap',
        'NativeModule vm',
        'NativeModule fs',
        'Binding fs',
        'Binding constants',
        'NativeModule readline',
        'Binding signal_watcher' ],
     versions:
      { http_parser: '1.0',
        node: '0.8.4',
        v8: '3.11.10.17',
        ares: '1.7.5-DEV',
        uv: '0.8',
        zlib: '1.2.3',
        openssl: '1.0.0f' },
     arch: 'x64',
     platform: 'darwin',
     argv: [ 'node' ],
     execArgv: [],
     env:
      { TERM_PROGRAM: 'Apple_Terminal',
        TERM: 'xterm-256color',
        SHELL: '/bin/bash',
        TMPDIR: '/var/folders/l8/fztfkhb92m9f928xlh6w8ck00000gn/T/',
        Apple_PubSub_Socket_Render: '/tmp/launch-Ry4HH6/Render',
        TERM_PROGRAM_VERSION: '309',
        TERM_SESSION_ID: 'A2FF9E88-5093-469C-A4B5-0077581189D1',
        USER: 'jr',
        COMMAND_MODE: 'unix2003',
        SSH_AUTH_SOCK: '/tmp/launch-PFoVUz/Listeners',
```

Figure 6-6 A portion of the global scope listed in a REPL session.

Instead, you have to explicitly expose the function you want to share, using `exports`:

```
exports.sayHello = function() {
  console.log('Hello World!');
};
```

Now you can call this function from `app.js`:

```
var myModule = require('say-hello');

myModule.sayHello(); // this works
```

Exporting the Entire Scope

Likewise, if your module is a "one trick pony," you can expose the function a little differently. For instance, say that this module has only the `sayHello()` function. You could expose this a bit differently:

```
module.exports = function() {
  console.log('Hello World!');
};
```

The only difference here is that you're using `module.exports` instead of `exports.sayHello`. That defines the export a little differently, which you can see when you reference the module in your app.js file:

```
var sayHello = require('say-hello');

sayHello();
```

As you can see here, the function is defined as the entire extent of the module. This technique can also be useful for exporting an entire object at once, rather than using a number of `exports` calls. For example:

```
// define an object for the module
var myModule = {
  var1: true,
  var2: false,

  func1: function() {
    console.log('Function 1');
  },

  func2: function() {
    console.log('Function 2');
  }
};

// export the entire object
modules.exports = myModule;
```

Rather than explicitly exporting every variable in this module, this script exports an object of variables at once. The various components of the module can then be accessed in `app.js`:

```
var myModule = require('my-module');

if ( myModule.var1 ) {
  myModule.func1();
}
else {
  myModule.func2();
}
```

Multiple Instances of a Module

This technique is also useful for exporting multiple instances of the same module. For example, create a module for users:

```
// user data module
modules.exports = function( name, age, gender ) {
  this.name = name;
  this.age = age;
  this.gender = gender;

  this.about = function() {
    return this.name + ' is a ' + this.age + ' year old ' + this.gender;
  }
}
```

Now you can create a new instance of User in `app.js` using the new keyword:

```
// include the module
var User = require('./user.js');

// create a new instance of the user, passing in appropriate arguments
var user = new User( 'Jon', 30, 'man' );

// use the module's about() method
console.log( user.about() );
```

This script pulls in the context you set in the module, so `user.about()` returns "Jon is a 30 year old man." Likewise, you can access other information defined in the module. For instance, to access the user's name directly you'd simply write `user.name`.

Asynchronous Patterns

Asynchronous requests are great for speeding up the Node server and improving the performance of your app. But they can also be more difficult to work with, especially when you are expecting functions to execute in a certain order. By their very nature, asynchronous methods are called as soon as possible, which means that even if you call function *a* before function *b*, you have no guarantee that it will be completed first. Without a guaranteed execution order, programming in Node can be challenging. That's especially true whenever you are depending on functions to execute sequentially.

Synchronous Calls

To avoid blocking execution, most of Node's native methods are asynchronous by default. That said, Node also provides synchronous versions of most of its methods. For example, you can read in the contents of a file using the `fs` (file system) module's `readFile()` method:

```
// include the fs module
var fs = require('fs');

// read in the file
fs.readFile('./path-to/my-file.txt', 'utf8', function(err, data) {
  if (err) throw err;

  console.log(data);
});
```

Since you haven't flagged this as a synchronous method, Node uses its default asynchronous pattern. However, reading a file can take a little while, which can produce unexpected problems if you're waiting on the results of this function. To get around this, use the `readFileSync()` method:

```
// include the fs module
var fs = require('fs');

// read in the file synchronously
var data = fs.readFileSync('./path-to/my-file.txt', 'utf8');

console.log(data);
```

This script blocks the thread while the file is read, so that no dependent functions can execute before the file is ready. However, the fact that files can take a while to read is often the exact reason *not* to use this approach. Remember, the longer the synchronous call takes to complete, the longer your entire Node server will be blocked. Thus, while you can use synchronous methods in certain situations, it's a good idea to avoid them whenever possible.

> Most Node methods come with a synchronous counterpart you can access by appending `Sync`—for example, `readFile()` becomes `readFileSync()`.

Nested Callbacks

Fortunately, you can get all the benefits of synchronous calls, without blocking the main thread. The trick is to use nested callbacks. For example, you can read all the files in a directory using the following script:

```
var fs = require('fs');

// get directory listing
fs.readdir('./my-dir', function(err, files) {
  var count = files.length,
      results = {};

  // loop through and read all the files
  files.forEach(function(filename) {
    fs.readFile('./my-dir/' + filename, 'utf8', function(err, data) {
      results[filename] = data;

      count--;
      if ( count <= 0 ) {
        console.log(results);
      }
    });
  });
});
```

This script first uses the `fs` module's `readdir()` to get a directory listing. It then loops through all the files in that directory, reading their contents. Since each of the individual calls is asynchronous, the files can all be read in parallel, and the script won't block the main thread from accomplishing other tasks. But the nesting ensures that the critical functions still execute serially.

However, you may have already noticed the downside of this approach: callback spaghetti, a.k.a. "the pyramid of doom." Each nested callback indents the chain further, and makes it easier to get lost in your code. This example isn't too bad with only two nested callbacks, but they can really start to pile up. And when you get a lot of them, it can be difficult to track which closure ends where.

There are a number of ways to minimize the level of nesting in your function. One simple technique is to chunk off portions of the script and pass them as separate callbacks. Alternatively, you can use a module to handle execution order, such as Async: `https://github.com/caolan/async`.

Streams

You've already learned how to use the `fs.readFile()` to fetch the contents of files on your server. However, that's not always the best way to read in file data because the server has to wait for the entire file to buffer into memory before executing the callback. If the file is very large this technique can present two problems. First, it can create latency issues if you are relaying the file to the client, since users will have to wait for the entire file to buffer before they start receiving any contents. Second, this approach can create memory issues if the program is handling lots of concurrent requests for the file.

A better solution is to use streams to process the file data while it buffers:

```
var http = require('http'),
    fs = require('fs');

var server = http.createServer(function(request, response) {
  // create the stream
```

```
var stream = fs.createReadStream('my-file.txt');

// handle any errors
stream.on('error', function(err) {
  response.statusCode = 500;
  response.end(String(err));
});

// pipe the response to the client
stream.pipe(response);
});

server.listen(8000);
```

This script first uses `fs.createReadStream()` to create the stream and then sets up basic error handling. Next, `pipe()` relays the data in the stream to the client. To test this functionality, create an extremely long chunk of text in `my-file.txt`, and then navigate to `http://localhost:8000`. You should see the contents of the file stream into the page.

`fs.createReadStream()` is just the beginning when it comes to streaming in Node. There are a variety of other built in streams, and you can even create your own. For more information visit `https://github.com/substack/stream-handbook`.

Events

As Node's website puts it, "Node.js uses an event-driven, non-blocking I/O model." Events are clearly a big part of Node, and the platform provides some useful techniques for setting up your own custom events. The main component for events in Node is `EventEmitter`. Whenever you see an event handled with `on()`, you're seeing the `EventEmitter` in action.

You can use the `EventEmitter` to create your own custom events and handlers throughout your app. First, include the `events` module, which is part of the Node core:

```
var events = require('events');
```

Next, create a new instance of `EventEmitter`:

```
var em = new events.EventEmitter();
```

Now, you can use the `EventEmitter` to handle two important tasks: creating an event handler and emitting the actual event. First, create the event handler using `on()`:

```
em.on( 'my-event', function(data) {
  // what to do when this event fires
});
```

Then, you can trigger this handler by firing the actual event. To do so, use `emit()`:

```
em.emit('my-event');
```

Using this technique, you can set up custom events and handlers throughout your app. For example, here's how to create an event that fires at every tick of an interval:

```
// include the events module
var events = require('events');

// create an instance of the EventEmitter
var em = new events.EventEmitter();

var counter = 0;

// emit the event every 5 seconds
var timer = setInterval(function() {
  em.emit('tick');
}, 5000);

// handle the event, logging either 'Tick' or 'Tock'
em.on('tick', function() {
  counter++;
  console.log( counter % 2 ? 'Tick' : 'Tock');
});
```

Here, an interval fires the `'tick'` event every five seconds. Each time it fires, the `'tick'` handler increments the counter and then logs either `'Tick'` or `'Tock'`.

Fire up your Node server, and you will see something similar to Figure 6-7:

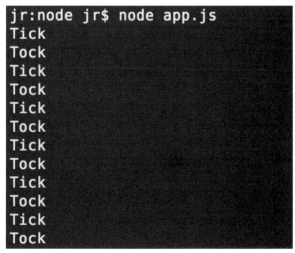

Figure 6-7 The custom event is logging every five seconds.

Child Processes

While client-side JavaScript is limited by whatever the browsers support, Node development is completely the opposite. In addition to the wide variety of modules available to Node, you can also access all of the functionality of the operating system that Node is running upon. That means you can build just about anything with Node.

Accessing the operating system commands is as simple as including the `child_process` module, which is part of the Node core. In particular, you'll want to use the `spawn` method, so call this as part of your `require` statement:

```
var spawn = require('child_process').spawn;
```

> Note that the examples in this section will only work with a Linux or UNIX system (such as Mac). If you're using Windows, you'll need to use Windows commands.

Using Child Processes

Now you can use this to call any OS commands you'd like. For instance, you can get a listing of the current directory using `ls`. The first step is to spawn a child process for `ls`:

```
// include the child_process module
var spawn = require('child_process').spawn;

// spawn a child process for ls
var ls = spawn('ls');
```

Next, set up a couple events. First, a handler for standard output (`stdout`):

```
// handle standard output
ls.stdout.on('data', function(data) {
  console.log(data.toString());
});
```

This outputs the result of `ls` to the Node console. However, that occurs only if there isn't an error. You should also set up a standard error (`stderr`) handler:

```
// handle error
ls.stderr.on('data', function(data) {
  console.log('Error: ' + data);
});
```

Finally, you should set up a handler for when the command exits. That way you can get a success or fail message depending on whether it crashes:

```
// handle exit
ls.on('exit', function(code) {
  console.log('child process exited with code ' + code);
});
```

Putting the script together:

```
// include the child_process module
var spawn = require('child_process').spawn;

// spawn a child process for ls
var ls = spawn('ls');

// handle standard output
ls.stdout.on('data', function(data) {
  console.log(data.toString());
});

// handle error
ls.stderr.on('data', function(data) {
  console.log('Error: ' + data);
});

// handle exit
ls.on('exit', function(code) {
  console.log('child process exited with code ' + code);
});
```

When you run this script, it will output a listing of the working directory in the Node console, as you can see in Figure 6-8.

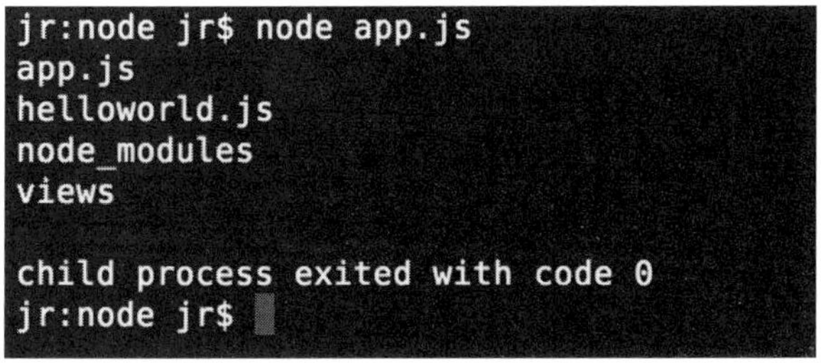

```
jr:node jr$ node app.js
app.js
helloworld.js
node_modules
views

child process exited with code 0
jr:node jr$
```

Figure 6-8 This directory listing has been output from Node using a child_process bridge to the operating system.

Passing Variables to a Child Process

You can also pass variables to your child process. For instance, to get a listing of all the files in the directory (including hidden files), enter the following into the command line:

```
ls -a
```

To execute the same command in Node, pass a second argument to `spawn()`. This second argument is an array of any arguments you want to pass with the command:

```
var ls = spawn('ls', ['-a']);
```

Now, when you restart your server, you see the expanded listing, like in Figure 6-9.

```
jr:node jr$ node app.js
.
..
.DS_Store
app.js
helloworld.js
node_modules
views

child process exited with code 0
jr:node jr$
```

Figure 6-9 This directory listing now includes hidden files, such as the Mac cache file `.DS_Store`.

Summary

In this chapter you got your first taste of Node development. You learned what types of apps are the best fit for Node, and why Node works so well for these apps. After installing Node on your machine, you built your first Hello World app. Then you learned about the Node module system, and how to install external modules with NPM. Finally, you armed yourself with a firm foundation in Node best practices. You learned how globals are handled in Node modules, and how to expose context between modules. You also discovered how to set up sequential behaviors in asynchronous functions and take advantage of streams. Then you learned how to create your own custom events, and access the operating system's command line from Node.

In the coming chapters, you learn how to use the Express framework to set up routes and views for your application. You also learn how to use a NoSQL database, MongoDB, to complement the high-speed scalability of the Node application you're building. Then, you'll tie it all together, creating a real-time app, that communicates with the client using WebSockets.

Additional Resources

Node Documentation: `http://nodejs.org/api/`

Books

Learning Node by Shelley Powers, (978-1449323073) published by O'Reilly, 10/2012

Mastering Node.js an open source book created by TJ Holowaychuk: `http://visionmedia.github.com/masteringnode/`

Smashing Node.js by Guillermo Rauch, (978-1119962595) published by Wiley 9/2012

Node.js in Action by Mike Cantelon and TJ Holowaychuk, published by Manning Publications

Tutorials

Node.js Step by Step: `http://net.tutsplus.com/tutorials/javascript-ajax/this-time-youll-learn-node-js/`

Let's Make a Web App: Nodepad: `http://dailyjs.com/2010/11/01/node-tutorial/`

A variety of good Node Tutorials: `http://howtonode.org/`

Video Tutorials

Introduction to Node.js with Ryan Dahl: `http://youtu.be/jo_B4LTHi3I`

Node.js: JavaScript on the Server: `http://youtu.be/F6k8lTrAE2g`

Node.js First Look: `http://www.lynda.com/Nodejs-tutorials/Nodejs-First-Look/101554-2.html`

Module Directories

The Node module wiki: `https://github.com/joyent/node/wiki/modules`

NPM registry: `https://npmjs.org/`

Nipster!: `http://eirikb.github.com/nipster/`

The Node Toolbox: `http://nodetoolbox.com/`

Best Practices

Node.js Style Guide: `http://nodeguide.com/style.html`

Stream Handbook: `https://github.com/substack/stream-handbook`

Chapter 7
Express Framework

Express is one of the most popular frameworks for Node development. It handles a number of common tasks for Node apps, and streamlines the development process. In this chapter you learn how to install Express and create your first Express app. You then set up routes to create the various paths your app needs.

Next you create handlers for these routes that display views using Underscore templates. By default, Express uses Jade templates, but you'll switch it to Underscore so that you don't have to learn a new template language. Finally, you handle posted form data with a special POST route. You then validate the form data, rendering messages for any errors that occur. If the form passes validation, you send an email to the server administrator. By the end of this chapter you'll be up and running with Express, and ready to build your own Node app.

Getting Started with Express

The main advantage to working with Express is that it makes development easier. Fortunately, that also means a gentle learning curve for using Express—getting set up for your first app is a piece of cake.

Installing Express

The first step to using Express is installing the module via NPM. Since you'll probably want to use Express for a number of different Node projects, it's a good idea to install it as a global module using the -g flag:

```
npm install express -g
```

If that fails, use a sudo:

```
sudo npm install express -g
```

Even though Express has a number of dependencies, the installation process should be pretty quick.

Creating an Express App

Next create a new folder for your Express app. Inside that folder, call the following command:

```
express --css less
```

This command creates a new Express app, with support for the CSS preprocessor LESS, which will be used by the app in this chapter.

You can include a number of different features when you instantiate your Express app. For example, you can include support for sessions using --sessions.

I strongly recommend using CSS preprocessing in any app you're building. I'm not going to go into too much detail about LESS in this chapter, but you can turn to Appendix A for more information about the preprocessor. Alternatively, if there's a different preprocessor you'd like to use with Express, simply call it out in this command: `--css sass` or `--css stylus`.

Before you can run the app, you need to install more dependencies using the following command:

```
cd . && npm install
```

Finally, start the app:

```
node app
```

If everything worked correctly, you should see it output `Express server listening on port 3000`, as shown in Figure 7-1.

```
jr:express-app jr$ node app
Express server listening on port 3000
```

Figure 7-1 The Express server is now running.

When you route to `http://localhost:3000` you should see a welcome message like in Figure 7-2.

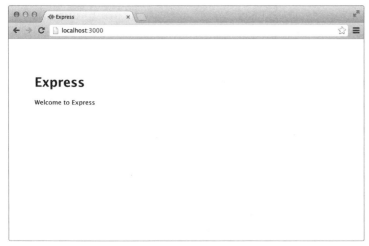

Figure 7-2 The Express server is running on localhost:3000.

Setting Up Routes

In Chapter 3 you set up routes in Backbone to map certain URLs to different states of your app. Routes work essentially the same in Express, except that they map to actual paths on the server.

Existing Routes

The best place to start learning about routes is to take a look at the routes that already exist in the Express build. Open up `app.js` and look for the lines:

```
app.get('/', routes.index);
app.get('/users', user.list);
```

These are two basic routes, one at the root (`http://localhost:3000/`) and another at `http://localhost:3000/users`.

The Routes Directory

Both of these basic routes tie a path to a particular callback found in the `./routes` directory of your app. For example, the second route binds the `http://localhost:3000/users` URL to a function found in `./routes/user.js`. Open up that file to see the following:

```
/*
 * GET users listing.
 */

exports.list = function(req, res){
  res.send('respond with a resource');
};
```

The route in `app.js` maps the /users path to `user.list`, which means that it looks in `./routes/user.js` for the `exports.list` callback. In this case, the list function prints a simple message to the screen, which you can see if you route your browser to `http://localhost:3000/users`, as shown in Figure 7-3.

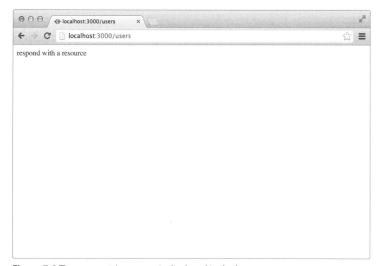

Figure 7-3 The `user.list` route is displayed in the browser.

> You might remember learning about the `exports` object in Chapter 6. It's used to relay variables between modules in Node. In this case it relays the `list` function so the router can use it.

Now take a look at the first route:

```
app.get('/', routes.index);
```

This route is a little more confusing, because `routes.index` doesn't refer to a file called `./routes/routes.js`. Rather, this route points to behavior found in `./routes/index.js`.

The Render Function

In the homepage route, you may have noticed the use of the render function, which Express uses to compile views. In this case, the render function is:

```
res.render('index', { title: 'Express' });
```

The first argument is the name of the template file. This corresponds to the `index.jade` file in the `./views` directory. By default, Express uses Jade templates, but don't worry about this too much. Later this chapter you'll switch these for Underscore templates, so that you don't have to learn a new template language. The second argument is an object of the variables you want to pass to the template.

Creating Additional Routes

Now that you know how routes work, you can create some of your own. Open up `app.js` and add the following routes:

```
app.get('/about', routes.about);
app.get('/contact', routes.contact);
```

Now open `./routes/index.js` and add behavior for these routes:

```
/*
 * GET about page.
 */

exports.about = function(req, res){
  res.render('about', { title: 'About' });
};

/*
 * GET contact page.
 */

exports.contact = function(req, res){
  res.render('contact', { title: 'Contact' });
};
```

Later on you'll customize these routes a bit further, but for now just leave them as is.

> When you modify the `app.js` file, make sure to restart the Express server to propagate the changes. These new paths won't work until you do. Or you can use Supervisor, a module you were introduced to in Chapter 6: `https://github.com/isaacs/node-supervisor`.

Post, Put, and Delete

So far you've used only `app.get()` which corresponds to a basic GET request—for example, getting a page to render in the browser. But Express is designed around REST patterns, and therefore provides methods for additional request types. You can take advantage of `app.post()`, `app.put()` and `app.delete()` in the exact same way as `app.get()`, to provide routes for whatever requests your app needs. You'll see `app.post()` later this chapter, when you learn how to process form data.

Rendering Views

So far you've set up some routes, but if you navigate to `http://localhost:3000/about` or `http://localhost:3000/contact`, you will get a 500 error. That's because you still need to set up the views.

Enabling Underscore Templates

By default, Express comes with a baked-in template engine called Jade. Jade is a minimalist template engine created by TJ Holowaychuk (who also created Express).

Jade Templates

To get an idea of how Jade works, open up `layout.jade` in the views folder of your Express app's directory. You should see something like this:

```
doctype 5
html
  head
    title= title
    link(rel='stylesheet', href='/stylesheets/style.css')
  body
    block content
```

As you can see, Jade's templates are very minimalist. There are no angular brackets around tag names, and attributes are defined in parentheses.

You can also define IDs and classes in Jade using CSS-style selectors—for example:

```
#my-id
  p.my-class Text content
```

This snippet compiles as follows:

```
<div id="my-id">
  <p class="my-class">Text content</p>
</div>
```

While Jade templates are great for reducing the number of characters in a template file, they can be difficult to read, and come with a steeper learning curve than other template engines.

Underscore Templates and uinexpress

You're already comfortable using Underscore templates after reading Chapter 4, so why not use them in Express? Fortunately, there's a Node module called uinexpress, which makes it easy to enable Underscore templates in Express. First install uinexpress and Underscore via NPM:

```
npm install uinexpress
npm install underscore
```

Next open up `app.js` and modify the Express configuration. Add the following lines beneath the `// all environments` line:

```
app.engine('html', require('uinexpress').__express);
app.set('view engine', 'html');
```

And then comment out the line for the Jade view engine:

```
//  app.set('view engine', 'jade');
```

Finally, restart your Express server to put the changes into effect.

Converting Jade Templates

If you route to `http://localhost:3000` you will see that the page is now broken. That's because the Jade templates are no longer working. But don't worry—you can easily modify the existing Jade templates to get a base state for views in your app. First, in the views directory, open up `layout.jade`, which should look like this:

```
doctype 5
html
  head
    title= title
    link(rel='stylesheet', href='/stylesheets/style.css')
  body
    block content
```

Now, convert this template into an Underscore version that's a bit more familiar:

```
<!DOCTYPE html>
<html>
<head>
    <title><%=title %></title>
```

```
        <link rel="stylesheet" href="/stylesheets/style.css" />
</head>

<body>
<%=body %>
</body>
</html>
```

Here you see some familiar Underscore patterns, such as variables delimited by `<% %>`. Save this new Underscore template as `layout.html`.

Next, open up `index.jade`, which should look like this:

```
extends layout

block content
  h1= title
  p Welcome to #{title}
```

You can also convert this into an Underscore template:

```
<h1><%=title %></h1>
<p>Welcome to <%=title %></p>
```

Save this new file as `index.html`, and you're done. Reload the page on `http://localhost:3000`, and you should see the same welcome message as before.

You may have noticed that the `extends layout` and `block content` calls were removed from these templates. But don't worry, the new Underscore templates function exactly like their Jade predecessors.

When the index view is rendered, it compiles the content in `index.html` and passes that to the `<%=body %>` variable in `layout.html`.

One of the best parts of working with Node is that you can reuse the same template files on the client-side. That means you can create a static version of the page using Node, and also load the exact same page using Ajax.

In Chapter 3, you read about loading Backbone views with `pushState`. There I explained why it was important to have a static backup for each page. There's no easier way to accomplish that than using a Node server that leverages the exact same Underscore templates on the frontend.

Creating Views

Once you've enabled Underscore templates, you can start building views for the various pages. I'm going to keep these views really simple, but feel free to embellish them with your Underscore skills.

The Homepage

First, start with the template for the homepage. In the `./views` directory add the following to `index.html`:

```
<h1><%=title %></h1>
<% if ( typeof subtitle !== 'undefined' ) { %>
<h2><%=subtitle %></h2>
<% } %>

<p><%=description %></p>
```

Here a few new variables have been added to the function: an optional subtitle and a description.

Now open up `index.js` in the `./routes` directory. The route for the homepage is already pointing to this template; you just have to change the variables that are passed into it:

```
/*
 * GET home page.
 */

exports.index = function(req, res){
  res.render('index', {
    title: 'My First Express App',
    description: 'This is my first Express app, so go easy on me'
  });
};
```

Now, if you reload the page at `http://localhost:3000`, you'll see the new homepage as shown in Figure 7-4.

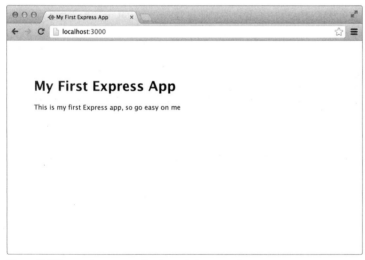

Figure 7-4 The new homepage view is rendering correctly.

The About Page

Next you need to create a view for the about page. However, the template for the about page is going to look pretty much like the one for the homepage. There's no sense in duplicating the homepage template, when all you need to do is reference the existing template and pass in new variables. That said, it also doesn't make much sense to continue calling it the `index.html` template. Rename the template to `main.html`, and modify the route for the homepage:

```
/*
 * GET home page.
 */

exports.index = function(req, res){
  res.render('main', {
    title: 'My First Express App',
    description: 'This is my first Express app, so go easy on me'
  });
};
```

Then, set up the view in the about page route:

```
/*
 * GET about page.
 */

exports.about = function(req, res){
  res.render('main', {
    title: 'About',
    subtitle: 'All about my Express app',
    description: 'I built this app using Node and the Express framework'
  });
};
```

As you can see, this time the template is using the optional subtitle variable.

Finally, make sure to restart your Express server, to empty the cache from the previous templates. Now when you route to `http://localhost:3000/about`, you see the new content, as shown in Figure 7-5.

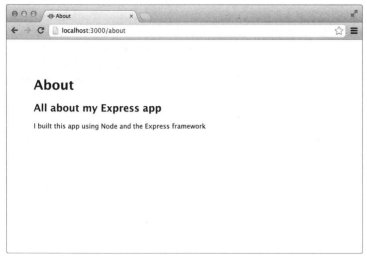

Figure 7-5 The about page view is rendering properly.

The Contact Page

Last but not least, you need to set up a view for the contact page. This view will be a little different, so you need to create a new template. Create a file named `contact.html` in the `./views` directory and add the following markup:

```
<h1><%=title %></h1>

<p><%=description %></p>

<form method="post">
  <div class="form-item">
    <label for="name">Name:</label>
    <input type="text" name="name" id="name" required />
  </div>

  <div class="form-item">
    <label for="email">Email:</label>
    <input type="email" name="email" id="email" required />
  </div>

  <div class="form-item">
    <label for="message">Message:</label>
    <textarea name="message" id="message" required></textarea>
  </div>

  <div class="form-item">
    <input type="submit" value="Send" />
  </div>
</form>
```

Next, adjust the route handler:

```
/*
 * GET contact page.
 */

exports.contact = function(req, res){
  res.render('contact', {
    title: 'Contact Us',
    description: 'Send us a message and we\'ll get back to you'
  });
};
```

Now, if you route to `http://localhost:3000/contact`, you'll see that the page is looking pretty ugly. It's time to add some basic CSS to improve the styling. Go to the `./public/stylesheets` directory and open up `style.less`. In here, add the following LESS styling:

```
.form-item {
  @labelWidth: 100px;
  @formPadding: 5px;

  padding: 5px 0;

  label {
    display: inline-block;
    width: @labelWidth - 10px;
    padding-right: 10px;
    text-align: right;
    vertical-align: top;
  }

  input[type=text], input[type=email] {
    width: 250px;
    padding: @formPadding;
  }

  textarea {
    width: 400px;
    height: 150px;
    padding: @formPadding;
  }

  input[type=submit] {
    margin-left: @labelWidth;
    font-size: 36px;
  }
}
```

When you save `style.less`, Express automatically compiles it to `style.css`. Now, navigate to `http://localhost:3000/contact` and you will see the rendered form, as in Figure 7-6.

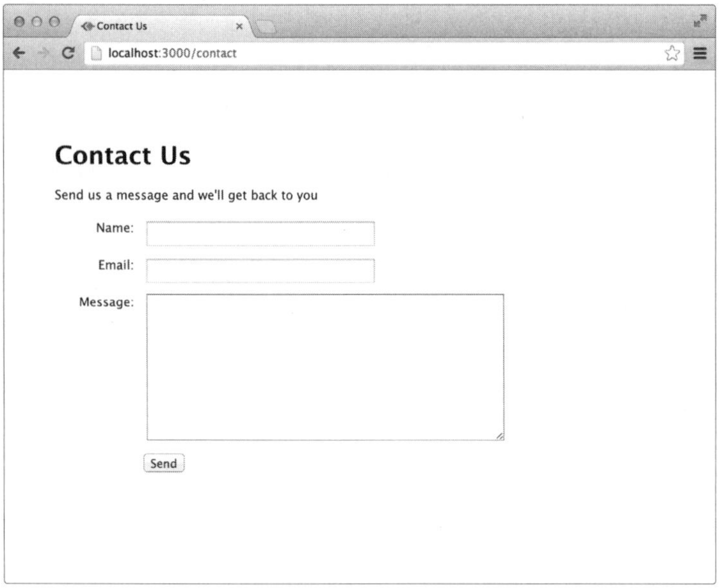

Figure 7-6 The contact view is being rendered nicely with the additional styling.

LESS styling looks pretty much like regular CSS, with a few extra things mixed in, such as the `@labelWidth` and `@formPadding` variables.

Additionally, notice how the styles are all nested under `.form-item`, which makes for better stylesheet organization, but don't worry, it still compiles to regular CSS. For example, the nested `label` becomes `.form-item label`.

> **Read Appendix A to learn more about LESS and CSS preprocessing.**

The Layout Template

When creating the templates for these different views, don't forget about `layout.html`. You can use this template to add anything you want to exist on every page of your app—for instance, a Google Analytics tracking code, or footer for the site.

For example, you've already set up routes for different pages of the app, but how are users supposed to get to those pages? Better add some navigation to `layout.html`:

```
<!DOCTYPE html>
<html>
<head>
  <title><%=title %></title>
  <link rel="stylesheet" href="/stylesheets/style.css" />
</head>

<body>
```

```
<nav>
  <ul>
    <li>
    <a href="/">Home</a>
    </li>

    <li>
    <a href="/about">About</a>
    </li>

    <li>
    <a href="/contact">Contact</a>
    </li>
  </ul>
</nav>

<%=body %>
</body>
</html>
```

Next add some more styling to `style.less`:

```
nav {
  background-color: tomato;
  padding: 0 50px;
  position: absolute;
  top: 0;
  left: 0;
  right: 0;

  > ul {
    list-style: none;
    margin: 0;
    padding: 0;
  }

  li {
    > a {
      color: papayawhip;
      text-decoration: none;
      float: left;
      padding: 20px;

      &:hover {
        color: tomato;
        background-color: papayawhip;
      }
    }
  }
}
```

Now that the navigation has been added, the page is looking a lot nicer, as shown in Figure 7-7.

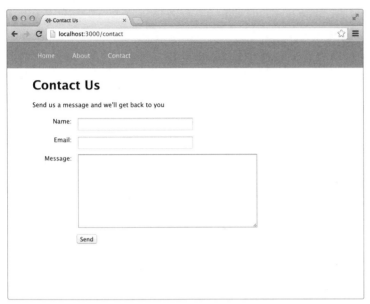

Figure 7-7 Navigation has been added to `layout.html`, which adds it to all the views in the app.

Don't worry too much about the LESS code—Express will compile it automatically to regular CSS, and if you want to learn more about LESS, read Appendix A.

Handling Form Data

At this point, a few basic routes and views are set up in the Express app, but you still need to handle the form data. In this section, you first learn how to set up post routes to handle the post data from the form. Then you validate the form data on the server side, rendering any validation errors on the client.

Creating a Post Route

Just for fun, try submitting the contact form as it currently stands. You should see an error `Cannot POST /contact`, as shown in Figure 7-8.

That might seem a bit strange, since you already set up a route for `/contact`. However, you still can't post form data to that route, because it's set up as a GET route:

```
app.get('/contact', routes.contact);
```

To process a POST request, you'll need to set up a different POST route in `app.js`:

```
app.post('/contact', routes.contactPostHandler);
```

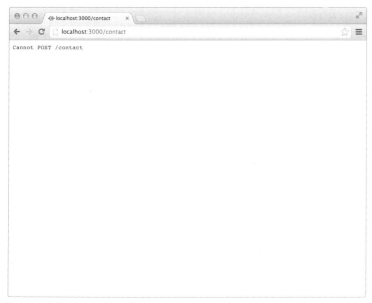

Figure 7-8 Posting the form triggers an error.

Now, add the handler in `./routes/index.js`:

```
/*
 * POST contact page.
 */

exports.contactPostHandler = function(req, res){
  console.log('Name: ' + req.body.name);
  console.log('Email: ' + req.body.email);
  console.log('Message: ' + req.body.message);

  res.send('Form posted successfully');
};
```

Although this handler is very basic, there are a few important patterns to note. Mainly, notice how the script drills into the request object `req` to pull the different fields that were posted. For example `req.body.name` pulls the data that was posted in the `<input type="text" name="name" />` field.

Restart your Express server, and submit the form. You should see the completion message displayed in the browser. Additionally, the form data is output in the Node console like in Figure 7-9.

```
Name: Jon Raasch,Test message
Email: jr@localhost
Message: undefined
POST /contact 200 2ms - 24
```

Figure 7-9 The form data is being output in the console.

Sending Feedback to the Template

The form is already outputting a basic success message, but that still leaves a lot of room for improvement. If there are any errors with the form, those should be output to the user, to provide an opportunity to resubmit the form.

Validation

The form markup already includes HTML5 form validation hooks, such as the email field and `required` attribute. Assuming the user has an HTML5 compliant browser, these fields will be validated before the form is ever posted to your Express server.

However, it's important to remember that some malformed data might get through despite these checks. For example, the validation won't work if the user has an older browser, or in the unlikely event that a hacker tries to post directly into the form. Fortunately, you can build additional validation into the backend to sanitize the form data, and send meaningful responses to the user. First, build validation to make sure all the required fields are filled in:

```
// validate required fields
function isFilled(field) {
  return field !== undefined && field !== '';
}

exports.contactPostHandler = function(req, res) {
  var response = 'Form posted successfully',
      required = [ 'name', 'email', 'message' ],
      missing = [];

  // check required fields
  missing = required.filter(function(prop) {
    return !isFilled(req.body[prop]);
  });

  if ( missing.length ) {
    response = 'Please fill out all required fields (' + missing.join(',
') +
')';
  }

  // send the success or error message
  res.send( response );
};
```

There are a couple things going on here:

- The script defines an `isFilled()` function, which checks to make sure the fields aren't empty or undefined. It's important to do both checks, in case someone posts directly into the form.

- The items in the `required` array are filtered against the `isFilled()` test. If any are missing, an appropriate error message is created.

- If errors exist, the error is printed to the screen, otherwise the success message is printed.

This is a pretty basic form, so the only other thing you have to validate is the email address. You can do so using a simple email regex:

```
// validate required fields
function isFilled(field) {
  return field !== undefined && field !== '';
}

// validate email address
var emailRegex = /^(([^<>()[\]\\.,;:\s@\"]+(\.[^<>()[\]\\.,;:\s@\"]+)*)|
(\".+\"))@((\[[0-9]{1,3}\.[0-9]{1,3}\.[0-9]{1,3}\.[0-9]{1,3}\])|
(([a-zA-Z\-0-9]+\.)+[a-zA-Z]{2,}))$/;

function isValidEmail(email) {
  return emailRegex.test(email);
}

exports.contactPostHandler = function(req, res) {
  var response = 'Form posted successfully',
      required = [ 'name', 'email', 'message' ],
      missing = [];

  // check required fields
  missing = required.filter(function(prop) {
    return !isFilled(req.body[prop]);
  });

  if ( missing.length ) {
    response = 'Please fill out all required fields (' + missing.join(',
') +
')';
  }

  // check email
  else if ( !isValidEmail( req.body.email ) ) {
    response = 'Please enter a valid email address';
  }

  // send the success or error message
  res.send( response );
};
```

The email test is fairly straightforward. Look at the bolded parts of the script to see an `isValidEmail` function, which uses a basic regular expression to validate the email address.

The validation for this form is pretty simple. But if you're working on a more intense form, consider using the Node Validator module: `https://github.com/chriso/node-validator`.

Rendering Feedback in the Template

So far the script just prints a basic error or success message when the form is submitted. But it would be much better to output that feedback in the template. Not only will it look better, but it will also give the user the opportunity to correct any issues with the form. Open up `contact.html` in the `./views` directory, and make the following changes:

```
<h1><%=title %></h1>

<% // error message
if (typeof success != 'undefined' && !success) { %>
<p style="color: red"><%=description %></p>
<% }

else { %>
<p><%=description %></p>
<% } %>

<% // only output the form if not posted, or unsuccessful
if (typeof success == 'undefined' || !success) { %>

<form method="post">
  <div class="form-item">
    <label for="name">Name:</label>
    <input type="text" name="name" id="name" required <%= typeof name !=
'undefined' ? 'value="' + name + '"' : '' %>/>
  </div>

  <div class="form-item">
    <label for="email">Email:</label>
    <input type="email" name="email" id="email" required
<%= typeof email != 'undefined' ? 'value="' + email + '"' : '' %>/>
  </div>

  <div class="form-item">
    <label for="message">Message:</label>
    <textarea name="message" id="message" required><%= typeof message !=
'undefined' ? message : '' %></textarea>
  </div>

  <div class="form-item">
    <input type="submit" value="Send" />
  </div>
</form>

<% } %>
```

Here a few basic changes, which are highlighted in bold, have been made to the template:

- Error styling has been added if the form is posted unsuccessfully.

- The form is set to only render when the posting is unsuccessful (or hasn't been posted at all).

- The value for each field is being added if it exists. That way the user won't lose anything he or she has entered into the form when there is an error.

The changes here are all straightforward, but pay attention to the `typeof` checks. Underscore templates throw errors if you try to reference a variable that doesn't exist, so it's important to check for undefined variables.

Passing New Variables to the Template

Finally, modify the view controller to pass the appropriate variables to the template when the form is submitted:

```
// validate required fields
function isFilled(field) {
  return field !== undefined && field !== '';
}

// validate email address
var emailRegex = /^(([^<>()[\]\\.,;:\s@\"]+(\.[^<>()[\]\\.,;:\s@\"]+)*)|
(\".+\"))@((\[[0-9]{1,3}\.[0-9]{1,3}\.[0-9]{1,3}\.[0-9]{1,3}\])|
(([a-zA-Z\-0-9]+\.)+[a-zA-Z]{2,}))$/;

function isValidEmail(email) {
  return emailRegex.test(email);
}

exports.contactPostHandler = function(req, res) {
  var response = 'Thank you for contacting us, we will get
back to you as soon as possible',
      required = [ 'name', 'email', 'message' ],
      missing = [],
      success = false;

  // check required fields
  missing = required.filter(function(prop) {
    return !isFilled(req.body[prop]);
  });

  if ( missing.length ) {
    response = 'Please fill out all required fields (' + missing.join(',
') + ')';
  }
```

```
      // check email
      else if ( !isValidEmail( req.body.email ) ) {
        response = 'Please enter a valid email address';
      }

      else {
        success = true;
      }

      // build the template variables
      var templateVars = {
        description: response,
        success: success
      };

      // error output
      if ( !success ) {
        console.log( response );

        templateVars.title = 'Contact Us';
        templateVars.name = req.body.name;
        templateVars.email = req.body.email;
        templateVars.message = req.body.message;
      }

      // else success output
      else {
        templateVars.title = 'Form posted successfully';
      }

      // render the view
      res.render('contact', templateVars);
    };
```

The changes in the script are highlighted in bold:

- A success flag has been added—it's initially false, then set to true if there are no errors. This controls the styling of the message in the template.

- The script begins building the universal template variables for all cases.

- On error, the script adds extra template variables including posted field values, so that they can be passed back into the form.

- On success, it adds a different `title` for the success page (the `description` variable has already been set with the `response` variable).

- The view is rendered with the new template variables.

As you can see in Figure 7-10, the contact form is now being rerendered with the form error.

The error message here is pretty basic. But if you want to, you can build in inline validation messages, or any other kind of feedback your form needs.

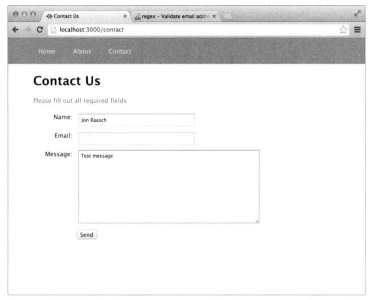

Figure 7-10 The form displays an error message when the user tries to submit it without an email address.

Sending an Email

Finally, you're going to want to do something with the data that's submitted to this contact form. You could simply log it to a file on the server, and check that every so often. But it's a better idea to send it to yourself in an email—after all, this is a *contact* form.

There are a few modules out there for sending emails from a Node server, but the easiest to use is EmailJS. First, install EmailJS with NPM:

```
npm install emailjs
```

Now you can use the module to send the contact form data to your email address.

Connecting to an SMTP Server

The EmailJS module doesn't create its own SMTP server. Instead, you need to connect to an existing one, like Gmail. First include the module and then connect to your SMTP server (all of the code in this section should be in the success portion of your form handler):

```
// connect to your smtp server
var emailjs = require('emailjs');
var server = emailjs.server.connect({
  user: 'username',
  password: 'password',
  host: 'smtp.gmail.com',
  ssl: true
});
```

Here EmailJS connects securely to the SMTP server you specify. Make sure to fill in your username and password, as well as the host if you want to use something other than Gmail.

> You can also build your own SMTP server in Node. Check out the SimpleSMTP module: `https://github.com/andris9/simplesmtp`.

Building the Email Message

Next, build a message using the form data:

```
// build the email body with a datestamp
var emailBody = 'From: ' + req.body.name + ' <' + req.body.email + '>' +
  "\n";
emailBody += 'Message: ' + req.body.message + "\n\n";
emailBody += 'Sent automatically from Node server on ' + Date();
```

Here, the script builds the body of the email using the name, email, and message that are entered into the form. It also adds a datestamp. I kept this example simple, but feel free to use a template for the email message if you'd prefer.

Sending the Email

Finally, send the email using EmailJS:

```
// send the email to the server admin
server.send({
    from:    'Node Server <no-reply@localhost>',
    to:      'Server Admin <admin@localhost>',
    subject: 'Contact form submission',
    text: emailBody
}, function(err, message) {
    console.log(err || message);
});
```

Here, the script sends the email you built to the server administrator. Make sure to change the *to* and *from* addresses.

Gmail prevents you from spoofing another email address, so you can't set the *from* address to the email address entered into the form. But if you're using another SMTP server, you might consider sending it from the user's email address, so you can respond directly to them.

> For more information about EmailJS, visit `https://github.com/eleith/emailjs`. Alternatively, if you need more robust email support, check out Node Email Templates: `https://github.com/niftylettuce/node-email-templates`.

Wrapping Up

Finally, on the off-chance the email fails, it's a good idea to relay that to the user. To do so, you can print a basic error message in the EmailJS callback. However, since the callback is asynchronous, it won't actually display to the user because the success message will have already printed on the screen. Thus, the script has to be reworked a bit:

```
// validate required fields
function isFilled(field) {
  return field !== undefined && field !== '';
}

// validate email address
var emailRegex = /^(([^<>()[\]\\.,;:\s@\"]+(\.[^<>()
[\]\\.,;:\s@\"]+)*)|(\".+\"))@((\[[0-9]{1,3}\.[0-9]{1,3}\.[0-9]{1,3}\.
[0-9]{1,3}\])|(([a-zA-Z\-0-9]+\.)+[a-zA-Z]{2,}))$/;

function isValidEmail(email) {
  return emailRegex.test(email);
}

exports.contactPostHandler = function(req, res) {
  var response = 'Thank you for contacting us, we will get back to you as
soon as possible',
      required = [ 'name', 'email', 'message' ],
      missing = [],
      success = false;

  // check required fields
  missing = required.filter(function(prop) {
    return !isFilled(req.body[prop]);
  });

  if ( missing.length ) {
    response = 'Please fill out all required fields (' + missing.join(',
') + ')';
  }

  // check email
  else if ( !isValidEmail( req.body.email ) ) {
    response = 'Please enter a valid email address';
  }

  else {
    success = true;
  }

  // build the template variables
  var templateVars = {
    description: response,
    success: success
  };

  // error output
```

```
    if ( !success ) {
      console.log( response );

      templateVars.title = 'Contact Us';
      templateVars.name = req.body.name;
      templateVars.email = req.body.email;
      templateVars.message = req.body.message;

      // render the template
      res.render('contact', templateVars);
    }

    // else success output
    else {
      // connect to your smtp server
      var emailjs = require('emailjs');
      var server = emailjs.server.connect({
        user: 'username',
        password: 'password',
        host: 'smtp.gmail.com',
        ssl: true
      });

      // build the email body with a datestamp
      var emailBody = 'From: ' + req.body.name + ' <' + req.body.email + '>'
+
        "\n";
      emailBody += 'Message: ' + req.body.message + "\n\n";
      emailBody += 'Sent automatically from Node server on ' + Date();

      // send the email to the server admin
      server.send({
        from:     'Node Server <no-reply@localhost>',
        to:       'Server Admin <admin@localhost>',
        subject: 'Contact form submission',
        text: emailBody
      }, function(err, message) {
        console.log(err || message);

        // if smtp error
        if ( err ) {
          res.send('Sorry, there was an error sending your message, please
try again later');
        }
        // otherwise show success message
        else {
          templateVars.title = 'Message sent successfully'

          // render the template
          res.render('contact', templateVars);
        }
      });
    }
};
```

Here a few basic changes have been made:

- The render function is pulled into the error handler to render any validation errors.

- If the SMTP emailer fails, a basic error is simply printed to the screen. It's a good idea not to rerender the form in this case, since the user will most likely not be able to use it.

- If the SMTP emailer is successful, the success message is displayed from within the callback. This way the success message won't overwrite the error message.

Summary

In this chapter you learned the basics of the Express framework. You learned how to install Express and start an Express server. You then learned how to set up routes to define the paths for your app.

Next you set up controllers on those routes to render views using Underscore templates. Then, you learned how to create a POST route to handle form data from your app. You validated the data, and displayed error messages when they occurred. On successful form submission, the server sent an email to the admin. To do so, it used the EmailJS module to connect to an external SMTP server.

You now have a pretty firm foundation in Node development. In the next chapter, you learn how to use a NoSQL database called MongoDB. This will support the data component of your Node app. Then in Chapter 9 you learn how to create even faster I/O communication with the client-side using WebSockets, and tie everything together to build a real-time app.

Additional Resources

Express Documentation: `http://expressjs.com/api.html`

Tutorials

Getting Started with Express: `http://howtonode.org/getting-started-with-express`

Express.js Tutorial: `http://www.hacksparrow.com/express-js-tutorial.html`

Template Resources

uinexpress Documentation: `https://github.com/haraldrudell/uinexpress`

Underscore Template Documentation: `http://underscorejs.org/#template`

Jade Documentation: `https://github.com/visionmedia/jade#readme`

Form Resources

Node Form Validation Module: `https://github.com/chriso/node-validator`

Email Resources

EmailJS Documentation: `https://github.com/eleith/emailjs`

Node Email Templates: `https://github.com/niftylettuce/node-email-templates`

Node SMTP Server: `https://github.com/andris9/simplesmtp`

Other Notable Frameworks

Geddy: `http://geddyjs.org/`

Ember: `http://emberjs.com/`

Flatiron: `http://flatironjs.org/`

Chapter 8

MongoDB

In this chapter, you first discover the advantages of NoSQL databases and why so many new projects are using them. Then you find out how to install MongoDB, along with a native MongoDB driver for Node.

Next you learn how to use the MongoDB driver to create a database. You also find out how to read entries from the database using MongoDB's robust query options, such as regular expressions and operators. Furthermore, you learn how to update and delete database entries, completing the CRUD system.

After determining how to use the native MongoDB driver, you learn about Mongoose, an object modeling package for Node and MongoDB. Mongoose provides the familiar ability to save data in models and then sync these models to a MongoDB server, much like you do with Backbone in Chapter 3. Finally, you find out about other database modules for Node, such as the MySQL module and another NoSQL database called Redis.

What's So Good About NoSQL?

For a good 30 years, the dominant model for database design has been relational databases such as MySQL. However, a recent trend is moving away from conventional relational database models. This trend is known as *NoSQL* (or Not Only SQL). Non-relational, NoSQL databases are an attractive alternative for a variety of reasons, mainly scalability and simplicity. Considering that Node.js projects often share the same goals, it makes sense that many use a NoSQL database.

Scalability

One of the main reasons to use a NoSQL database like MongoDB is its built-in sharding capabilities. Sharding allows you to distribute a single database across a cluster of machines, which means you can *scale out* (distribute the load) rather than *scale up* (purchase a larger server). Scaling horizontally complements the cloud model, since your NoSQL cloud can ramp up resources as needed to handle load, as opposed to having one really powerful server that sits unused for long periods of time.

Beyond load, sharding also helps the server handle big data. The volume of data stored in databases is increasing exponentially, to the point that some databases are too large for an individual server. With these databases, distribution across a cluster becomes a necessity. Traditional relational databases on the other hand were built before we ever had the need to work with large-scale data. It's not impossible to distribute a database like MySQL, but it is significantly more challenging than distributing a database that was designed to be sharded.

Simplicity

Part of the reason NoSQL databases scale so well is that they were built from the ground up for simplicity. Besides sharding, this simplicity also brings additional advantages. Mainly, NoSQL databases are a lot easier to manage thanks to administration tools that solve many of the admin problems we face today. These tools allow many NoSQL implementations to forgo the army of database administrators (DBAs) that is commonly associated with relational databases. Of course, this simplicity comes at the price of functionality. But if you need relatively simple features in your database software, non-relational databases can't be beat.

Getting Started with MongoDB

MongoDB is a NoSQL database that is very popular for Node development. Fortunately, getting started with MongoDB is relatively easy. In this section you learn how to install MongoDB along with a couple drivers for Node. Then you run the database server and create your first database.

Installing MongoDB

Before you can use MongoDB, you have to install it. Unlike other Node modules, the MongoDB module is only a driver. That means you'll have to install MongoDB on your system before you use it.

Mac Installation

The easiest way to install MongoDB on Mac is by using a package manager like MacPorts or Homebrew. If you're using MacPorts (`http://www.macports.org/install.php`), simply type the following command:

```
sudo port install mongodb
```

Likewise, if you're using Homebrew (`http://mxcl.github.com/homebrew`), type the following:

```
sudo brew install mongodb
```

Alternatively, you can install MongoDB yourself. First, download the tarball from `http://downloads.mongodb.org/osx/mongodb-osx-x86_64-2.2.2.tgz` and extract the contents. Then set up the `PATH` variable to wherever you extracted the MongoDB core—that way, you can use its commands easily. Add the MongoDB directory to the `PATH` declaration in `~/.bash_profile`.

Regardless of how you install MongoDB on Mac, you'll also need to set up the data directory:

```
sudo mkdir -p /data/db
sudo chown `id -u` /data/db
```

These commands set up the directory with the appropriate permissions.

There's a nice GUI tool for Mac called MongoHub, which you can download from `http://mongohub.todayclose.com`. This tool, shown in Figure 8-1, helps you manage the database.

MongoHub is great for managing complex aspects of a database, when you don't want to bother to learn how to do so with the API. It also provides a monitor you can use to view activity on a database in real time.

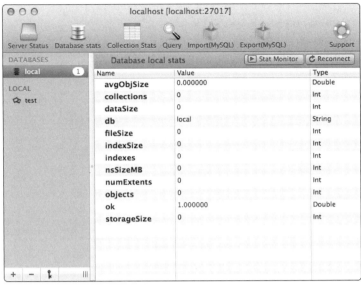

Figure 8-1 The MongoHub GUI tool for Mac.

Ubuntu Installation

First, to authenticate the `apt-get` package, install the public GPG key from the MongoDB creators:

```
sudo apt-key adv --keyserver keyserver.ubuntu.com --recv 7F0CEB10
```

Next create a file called `/etc/apt/sources.list.d/10gen.list`, and add the following text:

```
deb http://downloads-distro.mongodb.org/repo/ubuntu-upstart dist 10gen
```

Then back in the terminal, reload your repository and install the latest stable build of MongoDB:

```
sudo apt-get update
sudo apt-get install mongodb-10gen
```

Windows Installation

First, download the latest stable build from `http://www.mongodb.org/downloads`. Make sure to get the appropriate version for your Windows install (64-bit or 32-bit). Extract the contents of that file and move it to `C:\mongodb`. You can move it from the Window's Command Prompt:

```
cd \
move C:\mongodb-win32-* C:\mongodb
```

Finally, create the data directory for MongoDB:

```
md data
md data\db
```

> **MongoDB has installation instructions for other operating systems in its docs. Visit** `http://docs.mongodb.org/manual/installation` **for information.**

Running MongoDB

After installing MongoDB, you're ready to run it. You can do so using the following command in Mac:

```
mongod
```

Or in Ubuntu, use

```
sudo service mongodb start
```

Or in Windows, run the `.exe` file from the Command Prompt:

```
C:\mongodb\bin\mongod.exe
```

If you see some output in the terminal and the command is still running, you'll know that everything is working. See Figure 8-2.

```
jr:node jr$ sudo mkdir /data
jr:node jr$ sudo mkdir /data/db
jr:node jr$ sudo mongod
mongod --help for help and startup options
Thu Dec 20 11:00:01 [initandlisten] MongoDB starting : pid=55346 port=27017 dbpath=/data/db/ 64-bit host=jr.
local
Thu Dec 20 11:00:01 [initandlisten]
Thu Dec 20 11:00:01 [initandlisten] ** WARNING: soft rlimits too low. Number of files is 256, should be at l
east 1000
Thu Dec 20 11:00:01 [initandlisten] db version v2.2.2, pdfile version 4.5
Thu Dec 20 11:00:01 [initandlisten] git version: nogitversion
Thu Dec 20 11:00:01 [initandlisten] build info: Darwin teneight-slave.macports.org 12.2.0 Darwin Kernel Vers
ion 12.2.0: Sat Aug 25 00:48:52 PDT 2012; root:xnu-2050.18.24~1/RELEASE_X86_64 x86_64 BOOST_LIB_VERSION=1_49
Thu Dec 20 11:00:01 [initandlisten] options: {}
Thu Dec 20 11:00:01 [initandlisten] journal dir=/data/db/journal
Thu Dec 20 11:00:01 [initandlisten] recover : no journal files present, no recovery needed
Thu Dec 20 11:00:01 [websvr] admin web console waiting for connections on port 28017
Thu Dec 20 11:00:01 [initandlisten] waiting for connections on port 27017
```

Figure 8-2 If your terminal looks like this, MongoDB is running.

> **If you're having trouble getting the** `mongod` **command to work, make sure MongoDB has been added to your** `PATH` **variable. Package managers will handle that automatically, but you must set it up manually if you installed MongoDB yourself.**

Installing MongoDB Modules

Once MongoDB is running on your system, you need to install a module to communicate with the database. In this chapter, you learn how to use two different modules:

▨ **The MongoDB Native Node.js Driver:** Basic MongoDB support in JavaScript

▨ **Mongoose:** An object modeling tool that provides object-relational mapping (ORM)

But for now, just install the native driver using NPM:

```
npm install mongodb
```

Creating a Database

Once MongoDB is running and the Node.js driver is installed, you're ready to create a database. First, require the MongoDB module in Node:

```
var mongodb = require('mongodb');
```

Then create a new database:

```
var dbServer = new mongodb.Server('localhost', 27017, {auto_reconnect:
  true}),
var db = new mongodb.Db('mydb', dbServer, {w: 1});
```

A few things are going on here:

1. `new mongodb.Server('localhost', 27017, {auto_reconnect: true})`, connects to the MongoDB server. It uses the default host (`localhost`) and default port (`27017`). `auto_reconnect` allows it to reconnect automatically if the connection is interrupted.

2. `new mondodb.Db()` creates a new database, in this case called `mydb`. If this database already exists, it simply references the existing database.

3. The third argument of `mongodb.Db()`, `{w: 1}`, sets the write concern, indicating that this is the primary `mongod` instance. This works just fine so long as you don't have more than one instance of MongoDB on your server. But if you'd like to learn more about other options, visit `http://docs.mongodb.org/manual/core/write-operations/#write-concern`.

> **If you need to authenticate your database, you can do so using** `db.authenticate(user, password, function() { /* callback */ }).`

CRUD with MongoDB

In this section, you find out how to use CRUD in MongoDB to *create*, *read*, *update*, and *delete* documents. These four operations represent the basic needs of any persistent storage system, such as a database.

So far you've included the MongoDB module, and created a new database. However, if you look at the server on MongoHub or another GUI tool, you'll see that the database doesn't exist. That's because you still need to add collections before it will be created.

MongoDB is a document-based database, so entries are called *documents*.

Creating Collections

Whereas other databases, such as MySQL, represent data using tables, MongoDB uses collections, which are represented with simple JSON objects. As a JavaScript developer, that should be music to your ears. But before adding a collection, you first need to connect to the database, using the db variable defined earlier:

```
db.open( function(err, conn) {

});
```

Here you can see a familiar pattern in Node: an asynchronous callback, with an error object as the first argument.

Adding a Collection

Next, in this callback, add a collection to the database:

```
db.open( function(err, conn) {
  // add a collection to the db
  db.collection('myCollection', function(err, collection) {
    // insert a document into the collection
    collection.insert({
      a: 'my item'
    }, function(err, result) {
      // log the result
      console.log(result);

      // close the connection
      db.close();
    });
  });
});
```

Here's what's going on:

1. db.collection() creates a new collection called myCollection.

2. In the next callback, a document is added to the collection using collection.insert(). This uses the collection object that is passed into the callback. As you can see, the structure of the insert is a simple JSON object, {a: 'my-item'}.

3. Finally, in the callback for the insert, the result is logged to the console, and the database connection is closed with db.close(). Don't forget to close the MongoDB connection when you finish using it.

Now run the script in Node. Figure 8-3 shows the database and collection created.

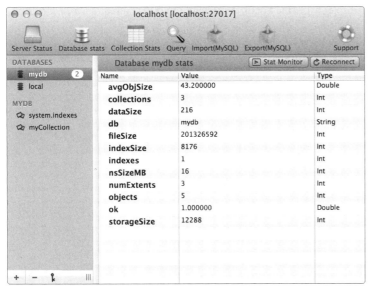

Figure 8-3 MongoHub shows the new database and collection.

> To make the example shorter, I avoided catching any of the errors. But you should use `console.log()` to find errors if you're having problems with this script.

The Unique Identifier

When you run this script, you may notice in the Node console that the database entry doesn't wind up as simple as `{a: 'my item'}` (see Figure 8-4). That's because MongoDB added an identifier, `_id`, to the document. MongoDB needs these unique identifiers for everything stored in the database, so by default, it will add them automatically whenever you create new documents.

```
jr:node jr$ node db.js
[ { a: 'my item', _id: 50dc7a36435e8a0000000001 } ]
```

Figure 8-4 The result of the database entry in the console.

But, as you can see, the identifiers are pretty long and unwieldy. Although they work well for MongoDB internally, you usually want to avoid using them to reference the documents in your database. Just as with other databases, it's a good idea to add your own key when you need to reference an identifier— for instance, `{id: 1}`.

Reading Data

After adding documents to the database, you can read them using `find()`. This API provides a number of useful selection capabilities, allowing you to select specific documents, leverage query selectors, and sort the data that is returned.

But before using the `find()` API, create a new collection to work with:

```
// open database connection
db.open( function(err, conn) {
  // select the collection
  db.collection('myNewCollection', function(err, collection) {
    // cache a count variable
    var count = 0;

    // insert numbers into the collection
    for ( var i = 0; i < 5; i++ ) {
      collection.insert({
        num: i
      }, function(err, result) {
        // log the result
        console.log(result);

        // increment the count value
        count++;

        // if the count is high enough, close the connection
        if ( count > 4 ) {
          db.close();
        }
      });
    }
  });
});
```

This script creates a new collection called `myNewCollection` and adds five new documents to it in a loop.

Here you can see an important pattern in Node development. Even though the script uses a for loop with an increment, it can't use that same increment to determine when to close the database connection. That's because all of the Node calls are asynchronous. As you may have noticed in the output, the different `collection.insert()` statements fired in a fairly random order:

```
[ { num: 0, _id: 50dc93c946f8df0000000001 } ]
[ { num: 4, _id: 50dc93c946f8df0000000005 } ]
[ { num: 3, _id: 50dc93c946f8df0000000004 } ]
[ { num: 2, _id: 50dc93c946f8df0000000003 } ]
[ { num: 1, _id: 50dc93c946f8df0000000002 } ]
```

However, it's still important to close the database connection at the right time. If you use the increment from the for loop, it will most likely close the connection too early (which will, in turn, reopen the connection in the next `insert()`, and then leave it open). To get around this issue, the script uses a separate `count` value, which is incremented as each asynchronous call completes. Once this value is high enough, you can safely close the connection.

Selecting All Entries in a Collection

Now that a collection has been created, you can select all the data in the database:

```
db.open( function(err, conn) {
  // select the collection
  db.collection('myNewCollection', function(err, collection) {
    // select all the documents in the collection
    collection.find().toArray(function(err, result) {
      // log the data
      console.log(result);

      // close the connection
      db.close();
    });
  });
});
```

This script selects the collection that was created earlier and then uses `collection.find()` to select all the documents in the collection. As you can see, all the entries are output to the console:

```
[ { num: 0, _id: 50dc93c946f8df0000000001 },
  { num: 1, _id: 50dc93c946f8df0000000002 },
  { num: 2, _id: 50dc93c946f8df0000000003 },
  { num: 3, _id: 50dc93c946f8df0000000004 },
  { num: 4, _id: 50dc93c946f8df0000000005 } ]
```

You may have noticed that the documents in this collection are now in the correct order, although you just saw them being inserted out of order. Even though the asynchronous insertion calls completed at different times, MongoDB's IDs are still in the correct order.

Selecting Specific Entries

Since you didn't pass any arguments into `collection.find()`, it selected all the documents in the database. But you can also select specific documents. For example:

```
db.collection('myNewCollection', function(err, collection) {
  // select all documents where num is 2
  collection.find({num: 2}).toArray(function(err, result) {
    // log the data
    console.log(result);

    // close the connection
    db.close();
  });
});
```

This script selects the document with a `num` value of 2, as seen in the output here:

```
[ { num: 2, _id: 50dc93c946f8df0000000003 } ]
```

> Because only one document has a `num` value of 2, the preceding search returned only one value. If there were more than one match, it would return an array of all the matching documents.

More Advanced Query Selectors

You can also use more advanced selectors. For example, to select all values that are greater than 1, use the `$gt` operator:

```
// select the collection
db.collection('myNewCollection', function(err, collection) {
  // select numbers greater than 1
  collection.find({num: {$gt: 1}}).toArray(function(err, result) {
    // log the data
    console.log(result);

    // close the connection
    db.close();
  });
});
```

Here the script passes in a query object, `{$gt: 1}`, for the `num` value to match against, which selects all values that are greater than 1, as shown in this output:

```
[ { num: 2, _id: 50dc93c946f8df0000000003 },
  { num: 3, _id: 50dc93c946f8df0000000004 },
  { num: 4, _id: 50dc93c946f8df0000000005 } ]
```

You can combine additional parameters in the query object. For instance, you can match all values that are greater than 1 but also less than 4:

```
db.collection('myNewCollection', function(err, collection) {
  // select numbers greater than 1 but less than 4
  collection.find({num: {$gt: 1, $lt: 4}}).toArray(function(err, result) {
    // log the data
    console.log(result);

    // close the connection
    db.close();
  });
});
```

This script adds a `$lt` operator to pull values that are also less than 4, as shown here:

```
[ { num: 2, _id: 50dc93c946f8df0000000003 },
  { num: 3, _id: 50dc93c946f8df0000000004 } ]
```

For a full list of the operators you can use in the query object, visit `http://docs.mongodb.org/manual/reference/operators`.

> You can even use regular expressions to select particular strings in MongoDB. Simply pass the regex into the selector; for example, you can select all names that start with "a" using `collection.find({name: /^a/})`.

Limiting Entries
You can also limit the number of documents the search returns:

```
db.collection('myNewCollection', function(err, collection) {
  // select all the data in the collection, limited to 3 entries
  collection.find({}, {limit: 3}).toArray(function(err, result) {
    // log the data
    console.log(result);

    // close the connection
    db.close();
  });
});
```

Here a second argument is passed to `collection.find()`, which defines additional information about the search. In this case, `{limit: 3}` limits the search to return at most three documents, as shown in this output:

```
[ { num: 0, _id: 50dc93c946f8df0000000001 },
  { num: 1, _id: 50dc93c946f8df0000000002 },
  { num: 2, _id: 50dc93c946f8df0000000003 } ]
```

> You can also use `findOne()` instead of `find()` as a shorthand to return a single document.

Sorting Entries
Additionally, you can sort the documents in the collection when selecting them.

```
db.collection('myNewCollection', function(err, collection) {
  // sort the collection in reverse order
  collection.find({}, {sort:[['num', 'desc']]}).toArray(function(err,
result) {
    // log the data
    console.log(result);

    // close the connection
    db.close();
  });
});
```

Here the script defines a sort parameter, which sorts by the num field, in descending order. This sort parameter accepts an array, which means that you can sort by multiple columns as needed. You also can combine it with limit values. You can see the result here:

```
[ { num: 4, _id: 50dc93c946f8df0000000005 },
  { num: 3, _id: 50dc93c946f8df0000000004 },
  { num: 2, _id: 50dc93c946f8df0000000003 },
  { num: 1, _id: 50dc93c946f8df0000000002 },
  { num: 0, _id: 50dc93c946f8df0000000001 } ]
```

Updating Data

So far you know how to handle the C and R of CRUD; now let's talk about the U. In this subsection you discover a variety of techniques for modifying the existing documents in your database. You learn how to select particular documents for updating, as well as how to take advantage of special update methods such as upsert and find and modify.

Updating an Entire Entry

To update a value, simply use the update() method:

```
db.collection('myNewCollection', function(err, collection) {
  // update one of the documents
  collection.update({num: 2}, {num: 10}, {safe: true}, function(err) {
    if (err) {
      console.log(err);
    }
    else {
      console.log('Successfully updated');
    }

    db.close({});
  });
});
```

As you can see, collection.update() accepts four arguments:

▪ **The criteria for the update, meaning a query for which documents to update** —In this case, it will update all entries with a num value of 2. This can also use any of the advanced query operators you learned about with find(). For instance, to update all num values less than 2, you pass {num: {$lt: 2}}.

▪ **The changes you want to make** —In this case, the num value is changed to 10.

▪ **An options object** —Here {safe: true} sets safe mode, which you should probably always use. Another useful option is {multi: true}, which allows the update to modify multiple documents.

▪ **An optional callback** —You can use this to output any error that occurs.

Upserting

You can also *upsert* values into your collection, which *updates* the document if it exists; otherwise it *inserts* a new document with the values you're updating. To use `upsert`, simply set `{upsert: true}` in the options object:

```
db.collection('myNewCollection', function(err, collection) {
  // upsert one of the documents
  collection.update({num: 8}, {num: 7}, {safe: true, upsert: true},
function(err) {
    if (err) {
      console.log(err);
    }
    else {
      console.log('Successfully updated');
    }

    db.close({});
  });
});
```

Here, even though a document matching `{num: 8}` can't be found in the collection, a new document with `{num: 7}` is inserted. Had the `{num: 8}` entry existed, MongoDB would have simply updated that document.

Setting a Particular Field

The previous examples all update the entire document, but you can also update an individual field using the `$set` modifier:

```
db.collection('myNewCollection', function(err, collection) {
  // set an individual field
  collection.update({num: 3}, {$set: {desc: 'favorite number'}}, {safe:
true}, function(err) {
    if (err) {
      console.log(err);
    }
    else {
      console.log('Successfully updated');
    }

    db.close({});
  });
});
```

Here, instead of passing an object for the second argument, the script uses a `$set` modifier. That sets the `desc` field of the document, while preserving any existing fields.

For information about other MongoDB update modifiers, visit `http://docs.mongodb.org/manual/applications/update`.

Find and Modify

Finally, you can use a special API if you want to do anything with the document you're updating. If that's the case, use `findAndModify()`, which returns the affected document in the callback. However, be careful because the API signature is slightly different; it inserts an additional argument after the first:

```
db.collection('myNewCollection', function(err, collection) {
  // find and modify
  collection.findAndModify({num: 4}, [['_id', 'asc']], {num: 25}, {safe:
true}, function(err, result) {
    if (err) {
      console.log(err);
    }

    // log the affected document
    else {
      console.log(result);
    }

    db.close({});
  });
});
```

As you can see here, `findAndModify()` accepts five arguments:

- The criteria for the search, `{num: 4}`
- The sort order (this argument doesn't exist in `update()`), `[['_id', 'asc']]`
- The change you want to make, `{num: 25}`
- An options object, `{safe: true}`
- The callback function, which also passes the result of the query, `function() { ... }`

Another caveat of using `findAndModify()` is that the callback returns the document as it stood *before* the modification. For example, in this case, `findAndModify()` returns `{num: 4}` instead of the new `{num: 25}`, which you can see in this output:

```
{ _id: 50dc93c946f8df0000000005, num: 4 }
```

Deleting Data

Lastly, you still need to know the D in CRUD before your knowledge of MongoDB is complete. This subsection teaches you how to remove documents and collections from your database.

Removing Documents

First, you can delete documents from a collection using `remove()`. `remove()` is pretty straightforward; you just pass in the criteria of the documents you want to remove, followed by a callback:

```
db.collection('myNewCollection', function(err, collection) {
  // remove a document
```

```
collection.remove({num: 1}, function(err) {
  if (err) {
    console.log(err);
  }
  else {
    console.log('Successfully removed');
  }

  db.close({});
});
});
```

If you want to do anything with the entry you're removing, use `findAndRemove()`. However, be careful—just like with `findAndModify()`, a sort argument has been added to the API:

```
db.collection('myNewCollection', function(err, collection) {
  // find and remove
  collection.findAndRemove({num: 0}, [['_id', 'asc']], function(err,
result) {
    if (err) {
      console.log(err);
    }

    // log the affected document
    else {
      console.log (result);
    }

    db.close({});
  });
});
```

This works exactly like `remove()`, except that a second argument for sort order is added. Additionally, the result of the query is passed to the callback, which allows you to output the document as it existed before deletion.

Dropping Collections

You can also delete an entire collection. To do so, use `db.dropCollection()`:

```
// open database connection
db.open( function(err, conn) {
  // drop a collection
  db.dropCollection('myNewCollection', function(err, result) {
    if (err) {
      console.log(err);
    }
    else {
      console.log(result);
    }

    db.close();
  });
});
```

This script drops the collection you've been working with. But be careful; as with all the database changes in this chapter, there's no magical undo button.

Mongoose

Mongoose is an object-modeling tool for Node that connects to MongoDB. You're already familiar with Backbone, so using Mongoose will be a piece of cake, because Mongoose models data similarly to Backbone, with models and collections. Mongoose then takes these models and maps them to a MongoDB database, saving you a lot of extra leg work.

This section teaches you how to install Mongoose and create models to store data. You then learn techniques for reading the data and how to select specific documents and fields from those documents.

Getting Started with Mongoose

Installing Mongoose is easy with NPM:

```
npm install mongoose
```

After Mongoose and its dependencies install, include it in Node:

```
var mongoose = require('mongoose');
```

Next connect to a MongoDB database:

```
mongoose.connect('localhost', 'mydb');
```

Here Mongoose will connect to the database `mydb` on `localhost`.

You may have noticed that the `connect()` call doesn't include a callback. That's because you have to set up these callbacks manually:

```
// connect to a MongoDB database
mongoose.connect('localhost', 'test');

// database connection
var db = mongoose.connection;

// error callback
db.on('error', function(msg) {
  console.log(
    'Connection Error: %s', msg
  );
});

// success callback
db.once('open', function callback () {
  // on success
  console.log('Database opened succesfully');
});
```

This script first creates a connection object and then binds two callbacks: One to fire on any connection error and another to fire once when the connection is successfully opened.

Pretty much everything you do in Mongoose will exist in the success callback. For the sake of brevity, I've omitted it from the following examples, but just assume that all of the code exists in this callback.

Creating Models

You use models to define all the documents in Mongoose. Models allow you to abstract away the database system and focus on what you really want: the data. In this section you learn how to create a schema to define the structure of a model, and then create and save models according to that structure.

Creating a Schema

The first step to creating a model is creating a schema to define the data types and structure that the model will use. For example, create a schema for different types of fruit:

```
// define the schema
var fruitSchema = mongoose.Schema({
  name: String,
  color: String,
  quantity: Number,
  ripe: Boolean
});
```

Here a schema is defined with different fields, setting a primitive data type for each.

You can also set more information along the schema by passing an object instead of a primitive, as in this example:

```
// define the schema
var fruitSchema = mongoose.Schema({
  name: {type: String, require: true, trim: true, unique: true},
  color: {type: String, require: true},
  quantity: Number,
  ripe: Boolean
});
```

Here a few extra properties are set for the schema's name field. It's now a required field that will be trimmed for any extra whitespace. Additionally, the name values must all be unique.

Creating a Model

Next, use this schema to define a model:

```
// define the model
var Fruit = mongoose.model('fruit', fruitSchema);
```

Here the model is created using the fruitSchema that was defined earlier. The first argument, 'fruit', sets the name for the model. This value corresponds to the name that will be used to save the collection, in this case fruits.

> **Pay careful attention to the API here: In** `mongoose.Schema` *Schema* **is capitalized, whereas in** `mongoose.model` *model* **isn't capitalized.**

After creating the structure, create a new instance of the model:

```
// create a new instance of the model
var apple = new Fruit({
  name: 'apple',
  color: 'red',
  quantity: 3,
  ripe: true
});
```

This snippet creates a new fruit along the schema that was defined earlier.

Saving the Model

Simply creating the model in Mongoose isn't enough—you still have to save it to MongoDB. To do so, use the `save()` method:

```
// save the model
apple.save(function (err, apple) {
  if (err) {
    console.log(err);
  }
  else {
    console.log(apple);
  }
});
```

This saves the model as a document in MongoDB. Anytime you create or modify the data in the model, simply use the `save()` method to sync those changes to the database.

Putting all the preceding code together:

```
// include the mongoose module
var mongoose = require('mongoose');

// connect to a MongoDB database
mongoose.connect('localhost', 'mydb');

// connection
var db = mongoose.connection;
db.on('error', console.error.bind(console, 'Connection error:'));
db.once('open', function callback () {
  // define the schema
  var fruitSchema = mongoose.Schema({
    name: String,
    color: String,
    quantity: Number,
```

```
      ripe: Boolean
    });

    // define the model
    var Fruit = mongoose.model('fruit', fruitSchema);

    // create a new instance of the model
    var apple = new Fruit({
      name: 'apple',
      color: 'red',
      quantity: 3,
      ripe: true
    });

    // save the model
    apple.save( function(err, apple) {
      if (err) {
        console.log(err);
      }
      else {
        console.log(apple);
      }
    });
  });
```

Just to recap what's going on here:

1. The script starts by including the Mongoose module.

2. It then creates a connection to the database with error and success callbacks.

3. In the open callback, the script defines a schema.

4. It uses the schema to define a model and creates a new instance of that model.

5. The model is saved as a MongoDB collection.

Reading Data

Reading data from a Mongoose collection is easy. But first add some more data to the collection so you have something to work with:

```
var orange = new Fruit({
  name: 'orange',
  color: 'orange',
  quantity: 5,
  ripe: true
});

var banana = new Fruit({
  name: 'banana',
  color: 'green',
  quantity: 1,
```

```
    ripe: false
});

orange.save( function(err, orange) {
  if (err) {
    console.log(err);
  }
  else {
    console.log(orange);
  }
});

banana.save( function(err, banana) {
  if (err) {
    console.log(err);
  }
  else {
    console.log(banana);
  }
});
```

Finding All Models

To read the data that has been saved to a collection, use the `find()` method on the corresponding model:

```
// define the model
var Fruit = mongoose.model('fruit', fruitSchema);

// select all the fruit
Fruit.find( function(err, fruit) {
  if (err) {
    console.log(err);
  }
  else {
    console.log(fruit);
  }
});
```

This code selects all the models in the collection, as shown in this output:

```
[ { name: 'apple',
    color: 'red',
    quantity: 3,
    ripe: true,
    _id: 50dcd5b8e890ee50000000001,
    __v: 0 },
  { name: 'orange',
    color: 'orange',
    quantity: 5,
    ripe: true,
    _id: 50dcd5b8e890ee0000000001,
    __v: 0 },
  { name: 'banana',
```

```
    color: 'green',
    quantity: 1,
    ripe: false,
    _id: 50dcd5b8e890ee0000000002,
    __v: 0 } ]
```

Finding Specific Models

You can also narrow down the models you select by passing a first argument to the `find()` method:

```
// select just the orange
Fruit.find({name: 'orange'}, function(err, fruit) {
  if (err) {
    console.log(err);
  }
  else {
    console.log(fruit);
  }
});
```

This snippet selects only those models with a `name` value of `'orange'`, as shown in this output:

```
[ { name: 'orange',
    color: 'orange',
    quantity: 5,
    ripe: true,
    _id: 50dcd5b8e890ee0000000001,
    __v: 0 } ]
```

Mongoose supports all of MongoDB's robust querying options. For example, you can select models using a regular expression:

```
// select fruits that end in 'e'
Fruit.find({name: /e$/}, function(err, fruit) {
  if (err) {
    console.log(err);
  }
  else {
    console.log(fruit);
  }
});
```

This example selects fruits that end in the letter 'e', using the regex /e$/, as shown here:

```
[ { name: 'apple',
    color: 'red',
    quantity: 3,
    ripe: true,
    _id: 50dcd5b8e890ee50000000001,
    __v: 0 },
  { name: 'orange',
    color: 'orange',
```

```
    quantity: 5,
    ripe: true,
    _id: 50dcd5b8e890ee0000000001,
    __v: 0 } ]
```

You can also use MongoDB's operators, for example:

```
// select quantities less than 4
Fruit.find({quantity: {$lt: 4}}, function(err, fruit) {
  if (err) {
    console.log(err);
  }
  else {
    console.log(fruit);
  }
});
```

This snippet selects fruits with a quantity less than 4, as you can see from this output:

```
[ { name: 'apple',
    color: 'red',
    quantity: 3,
    ripe: true,
    _id: 50dcd5b8e890ee50000000001,
    __v: 0 },
  { name: 'banana',
    color: 'green',
    quantity: 1,
    ripe: false,
    _id: 50dcd5b8e890ee0000000002,
    __v: 0 } ]
```

Accessing Fields from a Model

Once you've selected a model from the collection, drilling down into the individual fields is simple. You may have noticed that the output of the previous examples returns JSON objects. You can use the keys from these objects to get at whatever field data you need. For example:

```
// select all fruits
Fruit.find(function(err, fruits) {
  // loop through the results
  fruits.forEach(function(fruit) {
    // log the fruit's name
    console.log( fruit.name );
  }
});
```

This script loops through the results of the query, outputting the name of each fruit, like so:

```
apple
orange
banana
```

Using this, you can create any kind of output you need, for example:

```
// loop through the results
fruits.forEach(function(fruit) {
  // log info about the fruit
  console.log( 'I have ' + fruit.quantity + ' '
    + fruit.color + ' ' + fruit.name
    + ( fruit.quantity != 1 ? 's' : '' ) );
}
```

This script prints a more readable output:

```
I have 3 red apples
I have 5 orange oranges
I have 1 green banana
```

Other Database Options

If you're using Node, chances are that you'll also want to use MongoDB. But that said, MongoDB isn't for everything, and there are times when it's better to work with a relational database like MySQL. Fortunately, there's a MySQL module you can use with Node, which you can read about here: `https://github.com/felixge/node-mysql`.

Additionally, besides MongoDB, another popular NoSQL database for Node is Redis. Redis represents everything as key-value pairs and is ideal for really simple data that is updated frequently. To learn more about Redis, visit: `https://github.com/mranney/node_redis`.

Summary

In this chapter, you discovered how to create a lightning-fast, super-scalable database to match your Node deployment. You found out how to install the NoSQL database MongoDB and how to use the native MongoDB driver for Node. With that driver, you used CRUD techniques that would even make relational databases jealous. Next, you learned about the object modeling tool, Mongoose, which allows you to save data in models and then sync those models to a MongoDB. Finally, you were introduced to some MongoDB alternatives, such as the MySQL module for Node, as well as the NoSQL database Redis. In the next chapter, you combine your Node and MongoDB skills with WebSockets to build a real-time app.

Additional Resources
Documentation

MongoDB Documentation: `http://docs.mongodb.org/manual`

MongoDB Native NodeJS Driver Documentation: `https://github.com/mongodb/node-mongodb-native`

Mongoose Documentation: `http://mongoosejs.com/docs/guide.html`

GUI Tools

MongoHub (Mac OS X): `http://mongohub.todayclose.com`

UMongo (Linux, Windows & Mac): `http://edgytech.com/umongo`

Other Tools: `http://www.mongodb.org/display/DOCS/Admin+UIs`

Books

MongoDB: The Definitive Guide by Kristina Chodorow, published by O'Reilly Media, Inc. (2010): `http://bit.ly/mongodb-definitive-guide`

MongoDB In Action by Kyle Banker, published by Manning Publications (2011): `http://bit.ly/mongodb-in-action-book`

General NoSQL Info

NoSQL Databases: `http://nosql-database.org`

NoSQL Distilled (Book): `http://bit.ly/nosql-distilled`

Part IV

Pushing the Limits

Chapter 9

Going Real-Time with WebSockets

The main reason for using Node is real-time web apps, primarily because Node handles large amounts of I/O gracefully. But it doesn't matter how well your server handles I/O if messages can't be relayed to and from the client in real-time. That's where WebSockets come in—to create an open connection between the server and client, where messages can be streamed in both directions.

In this chapter, you learn why the WebSockets protocol was created and about the traditional approaches it replaces. You then dive right in and create a simple WebSockets app. You use Socket.IO both to create the socket server on Node and to connect to this server from the browser Next, you use Socket.IO to create a real-time chat room app. You find out how to relay messages to and from the server and how to communicate this information to the user. Then you add structure to this app with Backbone.js, adding in support for multiple usernames and timestamps in the chat room. Finally, you persist the data in the app with MongoDB.

This chapter ties together all of the concepts in Part III of this book: Node.js, the Express framework and MongoDB. By the end of the chapter, you'll be comfortable creating your own real-time apps in Node.

How WebSockets Work

To understand how WebSockets work, you first need to understand the conventional approach they were designed to replace. WebSockets are a solution to a long history of polling approaches with inadequate responses for real-time data.

Problems with Polling

Say that you're building the front end for a stock ticker web application. When the user hits the page, you first pull in the stock prices using an Ajax request. You then poll the server, say every five seconds, to see if a price change has occurred. However, rather than you having to check the server at regular intervals, wouldn't it be nicer if the server could let you know whenever a change occurs? That's essentially how WebSockets work: They create a two-way communication channel between the server and the client.

A Balancing Act

Without WebSockets, the polling approach forces developers to balance two problems:

- If you don't poll the server often enough, there can be a delay between when the change occurs and when that change is actually relayed to the user. For example, if a stock price changes before the five seconds are up, the user will have to wait for the next tic of the interval before seeing that change.

- On the other hand, if you poll the server too often, it produces unnecessary load for both the server and the client. If nothing has changed in the past five seconds, why slow down the browser with an extra Ajax request? Furthermore, why slow down the server to process the meaningless request?

The worst part is that these two problems feed off each other. Data isn't updating quickly enough, so you refresh more often, which causes unnecessary requests, so you refresh less often (and then you're back to where you started). As you can see, the issue can be tough to balance. Additionally, even if your server can handle the load, you're still going to run into HTTP latency issues. For a real-time solution, you could set the polling interval to something like 100 ms, but chances are it will take at least 200 ms for the complete round trip of the packets over HTTP.

Enter Long Polling

To tackle the problems with basic polling methods, long polling techniques (often referred as Comet applications) were created. One typical approach to long polling entails querying the server on a set interval, but unlike traditional polling approaches, the connection is kept open as the server sends a response only if there is new data. Long polling cuts down on unnecessary load but still doesn't address the fundamental latency issues with HTTP requests. Another major drawback to Comet applications is that they often violate the HTTP 1.1 spec, which states that a client should not maintain more than two simultaneous connections with the server (http://www.w3.org/Protocols/rfc2616/rfc2616-sec8.html#sec8.1.4).

> Long polling relies on iframe and MIME hacks, which should be reason enough to avoid it.

The WebSockets Solution

The WebSockets protocol provides an elegant solution for the polling dilemma. WebSockets create an open connection between the server and client, so the server can send content to the browser without being solicited by the browser requesting it. This open connection allows content to stream freely in both directions, much faster than it can over traditional HTTP connections.

Browser Support

Although you're probably chomping at the bit to get started with WebSockets, keep in mind that it's still a relatively new technology. And as such, browser support can be an issue. Fortunately, at the time of this writing, WebSockets are fully supported by all desktop browsers. However, Microsoft IE9 and earlier don't support sockets. Mobile support is also spotty. Although WebSockets are fully supported in most mobile browsers, such as iOS Safari, they aren't supported in Android Browser or Opera Mini. See the support table in Figure 9-1.

Unfortunately, if you want to support older versions of IE and any version of Android Browser, you'll need to use a mixed approach for polling. But don't get discouraged, in the next section, you learn about a sockets API that provides very robust fallbacks for all the browsers you want to support.

▶ Show options ▮ = Supported ▮ = Not supported ▮ = Partially supported ▮ = Support unknown

Web Sockets - Working Draft

Bidirectional communication technology for web apps

*Usage stats:	Global
Support:	67.25%
Partial support:	3.65%
Total:	70.9%

Show all versions	IE	Firefox	Chrome	Safari	Opera	iOS Safari	Opera Mini	Android Browser	Blackberry Browser
								2.1	
								2.2	
						3.2		2.3	
						4.0-4.1		3.0	
	8.0					4.2-4.3		4.0	
	9.0	20.0	26.0	5.1		5.0-5.1		4.1	7.0
Current	10.0	21.0	27.0	6.0	12.1	6.0-6.1	5.0-7.0	4.2	10.0
Near future	11.0	22.0	28.0		15.0				
Farther future		23.0	29.0						

Notes   Known issues (0)   Resources (6)   Feedback   Edit on GitHub

Partial support refers to the websockets implementation using an older version of the protocol and/or the implementation being disabled by default (due to security issues with the older protocol).

From caniuse.com

Figure 9-1 WebSockets support table.

Getting Started with Socket.IO

Socket.IO is a JavaScript library for the server and the client that makes WebSocket communication a piece of cake. The API provides useful methods for sending and receiving data using WebSockets. Best of all, Socket.IO automatically provides fallbacks for older browsers, using Adobe, Flash, Socket, and various long-polling techniques. It automatically selects the best transport method at runtime, using the appropriate protocol on the client, while also providing the appropriate API on the server. Combining these fallbacks ensures that you will have the best transport possible on just about any browser (even all the way back to IE 5.5). For more information about Socket.IO's browser support, visit `http://socket.io/#browser-support`.

> In this chapter, I'm assuming that you're using WebSockets with the Express framework and Underscore templates, as I explain in Chapter 7.

Socket.IO on the Server

In this subsection you combine Express with Socket.IO to create your first socket server. You learn how to track the number of connections to your socket, and emit messages to the client. First, install Socket.IO using NPM:

```
npm install socket.io
```

Next, make sure Express is installed for your app, and open the `app.js` file generated by Express. Scroll down to the bottom and replace the `http.createServer()` call with the following:

```
var server = http.createServer(app),
io = require('socket.io').listen(server);
```

```
server.listen(app.get('port'), function(){
  console.log("Express server listening on port " + app.get('port'));
});
```

This snippet modifies the HTTP server call so that it can be used to create the socket server.

Next, add the following lines:

```
var activeClients = 0;

// on connection
io.sockets.on('connection', function(socket) {
  activeClients++;
  io.sockets.emit('message', {clients: activeClients});

  // on disconnect
  socket.on('disconnect', function(data) {
    activeClients--;
    io.sockets.emit('message', {clients: activeClients});
  });
});
```

This is a very simple script that tracks the number of users connected to the socket server. First, an event is set up with `io.sockets.on('connection')` to track when a new user connects. When that event fires, it increments the number of `activeClients` and then emits a message using the socket connection. Likewise, another event is set up for when this particular user disconnects from the socket. A similar callback is fired, this time reducing the number of `activeClients` and emitting that data via the socket.

Socket.IO on the Client

You have now set up some very basic events to relay data about how many users are connected to the socket. But you still need to connect to the socket on the client-side and handle that data. This subsection teaches you how to set up a socket listener on the client-side to update the view in real-time.

Before handling the client-side of the socket connection, you need to create some markup for the page to set up the quick view. First, open `./routes/index.js` and make sure you have a route set up for the root of your app:

```
exports.index = function(req, res){
  res.render('index', { title: 'Socket.IO' });
};
```

Then open `./views/index.html` and add the following Underscore template:

```
<p>
Connected clients: <span id="client-count">0</span>
</p>
```

Finally, open `./views/layout.html` and add the necessary script tags right before the closing `</body>` tag:

```
<!DOCTYPE html>
<html>
<head>
  <title><%=title %></title>
  <link rel="stylesheet" href="/stylesheets/style.css" />
</head>

<body>
<%=body %>

<script src="/socket.io/socket.io.js"></script>
<script src="/javascripts/main.js"></script>
</body>
</html>
```

Now the view references two scripts: the Socket.IO core and a `main.js` file you can use for your client-side code. There's no need to add the `socket.io.js` file to your server, because the Socket.IO module handles that for you.

> Make sure to set up Express with Underscore templates as described in Chapter 7. Otherwise, simply convert the templates used in this chapter to the default Jade templates.

Now you're ready to connect to the socket from the browser. Create a file called `./public/javascripts/main.js` with the following code:

```
// connect to the socket on port 3000
var socket = new io.connect(null, {port: 3000});

// when data is received, update the count on the page
socket.on('message', function(data) {
    document.getElementById('client-count').innerHTML = data.clients;
});
```

Here the script first connects to the WebSocket using `http://localhost:3000`, since that is where the Node server is located. Once a user connects, it will fire the `io.socket.on('connection')` event on the server-side. Then a callback fires whenever data is received from the socket. The data is used to update the count on the page with the appropriate number of connected users.

Now that the WebSocket functionality for the server and client is created, you're ready to test the app. Fire up your Express server and open `http://localhost:3000`; you should see `Connected lients: 1`, as shown in Figure 9-2.

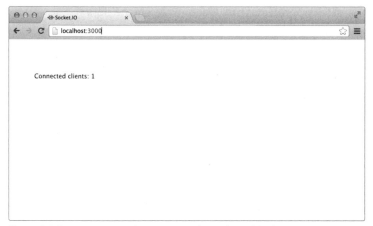

Figure 9-2 One connection is being registered over the WebSocket.

Now open up the same page in another tab, and you should see the count increase to 2. Because they are connected using WebSockets, the change will be reflected in real time on both pages. Next, close one of the pages, and you will see the count jump back down to 1. Congratulations, you've built your first WebSockets app!

Building a Real-Time Chat Room

You've gotten your feet wet with WebSockets, but so far the connection-counting app isn't all that impressive. Fortunately, it won't be too hard to take it to the next level. In this section, I explain how you can expand the app to build a chat room that people can use in real time.

Creating the Chat Room View

First, you need to create a new view for the chat room. Modify `./views/index.html` as follows:

```
<div id="chatroom"></div>

<form method="post" class="chatbox">
<input type="text" name="message" />
<input type="submit" value="Send" />
</form>

<p class="connected">
Connected users: <span id="client-count">0</span>
</p>
```

Here you can see a `<div id="chatroom"></div>`, which is used to display the messages, as well as a form to submit a new message to the chat.

Next, add some styling to `./public/stylesheets/style.less`:

```less
#chatroom {
  background: #DDD;
  width: 800px;
  height: 300px;
  margin-bottom: 10px;
  overflow-y: scroll;

  p {
    padding: 0 15px;
  }
}

.chatbox {
  input[type=text] {
    font-size: 14px;
    width: 700px;
    padding: 5px;
    float: left;
    margin-right: 10px;
  }

  input[type=submit] {
    -webkit-appearance: none;
    font-size: 14px;
    border: 1px solid rgba(0,0,0,0.3);
    background-color: tomato;
    color: papayawhip;
    text-shadow: 1px 1px 1px rgba(0,0,0,0.8);
    padding: 5px;
    width: 76px;
  }
}

.connected {
  font-size: 12px;
  color: gray;
}
```

This adds basic LESS styles.

I'm assuming you're already comfortable with LESS, but if not, check out Appendix A, or simply convert the styles to regular CSS.

The scripting becomes a little more intense from this point, so download jQuery to your `./public/javascripts/` directory. Then include it in `./views/layout.html`:

```html
<!DOCTYPE html>
<html>
```

```html
<head>
  <title><%=title %></title>
  <link rel="stylesheet" href="/stylesheets/style.css" />
</head>

<body>
<%=body %>

<script src="/javascripts/jquery-1.8.3.min.js"></script>
<script src="/socket.io/socket.io.js"></script>
<script src="/javascripts/main.js"></script>
</body>
</html>
```

Now, if you reload `http://localhost:3000`, the chat room view appears, as shown in Figure 9-3.

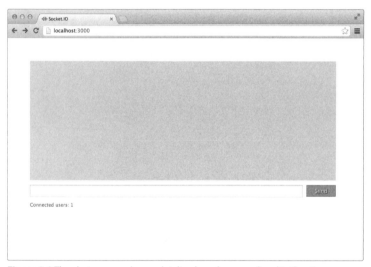

Figure 9-3 The chatroom markup and styling have been rendered in the view.

Submitting a Message to the Server

Now that the chat room view is set up, it's time to build the functionality. Starting with the client-side open `./public/javascripts/main.js`. The first step is to pass along messages that are submitted into the form:

```javascript
var socket,
    Chat = {};

Chat.init = function(setup) {
  // connect to the socket
  socket = new io.connect(setup.host);

  // when data is received, update the user count
  socket.on('message', function(data) {
    setup.dom.count.text(data.clients);
```

```
  });

  // bind submit for chat box
  setup.dom.form.submit(Chat.submit);
};

// submit a new chat to the server
Chat.submit = function(e) {
  e.preventDefault();

  // get the text of the input and empty it
  var $message = $(e.target.message),
  text = $message.val();

  $message.val('');

  // send the message over the socket
  socket.emit('newchat', {text: text});
};

$(function() {
  // initialize the chat app
  Chat.init({
    host: 'http://localhost:3000',
    dom: {
      count: $('#client-count'),
      form: $('.chatbox')
    }
  });
});
```

Here, a `Chat.init()` function is established, which accepts the socket host as well as reference to various DOM elements. The init function first connects to the socket server, then binds a handler, `Chat.submit()`, to the submit event for the chat form. `Chat.submit()` starts by preventing the form from being submitted over HTTP and then pulls the text of the message and empties the text input. Next, it sends that text to the socket, by emitting a new event called `newchat`.

Handling the Message on the Server

Next, set up the server to handle the `newchat` message. Modify `app.js` as follows:

```
var activeClients = 0;

// on connection
io.sockets.on('connection', function(socket) {
  activeClients++;
  io.sockets.emit('message', {clients: activeClients});

  // on disconnect
  socket.on('disconnect', function(data) {
    activeClients--;
    io.sockets.emit('message', {clients: activeClients});
```

```
  });

  // new chat received
  socket.on('newchat', function(data) {
    io.sockets.emit('chat', data);
  });
});
```

The changes on the server-side are pretty simple, as you can see from the bold section in the code. First, a handler is registered for the `newchat` event. That handler simply emits the data from that event back over the socket so that all the connected clients can register the new message.

Displaying the New Message on the Clients

Now, when a user submits a new message, it is passed over the socket to the server, which then passes it back over the socket to all the connected clients. You want to catch this new event and then display the message on the client-side, back in `main.js`:

```
var socket,
    Chat = {};

Chat.init = function(setup) {
  // connect to the socket
  socket = new io.connect(setup.host);

  // when data is received, update the user count
  socket.on('message', function(data) {
    setup.dom.count.text(data.clients);
  });

  // bind submit for chat box
  setup.dom.form.submit(Chat.submit);

  // handle new chats
  Chat.$chatroom = setup.dom.room;
  socket.on('chat', Chat.printChat);
};

// submit a new chat to the server
Chat.submit = function(e) {
  e.preventDefault();

  // get the text of the input and empty it
  var $message = $(e.target.message),
  text = $message.val();

  $message.val('');

  // send the message over the socket
  socket.emit('newchat', {text: text});
};
```

```
// print a new chat to the chat room
Chat.printChat = function(data) {
  var $newChat = $('<p>' + data.text + '</p>');

  $newChat.appendTo(Chat.$chatroom);

  // scroll to the bottom
  Chat.$chatroom.animate({ scrollTop: Chat.$chatroom.height() }, 100);
};

$(function() {
  // initialize the chat app
  Chat.init({
    host: 'http://localhost:3000',
    dom: {
      count: $('#client-count'),
      form: $('.chatbox'),
      room: $('#chatroom')
    }
  });
});
```

In the bold sections, this script defines a handler, `Chat.printChat`, for the `chat` event. That event simply creates a new <p> with the text and appends that to the chat room <div>. It then scrolls to the bottom of that <div> so that the newest message will always be displayed.

Now fire up `http://localhost:3000` in a couple different tabs. When you send a message from any one of them, you will see it displayed on each, as shown in Figure 9-4.

Figure 9-4 The chat app is now working, with messages being relayed to all connected users.

Adding Structure with Backbone.js

So far, the basic chat room app is working, but there's still a lot to add to it. However, before getting too deep into additional functionality, it's a good idea to work in some Backbone.

Adding Scripts to Layout.html

First, put the latest versions of Backbone.js and Underscore.js in the `./public/javascripts` directory. Then include the scripts in `layout.html`:

```html
<!DOCTYPE html>
<html>
<head>
  <title><%=title %></title>
  <link rel="stylesheet" href="/stylesheets/style.css" />
</head>

<body>
<%=body %>

<script src="/javascripts/jquery-1.8.3.min.js"></script>
<script src="/javascripts/underscore.min.js"></script>
<script src="/javascripts/backbone.min.js"></script>
<script src="/socket.io/socket.io.js"></script>
<script src="/javascripts/main.js"></script>
</body>
</html>
```

Models and Collections

When building with Backbone, always start with the models and collections. So add these to `main.js`:

```javascript
// Models & Collections

Chat.Message = Backbone.Model.extend({
  defaults: {
    text: ''
  }
});

Chat.Messages = Backbone.Collection.extend({
  model: Chat.Message
});
```

As you can see, the models are really basic for this app.

Views

Although the models are simple, the views are a little more complex. You may recall that in Chapter 3 you used Backbone to create nested views. A similar approach is covered in this chapter, because you need a main view for the chat room, which will be filled with child views for each message.

I move fairly quickly in this section, but the script almost exactly follows the example of nested views in Chapter 3. Feel free to flip back to Chapter 3 if you need a refresher for anything that's going on here.

Start with the child view, which is pretty basic. First, it builds a wrapper <p> for each message. Next, it defines a `render()` function that pulls in the text of the message and then appends that to the parent view:

```
Chat.MessageView = Backbone.View.extend({
  tagName: 'p',

  render: function() {
    // add the message text
    this.$el.text(this.model.get('text'));

    // append the new message to the parent view
    this.parentView.$el.append(this.$el);

    return this;
  }
});
```

Next, create the parent view:

```
Chat.MessagesView = Backbone.View.extend({
  el: '#chatroom',

  initialize: function() {
    // bind "this" context to the render function
    _.bindAll( this, 'render' );

    // register event handlers on the collection
    this.collection.on('change', this.render);
    this.collection.on('add', this.render);
    this.collection.on('remove', this.render);

    // render the initial state
    this.render();
  },

  render: function() {
    // empty out the wrapper
    this.$el.empty();

    // loop through the messages in the collection
    this.collection.each(function(message) {
      var messageView = new Chat.MessageView({
        model: message
      });

      // save a reference to this view within the child view
```

```
      messageView.parentView = this;

        // render it
        messageView.render();
    }, this);

    // scroll to the bottom
    this.$el.animate({ scrollTop: this.$el.height() }, 100);

    return this;
    }
});
```

There's a lot going on in this view:

1. First, it binds itself to the `<div id="chatroom">` in the markup.

2. Then the `initialize()` function binds the `render()` function to any changes in the collection. That way, when a message is added, deleted, or modified, it will be reflected in the view.

3. Next, the `render()` function starts by emptying out the `#chatroom` wrapper. Then it loops through each of the items in the collection, using the model from each to create a new instance of the child view. Finally, it scrolls to the bottom of the wrapper.

Attaching Backbone to the App

Now the models, collections, and views are set up in Backbone, but they still need to be connected to the app:

```
Chat.init = function(setup) {
  // connect to the socket
  socket = new io.connect(setup.host);

  // when data is received, update the user count
  socket.on('message', function(data) {
    setup.dom.count.text(data.clients);
  });

  // initialize the collection & views
  Chat.messages = new Chat.Messages();

  Chat.messagesView = new Chat.MessagesView({
    collection: Chat.messages
  });

  // bind submit for chat box
  setup.dom.form.submit(Chat.submit);

  // handle new chats
  Chat.$chatroom = setup.dom.room;
  socket.on('chat', Chat.addMessage);
};

// add a new message to the chat room
```

```
Chat.addMessage = function(data) {
  Chat.messages.add(data);
};
```

A couple of changes were made here:

- The `Chat.init()` function creates new instances of both the collection and parent view.
- The `Chat.printChat()` function is replaced with `Chat.addMessage()`. The new function simply adds the new message to the collection. It doesn't have to handle the rendering, because that is done automatically with Backbone.

Now, if you reload the page, you see it working as before, except now the page is built with better structure.

Putting all the code together:

```
var socket,
    Chat = {};

// Models & Collections

Chat.Message = Backbone.Model.extend({
  defaults: {
    text: ''
  }
});

Chat.Messages = Backbone.Collection.extend({
  model: Chat.Message
});

// Views

Chat.MessageView = Backbone.View.extend({
  tagName: 'p',

  render: function() {
    // add the message text
    this.$el.text(this.model.get('text'));

    // append the new message to the parent view
    this.parentView.$el.append(this.$el);

    return this;
  }
});

Chat.MessagesView = Backbone.View.extend({
  el: '#chatroom',

  initialize: function() {
    // bind "this" context to the render function
```

```javascript
    _.bindAll(this, 'render');

    // add various events for the collection
    this.collection.on('change', this.render);
    this.collection.on('add', this.render);
    this.collection.on('remove', this.render);

    // render the initial state
    this.render();
  },

  render: function() {
    // empty out the wrapper
    this.$el.empty();

    // loop through the messages in the collection
    this.collection.each(function(message) {
      var messageView = new Chat.MessageView({
        model: message
      });

      // save a reference to this view within the child view
      messageView.parentView = this;

      // render it
      messageView.render();
    }, this);

    // scroll to the bottom
    this.$el.animate({ scrollTop: this.$el.height() }, 100);

    return this;
  }
});

// init function
Chat.init = function(setup) {
  // connect to the socket
  socket = new io.connect(setup.host);

  // when data is received, update the user count
  socket.on('message', function(data) {
    setup.dom.count.text(data.clients);
  });

  // initialize the collection & views
  Chat.messages = new Chat.Messages();

  Chat.messagesView = new Chat.MessagesView({
    collection: Chat.messages
  });

  // bind submit for chat box
```

```
  setup.dom.form.submit(Chat.submit);

  // handle new chats
  Chat.$chatroom = setup.dom.room;
  socket.on('chat', Chat.addMessage);
};

// submit a new chat to the server
Chat.submit = function(e) {
  e.preventDefault();

  // get the text of the input and empty it
  var $message = $(e.target.message),
  text = $message.val();

  $message.val('');

  // send the message over the socket
  socket.emit('newchat', {text: text});
};

// add a new message to the chat room
Chat.addMessage = function(data) {
  Chat.messages.add(data);
};

$(function() {
  // initialize the chat app
  Chat.init({
    host: 'http://localhost:3000',
    dom: {
      count: $('#client-count'),
      form: $('.chatbox'),
      room: $('#chatroom')
    }
  });
});
```

Adding Users

Now that the chat room is built with more structure, it's time to add some more features. First, as it currently stands, the chat room isn't all that useful for communication, because users can't tell who is saying what. First, create a prompt for the user to enter his or her name:

```
Chat.init = function(setup) {
  // connect to the socket
  socket = new io.connect(setup.host);

  // when data is received, update the user count
  socket.on('message', function(data) {
    setup.dom.count.text(data.clients);
  });
```

```
// get username
Chat.username = Chat.getUsername();

// initialize the collection & views
Chat.messages = new Chat.Messages();

Chat.messagesView = new Chat.MessagesView({
  collection: Chat.messages
});

// bind submit for chat box
setup.dom.form.submit(Chat.submit);

// handle new chats
Chat.$chatroom = setup.dom.room;
socket.on('chat', Chat.addMessage);
};

// get the user's name
Chat.getUsername = function() {
  return prompt("What's your name?", '') || 'Anonymous';
};
```

Here the `Chat.getUsername()` function uses a basic DOM prompt to fetch the user's name, which you can see in Figure 9-5.

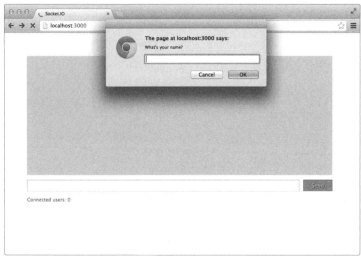

Figure 9-5 This prompt pulls in the user's name. The prompt is pretty basic, so feel free to replace it with a modal dialog or another implementation.

`Chat.getUsername()` returns what the user entered, or 'Anonymous' in the event that the user cancels out of the prompt.

Next, modify the `Chat.submit()` function to pass the user's name along via the WebSocket:

```
// submit a new chat to the server
Chat.submit = function(e) {
  e.preventDefault();

  // get the text of the input and empty it
  var $message = $(e.target.message),
  text = $message.val();

  $message.val('');

  // send the message over the socket
  socket.emit('newchat', {
    name: Chat.username,
    text: text
  });
};
```

Because the server simply relays whatever is sent to the socket back to all the users, you don't have to do anything on the server-side. The last step is to modify the message view to display the username:

```
Chat.MessageView = Backbone.View.extend({
  tagName: 'p',

  template: _.template('<strong><%=name %>:</strong> <%=text %>'),

  render: function() {
    // add the message html
    this.$el.html(this.template(this.model.toJSON()));

    // append the new message to the parent view
    this.parentView.$el.append(this.$el);

    return this;
  }
});
```

As you can see here, the view is now using an Underscore template to render the message. You'll need all the data in the model, so the model is converted to JSON and passed into the template when it compiles. Now fire up two different clients. As shown in Figure 9-6, the names are now displaying in the chat room.

> Consider saving the username in local storage so that the user doesn't have to reenter it. I omitted that from this example so that you can test the app in multiple tabs with different usernames.

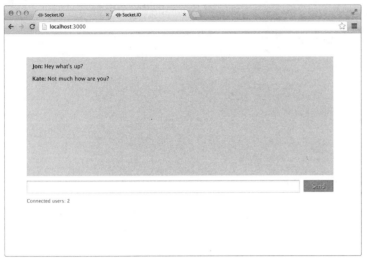

Figure 9-6 The chatroom has a much better UX now that names are being displayed.

Adding a Timestamp

It's also a good idea to add a timestamp to the messages so that users can see when each message is sent. First, install the Moment.js module, which makes formatting timestamps easy:

```
npm install moment
```

With Moment.js, you can create a timestamp for the chat messages, such as:

```
moment().format('h:mm');
```

This method returns a formatted time, such as $14:10$ for 2:10 PM. Although you could include this on the client-side, doing so isn't the best idea. Different chat room users may be in different time zones or have incorrect times set on their machines. If you include this function on the client-side, it will pull much less dependable values. So include this function on the server-side and add the timestamp to the message when it's received over the socket:

```
var moment = require('moment'),
    activeClients = 0;

// on connection
io.sockets.on('connection', function(socket) {
  activeClients++;
  io.sockets.emit('message', {clients: activeClients});

  // on disconnect
  socket.on('disconnect', function(data) {
    activeClients--;
    io.sockets.emit('message', {clients: activeClients});
  });
```

```
    // new chat received
    socket.on('newchat', function(data) {
      data.timestamp = moment().format('h:mm');
      io.sockets.emit('chat', data);
    });
  });
```

Finally, you just have to add the timestamp to the message template in `main.js`:

```
Chat.MessageView = Backbone.View.extend({
  tagName: 'p',

  template: _.template('<strong><%=name %> [<%=timestamp %>]:</strong>
<%=text %>'),

  render: function() {
    // add the message html
    this.$el.html(this.template(this.model.toJSON()));

    // append the new message to the parent view
    this.parentView.$el.append(this.$el);

    return this;
  }
});
```

Now the timestamps are displaying in the chat room, as you can see in Figure 9-7.

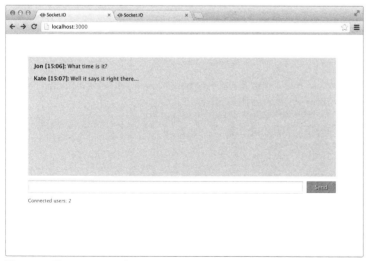

Figure 9-7 The messages in the chatroom now display a timestamp.

Persistence with MongoDB

As the app currently stands, messages are displayed in a real-time stream that is sent to all connected users. But it would be nice to save the messages to a persistence layer so that previous messages can be displayed when a user enters the chat room.

Connecting to MongoDB

First, make sure MongoDB is installed and running. Then install the Native MongoDB Driver module:

```
npm install mongodb
```

Then add a `require()` statement in the top of your Express app.js file:

```
var express = require('express')
  , routes = require('./routes')
  , user = require('./routes/user')
  , http = require('http')
  , path = require('path')
  , mongodb = require('mongodb');
```

Next, connect to the MongoDB server and create a collection for messages on your database:

```
// connect to mongodb
var db = new mongodb.Db('mydb', new mongodb.Server('localhost', 27017,
  {auto_reconnect: true}), {w: 1});

db.open( function(err, conn) {
  db.collection('chatroomMessages', function(err, collection) {
    // init the chatroom
    chatroomInit(collection);
  });
});
```

The `chatroomInit()` function is just a callback to make sure the socket functionality doesn't initialize before you're connected to MongoDB. So fold the chat room code into the callback:

```
var chatroomInit = function(messageCollection) {
  var moment = require('moment'),
      activeClients = 0;

  // on connection
  io.sockets.on('connection', function(socket) {
    activeClients++;
    io.sockets.emit('message', {clients: activeClients});

    // on disconnect
    socket.on('disconnect', function(data) {
      activeClients--;
      io.sockets.emit('message', {clients: activeClients});
```

```
    });

    // new chat received
    socket.on('newchat', function(data) {
      data.timestamp = moment().format('h:mm');
      io.sockets.emit('chat', data);
    });
  });
};
```

Saving Messages on MongoDB

Next, save any new chats that are received to the database by modifying the newchat callback:

```
// new chat received
socket.on('newchat', function(data) {
  data.timestamp = moment().format('h:mm');
  io.sockets.emit('chat', data);

  // save the new message to mongodb
  messageCollection.insert(data, function(err, result) {
    console.log(result);
  });
});
```

Here the script uses the messageCollection that was passed into the chatroomInit() callback to insert the new data into the database. If you restart your Node server and submit a new message, you see the database insertion logged in the console, as shown in this output:

```
[ { name: 'Anonymous',
    text: 'Test message',
    timestamp: '16:01',
    _id: 50e2274ded94e40000000001 } ]
```

Loading Messages from MongoDB

Now that messages are being saved in MongoDB, you just need to load those documents when a new user connects to the socket. In the callback for io.sockets.on('connection'), add the following code:

```
// get the last 10 messages from mongodb
messageCollection.find({}, {sort:[['_id', 'desc']], limit: 10}).
toArray(function(err, results) {
  // loop through results in reverse order
  var i = results.length;
  while(i--) {
    // send each over the single socket
    socket.emit('chat', results[i]);
  }
});
```

This script uses the `messageCollection` from MongoDB to get in the last ten messages. To do so, it sorts by `_id` in descending order, with a limit of ten documents. However, there are a couple important things to note:

1. Because the documents are requested in descending order, the script has to loop through them in reverse using the `while(i--)` loop. That way, it can get the latest ten entries, but still display them in the correct order.

2. The script then emits the data over the socket, almost exactly as when it receives a new message to the chatroom. However, instead of using the public socket, `io.sockets.emit()`, it uses the private socket, `socket.emit()`.

   That's crucially important, because you want to relay the saved messages only to the newly connected user. If you were to transmit these messages over the main public socket, all connected users would get a new set of recent messages every time a new user connected.

The script emits the same chat event over the socket, so there's no need to modify anything on the client-side. The script in `main.js` already handles displaying data that is sent over this socket. However, this approach can create a bit of a bottleneck, since it will emit as many as ten individual messages over the socket. Feel free to modify the client-side script to accept an array of messages if you'd like to optimize this portion a bit.

Closing the Connection

It's a good idea to close the database connection if there are no users actively using the chat room. So add a close call to the `disconnect` handler:

```
// on disconnect
socket.on('disconnect', function(data) {
  activeClients--;
  io.sockets.emit('message', {clients: activeClients});

  // if no active users close db connection
  if ( !activeClients ) db.close();
});
```

Now, when a user disconnects, the script will check the number of connected uses. If there are no `activeClients`, it closes the connection to MongoDB to save resources. But don't worry; when a new user connects and queries the database, the connection reopens automatically.

Wrapping Up

The chat room script is now complete, but I want to walk through the code one last time. Putting all the client-side code together from `main.js`:

```
var socket,
    Chat = {};

// Models & Collections

Chat.Message = Backbone.Model.extend({
  defaults: {
```

```
    text: ''
  }
});

Chat.Messages = Backbone.Collection.extend({
  model: Chat.Message
});

// Views

Chat.MessageView = Backbone.View.extend({
  tagName: 'p',

  template: _.template('<strong><%=name %> [<%=timestamp %>]:</strong>
<%=text %>'),

  render: function() {
    // add the message html
    this.$el.html(this.template(this.model.toJSON()));

    // append the new message to the parent view
    this.parentView.$el.append(this.$el);

    return this;
  }
});

Chat.MessagesView = Backbone.View.extend({
  el: '#chatroom',

  initialize: function() {
    // bind "this" context to the render function
    _.bindAll(this, 'render');

    // add various events for the collection
    this.collection.on('change', this.render);
    this.collection.on('add', this.render);
    this.collection.on('remove', this.render);

    // render the initial state
    this.render();
  },

  render: function() {
    // empty out the wrapper
    this.$el.empty();

    // loop through the messages in the collection
    this.collection.each(function(message) {
      var messageView = new Chat.MessageView({
        model: message
```

```
    });

    // save a reference to this view within the child view
    messageView.parentView = this;

    // render it
    messageView.render();
  }, this);

  // scroll to the bottom
  this.$el.animate({ scrollTop: this.$el.height() }, 100);

  return this;
}
});

// init function
Chat.init = function(setup) {
  // connect to the socket
  socket = new io.connect(setup.host);

  // when data is received, update the user count
  socket.on('message', function(data) {
    setup.dom.count.text(data.clients);
  });

  // get username
  Chat.username = Chat.getUsername();

  // initialize the collection & views
  Chat.messages = new Chat.Messages();

  Chat.messagesView = new Chat.MessagesView({
    collection: Chat.messages
  });

  // bind submit for chat box
  setup.dom.form.submit(Chat.submit);

  // handle new chats
  Chat.$chatroom = setup.dom.room;
  socket.on('chat', Chat.addMessage);
};

// submit a new chat to the server
Chat.submit = function(e) {
  e.preventDefault();

  // get the text of the input and empty it
  var $message = $(e.target.message),
```

```
    text = $message.val();

    $message.val('');

    // send the message over the socket
    socket.emit('newchat', {
      name: Chat.username,
      text: text
    });
  };

  // add a new message to the chat room
  Chat.addMessage = function(data) {
    Chat.messages.add(data);
  };

  // get the user's name
  Chat.getUsername = function() {
    return prompt("What's your name?", '') || 'Anonymous';
  };

  $(function() {
    // initialize the chat app
    Chat.init({
      host: 'http://localhost:3000',
      dom: {
        count: $('#client-count'),
        form: $('.chatbox'),
        room: $('#chatroom')
      }
    });
  });
```

To recap what's going on in this script:

1. It starts by creating models and collections for the messages in Backbone.

2. The script then creates views for each message as well as a parent view to display the list of messages. These are bound to changes in the collection so that any data changes automatically render on the page.

3. `Chat.init()` starts by connecting to the socket, then calls `Chat.getUsername()`, which allows the user to enter a name into a simple DOM `prompt()`.

4. Then `Chat.init()` initializes the collection and views in Backbone.

5. Next, the `Chat.submit()` function handles submission of the chat message form, transmitting the text and username over the WebSocket.

6. The last part of `Chat.init()` handles new chats that are received over the WebSocket. These are added to the `Chat.messages` collection, which in turn renders the changes in the view.

7. Finally, everything is started in the main `$(function)` init, which starts the socket connection and triggers `Chat.init()`.

To recap the server side, here are the relevant parts of `app.js`:

```
var server = http.createServer(app),
io = require('socket.io').listen(server);

server.listen(app.get('port'), function(){
  console.log("Express server listening on port " + app.get('port'));
});

// connect to mongodb
var db = new mongodb.Db('mydb', new mongodb.Server('localhost', 27017,
{auto_reconnect: true}), {w: 1});

db.open( function(err, conn) {
  db.collection('chatroomMessages', function(err, collection) {
    // init the chatroom
    chatroomInit(collection);
  });
});

var chatroomInit = function(messageCollection) {
  var moment = require('moment'),
      activeClients = 0;

  // on connection
  io.sockets.on('connection', function(socket) {
    activeClients++;
    io.sockets.emit('message', {clients: activeClients});

    // on disconnect
    socket.on('disconnect', function(data) {
      activeClients--;
      io.sockets.emit('message', {clients: activeClients});

      // if no active users close db connection
      if ( !activeClients ) db.close();
    });

    // pull in the last 10 messages from mongodb
    messageCollection.find({}, {sort:[['_id', 'desc']], limit:
10}).toArray(function(err, results) {
      // loop through results in reverse order
      var i = results.length;
      while(i--) {
        // send each over the single socket
        socket.emit('chat', results[i]);
      }
    });

    // new chat received
    socket.on('newchat', function(data) {
```

```
      data.timestamp = moment().format('h:mm');
      io.sockets.emit('chat', data);

      // save the new message to mongodb
      messageCollection.insert(data, function(err, result) {
        console.log(result);
      });
    });
  });
};
```

Now to go over the main points:

1. The server-side code starts by creating the HTTP and socket server.

2. It then connects to a collection on MongoDB, firing the `chatroomInit()` callback once it connects.

3. In `chatroomInit()`, it connects to the socket server, emitting a connection message over the socket and applying a handler to the `disconnect` event.

4. Then it gets the last ten messages from the MongoDB persistence layer, relaying each to the socket using a private connection for the user that just connected.

5. Finally, it sets up a handler for new messages that are sent from the client. It adds a timestamp to each of these and then relays it to all the users over the socket; then it saves the message to a MongoDB document.

Summary

In this chapter, you built a fast, real-time app using Node and WebSockets. You started by learning about traditional polling techniques and why WebSockets were created to replace them. Then you read about the WebSockets API Socket.IO. You used Socket.IO to create your first sockets server on Node and also to communicate with that server from the client-side.

Then you expanded the simple sockets app to create a real-time chat room application. You relayed data to and from the sockets server and displayed that information on the front end. Next, you hooked the chat room app into Backbone, to add a structure for the data, and used that structure to render changes in the browser. You then added a few features to the app, and finally you added a persistence layer using MongoDB.

This chapter wraps up all the server-side JavaScript concepts you learned in Part III. At this point, you should be comfortable enough with Node to create your own server-side applications. You know how to streamline Node development using the Express framework, persist data from Node using MongoDB, and finally how to connect to the Node server using WebSockets.

In the coming chapters, you'll continue to take your JavaScript skills to the next level, creating mobile apps, drawing in HTML5 canvas, and launching your app.

Additional Resources

Documentation

Socket.IO Wiki: `https://github.com/learnboost/Socket.IO/wiki` Moment.js Docs: `http://momentjs.com/docs/`

Tutorials

Getting Your Feet Wet with Node.js and Socket.IO: `http://thecoffman.com/2011/02/21/getting-your-feet-wet-with-node.js-and-Socket.IO`

Node.js & WebSocket. Simple Chat Tutorial: `http://martinsikora.com/nodejs-and-websocket-simple-chat-tutorial`

Nodechat.js. Using Node.js, Backbone.js, Socket.IO and Redis to Make a Real-Time Chat App: `http://fzysqr.com/2011/02/28/nodechat-js-using-node-js-backbone-js-socket-io-and-redis-to-make-a-real-time-chat-app/`

General WebSocket Info

Introducing WebSockets: Bringing Sockets to the Web: `http://www.html5rocks.com/en/tutorials/websockets/basics`

WebSockets Everywhere with Socket.IO: `http://howtonode.org/websockets-socketio`

WebSockets (MDN): `https://developer.mozilla.org/en-US/docs/WebSockets`

Chapter 10

Going Mobile

In recent years, users have been moving away from desktop computers and relying more and more on mobile devices to browse the web. The mobile growth rate has been staggering, especially outside of North America. In many developing countries, users are skipping over the desktop computer and browsing the web for the first time on a mobile device.

For instance, Asia saw a 192 percent growth rate in mobile traffic share from 2010 to 2012, according to Pingdom (`http://royal.pingdom.com/2012/05/08/mobile-web-traffic-asia-tripled`). And it's not just an Asian phenomenon: The worldwide increase in that period is over 162 percent.

Although desktop browsing still outpaces browsing on mobile devices, that is projected to change as early as 2014. That's an enticing opportunity, and many companies are positioning themselves to reap the rewards of mobile traffic. *Mobile-first* has become a common mantra among many developers, who are now gearing their apps toward mobile devices, with desktop support as an afterthought. That's a remarkable shift from a couple of years ago when mobile apps were tacked onto the primary offering: desktop web apps.

In this chapter, you find out how to position your web app in the mobile space. You first learn how to detect mobile devices and create responsive layouts that adjust for different screen sizes and device orientations. Then you learn about a couple of scripts you can employ to handle the mobile viewport and to serve responsive content, followed by a few mobile frameworks you can use to streamline your mobile development.

After building a firm foundation in mobile development, you dive right in, handling multi-touch events and complex finger gestures using the Hammer.js library. This library helps you to leverage the touch screen interface in your apps, which can respond to swipes, taps, and more user interaction.

Next you discover how to use the geolocation API to deliver localized content to your app users based on their devices' GPS. You also learn how to dial phone numbers and send text messages using JavaScript. Finally, you learn how to build native device apps with PhoneGap and JavaScript. PhoneGap allows you to bridge the gaps between your JavaScript app and the various APIs that are unavailable at the browser level. By the end of this chapter, you'll have a nice introduction to a variety of key skills for mobile development.

Setting Up a Mobile App

With the overwhelming popularity of mobile, it just doesn't make much sense to build a web app for only desktop browsers. Unless there's literally no way to get your app working on mobile, you should definitely build a version for smartphones and tablets. But that doesn't mean you have to start from scratch and build an entirely separate app. In fact, it's a good idea to avoid segmentation and create a more universal codebase for both desktop and mobile.

Detecting Mobile

The first challenge to setting up a mobile version of a site or app is detecting whether the user is on a mobile device in the first place. Normally, it's best to do this on the server-side so that you can send pared-down content and reduce the size of the markup for slower mobile connections. You can then send mobile-specific JavaScript and avoid any detection on the front end.

However, sometimes it makes sense to handle this detection with JavaScript. Unfortunately, that's going to mean browser-sniffing with user agents. There's just no reliable way to detect mobile without the user agent, since device manufacturers have derailed all the proposed methods.

> **Device manufacturers deliberately dodge mobile detection so they can display the full-scale desktop site and make their devices seem more impressive.**

Finding User Agents

Detecting mobile with the user agent presents its own challenges. With new devices and mobile browsers coming out regularly, it can be difficult to keep an up-to-date list of mobile user agents. Fortunately, there are a number of services that handle it for you.

- The simplest approach is to download the JavaScript implementation from `http://detectmobile browsers.com`. However, the script just provides a simple redirect—so you'll need to modify it to create a hook you can use in your JavaScript, such as setting a variable `isMobile`. Additionally, bear in mind that you'll have to update the script over time as user agents change.

- If you need finer-grained detection, you should use WURFL: `http://wurfl.sourceforge.net`. WURFL (Wireless Universal Resource FiLe) is a frequently updated XML file that lists not only mobile browsers but also a variety of their device-specific capabilities. Thus, although it relies on user-agent sniffing, it's still reasonably reliable for feature-detection.

  The only downside is that you'll have to set up an API to use it in your JavaScript. Fortunately, there are a few available, such as the Tera-WURFL remote client for PHP: `http://dbapi.scientiamobile.com/wiki/index.php/Remote_Webservice`.

Discovering Orientation

Once you know the user is on a mobile device, you can also check the device orientation with JavaScript. The trick is to use `window.orientation`, which outputs the orientation in degrees. You can use it to set up a simple switch for portrait and landscape modes:

```
switch( window.orientation ) {
  case 0:
  case 180:
    // portrait mode
  break;

  case 90:
  case -90:
```

```
     // landscape mode
   break;
 }
```

Landscape mode can be either 90 or -90 degrees, depending on which way the device has been rotated. Additionally, you can track when the orientation of the device changes, using `window.onorientationchange`:

```
window.onorientationchange = function() {
  alert('new orientation: ' + window.orientation + ' degrees');
};
```

> In iOS, you can tap into much more precise information about the device using `window.ondevice orientation`. It can tell you exact rotational measurements from the device's gyroscope and even tap into the accelerometer. For more information, visit `http://www.peterfriese.de/how-to- use-the-gyroscope-of-your-iphone-in-a-mobile-web-app`.

Using Media Queries to Resolve Layout Issues

Finally, you can use media queries with JavaScript if you're detecting layout-based issues. For instance, here's how to set up a switch based on the window size:

```
if (window.matchMedia('(max-device-width: 480px)').matches) {
  // devices that are 480px or smaller
}
```

However, bear in mind that this script detects any matching device, mobile or otherwise.

Styling a Mobile Site

In the past, mobile styling was an HTML/CSS thing. You used media queries, or back-end mobile detection to display different stylesheets and HTML techniques to display the modified site within the mobile viewport. However, recently there's been a trend to handle some of this with JavaScript. It's not that the traditional approaches don't work. It's that with a variety of device-specific issues, they don't work well enough.

Viewport Script

One such example is handling the mobile viewport, meaning the scale that the page is displayed on the mobile screen. In the past, you handled this with a basic HTML meta tag:

```
<meta name="viewport" content="width=device-width, initial-scale=1.0,
maximum-scale=1.0" />
```

In theory this approach should work reasonably well to show the page at a certain zoom level. However, in practice, it leaves a lot to be desired. The main issue is rotating. You've probably noticed on your device that when you rotate to landscape, the screen zooms to match the scale of the device in portrait mode. While that's good if you're reading a paragraph, it's not necessarily the best user experience for most sites.

Fortunately, the folks at Zynga released an open-source JavaScript that handles viewporting much better. You can download it here: `https://github.com/zynga/viewporter`.

The script handles the rotating issue much more gracefully and also provides some other niceties, such as removing the top bar of the browser.

Another Viewport Script

Another issue with viewports is that they can be pretty arbitrary when it comes to content. Why should the user's screen size determine the breakpoints of a page, potentially cutting off images and paragraphs onto the next screen?

When it comes to responsive designs and viewports, the conventional approach is to set fixed breakpoints. That approach works pretty well if you need to support only a couple of devices, but it fails miserably with the vast number of different mobile screen sizes out there. Fortunately, there's a script that sets up viewports according to the content on the page, which you can download here: `https://github.com/bradfrost/ish`. With this script, you define a few bucket sizes and let it automate the rest.

Responsive Images Script

Another common problem when serving a mobile version of a website is how to handle images. On the one hand, you want to display small images to mobile; on the other hand, you want to display high-res images to desktop browsers. You could handle that by serving completely different markup from the server, but that can be a bit difficult to build and maintain. There is an easier solution that uses some interesting tricks with the image paths, which you can download here: `https://github.com/filamentgroup/Responsive-Images`.

Basically, you define paths to both of the images you want to use, and the script uses JavaScript to determine the best one to use. However, the paths work only on an Apache server, so you'll need to explore other options if you're not using Apache. Fortunately, there are a number of different scripts out there, which you can read about here: `http://css-tricks.com/which-responsive-images-solution-should-you-use`.

Mobile Frameworks

As a result of the popularity of mobile devices, a large number of mobile libraries and frameworks are now available. These resources provide a giant head start for your mobile development efforts. However, just like with any third-party tool, it's important to select the one that best suits your project.

- **Sencha Touch:** Sencha Touch is probably the most robust mobile framework. It provides a number of useful mobile components, as well as an MVC and styling. It's a perfect fit for very interactive apps that need a lot of mobile-specific functionality. So if you're building a fully-featured mobile app, look at Sencha Touch. But if you're just building a mobile skin for a simple brochure website, Sencha Touch is major overkill. Of all the mobile frameworks, it has the highest learning curve and largest filesize. To learn more about Sencha Touch, visit `www.sencha.com/products/touch`.

- **jQuery Mobile:** jQuery Mobile is another framework that provides a variety of mobile components and themes. It's built on jQuery and jQuery UI, so most developers find it easy to pick up and hit the ground running. jQuery Mobile provides a lot of styling, and a themer similar to jQuery UI, so it can be really great for rolling out a mobile UI without design comps. But if you do have design direction, it can be a little more challenging to work with. jQuery Mobile is best for web apps that don't need all the functionality of SenchaTouch. To learn more about jQuery Mobile, visit `http://jquerymobile.com`.

Mobile libraries: If you're just building a mobile skin for a simple website, avoid the mobile frameworks. You'll be a lot happier with mobile libraries if you want to inject a small amount of mobile functionality to your site. In Chapter 2, you read a bit about Zepto.js. Zepto is a lightweight JavaScript library that includes a few basic touch gestures you can use for mobile. Find more about Zepto's touch events here: `http://zeptojs.com/#touch`. Additionally, in the next section, you discover how to use Hammer.js to add robust touch-gesture support to your app.

Touch Screen Integration

One of the particular challenges of mobile development is handling a different interface: the touch screen. But you shouldn't think of it as a challenge, so much as an opportunity to provide a higher quality UX.

At the time of this writing, touch screens are mostly a mobile phenomenon. But some touch-screen monitors have already been produced for desktop computers, and that trend is likely to continue in the coming years as the line blurs between desktop and mobile.

Basic Touch Events

To interface with the touch screen, you have to create handlers for a new type of event: the touch event. But you may be wondering why you'd even set up handlers for touch events. After all, mobile browsers still register click events when the user touches the screen. However, while a mouse can click only a single point on the screen, touch screens can register multiple touch events at a time—as many as users have fingers.

Creating a Single Touch Event

Creating a handler for a single touch event is simple:

```
var el = document.getElementById('my-element');

el.addEventListener('touchstart', function(e) {
  // what to do on touch
});
```

Here the script uses the standard JavaScript `addEventListener()` method to attach the `touchstart` event. This event fires the moment the user's finger touches the screen, similarly to `mousedown`.

Likewise, you can also bind `touchend`, which fires when the user removes his or her finger (similar to `mouseup`). There's also a third event, `touchmove`, which fires when the user places his or her finger on the device and then moves it.

Creating Multi-Touch Events

When using touch events, you can get the coordinates of the touch point from the event object:

```
el.addEventListener('touchstart', function(e) {
  var x = e.touch.pageX;
  var y = e.touch.pageY;
});
```

As you can see here, `touch.pageX` and `touch.pageY` give you the (x,y) coordinates of the point on the screen the user touches. But you can also get information about multiple touch points—if the user is touching the screen with more than one finger. For that, you need the `touches` array:

```
el.addEventListener('touchstart', function(e) {
  // first finger
  var x1 = e.touches[0].pageX;
  var y1 = e.touches[0].pageY;

  // second finger
  var x2 = e.touches[1].pageX;
  var y2 = e.touches[1].pageY;
});
```

Here the event relays the coordinates of the first finger on the screen in `touches[0]` and the second finger in `touches[1]`. Additional touch points will be added to this array (`touches[2]` for the third finger and so on).

Complex Touch Gestures

Probably the best part about coding for the touch screen is the opportunity to use touch gestures, such as swiping, pinching, and rotating. These gestures improve the UI of mobile apps, providing a much more interactive experience.

Although you can program your own gestures, doing so can get pretty complicated. Fortunately, a number of gesture libraries are available, most notably Hammer.js (`http://eightmedia.github.com/hammer.js`). Hammer.js makes it easy to include a wide variety of touch gestures for different mobile platforms such as iOS, Android, and Blackberry.

> iOS includes some native gesture support. But you'll most likely end up building fallbacks for other devices, so it's best to just stick to Hammer.js gestures.

Hammer.js Basics

Using Hammer.js is really easy. First, download the source and include it on your page. Next, bind it to an element:

```
var hammer = new Hammer( document.getElementById('my-element') );
```

Finally, define a touch event on that object:

```
hammer.ondoubletap = function(e) {
   console.log('Whoah the element has been double tapped');
}
```

This event fires whenever the user double taps the element. But `ondoubletap` is just the beginning. Hammer.js includes many different gestures, such as `ondrag`, `onhold`, and `ontransform`.

Slideshow with Hammer.js

One of the most common website elements is the image slideshow. To create a better mobile experience, you can enhance basic slideshows with gesture controls. That way the user can swipe left and right to change the image.

Creating the Slideshow

First, start with some markup:

```
<section class="slideshow">
  <div class="slides">
     <img src="images/my-image.jpg" alt="" class="slide" />
     <img src="images/my-image-2.jpg" alt="" class="slide" />
     <img src="images/my-image-3.jpg" alt="" class="slide" />
     <img src="images/my-image-4.jpg" alt="" class="slide" />
  </div>
</section>
```

As you can see here, the slideshow markup is kept very simple.

Next add some styling:

```
.slideshow {
  width: 500px;
  height: 300px;
  position: relative;
  overflow: hidden;
}

.slides {
  position: absolute;
  top: 0;
  left: 0;
  width: 10000px;
  -webkit-transition: left 0.3s ease;
     -moz-transition: left 0.3s ease;
       -o-transition: left 0.3s ease;
          transition: left 0.3s ease;
}

.slide {
```

```
        width: 500px;
        height: 300px;
        float: left;
    }
```

The idea with the styling here is to float all the .slide images within the .slides wrapper to make a long horizontal reel. This wrapper is then absolutely positioned in the parent .slideshow container.

That way you can move the .slides wrapper left and right to show different slides in the reel. And rather than animate the changes in the JavaScript, the code uses some simple CSS transitions.

> **When building for mobile, it's a good idea to animate with transitions since they are much better for performance.**

Finally, add some basic jQuery:

```
    function Slideshow($wrap) {
        this.currSlide = 0;

        // cache some variables
        var $slideWrap = $wrap.find('.slides');
        var slideWidth = $slideWrap.children(':first-child').width();
        var slideCount = $slideWrap.children().length;

        this.changeSlide = function() {
            // sanity check on currSlide
            var $kids = $slideWrap.children();
            if ( this.currSlide >= $kids.length ) this.currSlide = 0;
            else if ( this.currSlide < 0 ) this.currSlide = $kids.length - 1;

            // change the horizontal position of the slides
            $slideWrap.css('left', slideWidth * this.currSlide * -1);
        };

        // change slides on an interval
        var slideInterval = setInterval( $.proxy( function() {
            this.currSlide++;
            this.changeSlide();
        }, this), 4000);
    }

    var slideshow = new Slideshow( $('.slideshow') );
```

The slideshow script is really straightforward so far:

1. First it sets up a public this.currSlide variable and caches a few variables for later.

2. Then it creates a public this.changeSlide() function, which changes the displayed slide based on the this.currSlide variable.

3. `this.changeSlide()` checks to make sure the new slide isn't outside the bounds of the slideshow. Then it moves the `.slides` wrapper based on the index of the new slide and the width of the slides. The animation is then handled with the CSS transition that was established earlier.

4. Finally, an interval is set up to change the current slide every four seconds. One thing to pay attention to here is the use of `$.proxy()`, which passes the context of `this` into the interval callback.

The script changes the slides on an interval, but you can set up any type of functionality you want. Just use the `this.changeSlide()` function to create next and previous buttons, numbered navigation, and so on.

Adding Swipe Gestures

So far the slideshow is working on an interval, changing the slide every four seconds. The next step is to add swipe gestures for mobile. First, download Hammer.js from `http://eightmedia.github.com/hammer.js` and include the main script on your page. Hammer.js also includes a jQuery plugin, but for now you're just going to use the stand-alone script.

Using Hammer.js is pretty easy; first you create a new instance of Hammer on whichever element you want to bind the touch events and then define a handler. For example:

```
var hammer = new Hammer( document.getElementById('my-element') );

hammer.onswipe = function(e) {
  // whatever you want to do on swipe
};
```

In the slideshow example, you want to bind this event to the main wrapper, so add the following within the `Slideshow()` function:

```
var hammer = new Hammer( $wrap[0] );
```

`$wrap[0]` grabs the DOM reference of the jQuery object in the script and uses that to bind Hammer.js.

Next, bind the actual swipe event:

```
var hammer = new Hammer( $wrap[0] );

hammer.onswipe = $.proxy(function(e) {
  switch( e.direction ) {
    case 'left':
      this.currSlide++;
      this.changeSlide();
    break;

    case 'right':
      this.currSlide--;
      this.changeSlide();
    break;
  }
}, this);
```

The swipe event is first bound using the same $.proxy() method you saw earlier. That way the context of the slideshow instance is retained in the onswipe event handler. Next it uses the direction key from the event object to determine whether the user is swiping left or right. It then increments the currSlide variable accordingly and finally calls the changeSlide() function.

If you reload the slideshow in a mobile browser, you see that the swipe events are working. However, there is still more work to be done.

First, the swipes also move the page—you still need to prevent the default behavior of this touch event. Additionally, whenever you have a slideshow with an interval, it's a good idea to remove the interval once the user starts interacting with the controls—that way the script doesn't hijack whatever the user is trying to do. Making these changes is easy:

```
var hammer = new Hammer( $wrap[0] );

hammer.onswipe = $.proxy(function(e) {
  // clear any interval
  clearInterval( slideInterval );

  switch( e.direction ) {
    case 'left':
      this.currSlide++;
      this.changeSlide();
    break;

    case 'right':
      this.currSlide--;
      this.changeSlide();
    break;
  }

  // prevent default behavior
  return false;
}, this);
```

Here the interval is being cleared first. Then the default behavior is prevented with return false. Unfortunately, Hammer.js doesn't support preventDefault() at the time of this writing, except with a global option that is a little too heavy-handed here.

> If the swipes aren't working exactly as you want, consider changing some of the options for Hammer.js. You can find out more about these options here: https://github.com/eightmedia/hammer. js#defaults. Try adjusting the swipe_time and swipe_min_distance.

Rubber Banding

Now the swipe gestures are working, but the slideshow acts a bit weird at the top and bottom bounds because it loops around to the other side. That works well in the interval, but it's not the best experience for the swipe events. Fortunately, it's easy to prevent the looping on the swipe events:

```
var hammer = new Hammer( $wrap[0] );

hammer.onswipe = $.proxy(function(e) {
  // clear any interval
  clearInterval( slideInterval );

  switch( e.direction ) {
    case 'left':
      // stop if at the bounds
      if (this.currSlide >= slideCount - 1) {
        return false;
      }

      this.currSlide++;
      this.changeSlide();
    break;

    case 'right':
      // stop if at the bounds
      if (this.currSlide <= 0) {
        return false;
      }

      this.currSlide--;
      this.changeSlide();
    break;
  }

  // prevent default behavior
  return false;
}, this);
```

Now the script is stopping the loop, but that doesn't relay much information to the user—it just looks like the slideshow is broken. It's a much better idea to set up rubber banding—moving the slideshow slightly past the bounds and then snapping it back into place. Rubber banding is a very common paradigm in mobile UIs, and one with which the user will most likely be familiar. Fortunately, with the CSS transitions already set up, it isn't too difficult to accomplish:

```
var hammer = new Hammer( $wrap[0] );

hammer.onswipe = $.proxy (function(e) {
  // clear any interval
  clearInterval( slideInterval );

  switch( e.direction ) {
    case 'left':
      // stop if at the bounds
      if (this.currSlide >= slideCount - 1) {
        // rubberband it
        var thisPosLeft = slideWidth * -1 * (slideCount - 1);
        $slideWrap.css('left', thisPosLeft + slideWidth / 3 * -1)

        setTimeout(function() {
```

```
          $slideWrap.css('left', thisPosLeft);
        }, 200);

        return false;
      }

      this.currSlide++;
      this.changeSlide();
    break;

    case 'right':
      // stop if at the bounds
      if (this.currSlide <= 0) {
        // rubberband it
        $slideWrap.css('left', slideWidth / 3);

        setTimeout(function() {
          $slideWrap.css('left', 0);
        }, 200);

        return false;
      }

      this.currSlide--;
      this.changeSlide();
    break;
  }

  // prevent default behavior
  return false;
}, this);
```

Take a look at the rubber banding in the right swipe—because it's a little easier to follow. First, it moves the slide one third of the way out; then it sets a timeout to snap it back into place. The opposite is set up for the left swipe.

Wrapping Up

Now the slideshow is working with both the swipe gestures and rubber banding. Here's the entire script:

```
function Slideshow($wrap) {
  this.currSlide = 0;


  // cache some variables
  var $slideWrap = $wrap.find('.slides');
  var slideWidth = $slideWrap.children(':first-child').width();
  var slideCount = $slideWrap.children().length;

  this.changeSlide = function() {
    // sanity check on currSlide
    var $kids = $slideWrap.children();
    if ( this.currSlide >= $kids.length ) this.currSlide = 0;
```

```
    else if ( this.currSlide < 0 ) this.currSlide = $kids.length - 1;

    // change the horizontal position of the slides
    $slideWrap.css('left', slideWidth * this.currSlide * -1);
};

// change slides on an interval
var slideInterval = setInterval( $.proxy ( function() {
  this.currSlide++;
  this.changeSlide();
}, this), 4000);

// make swipeable
var hammer = new Hammer( $wrap[0] );

hammer.onswipe = $.proxy(function(e) {
  // clear any interval
  clearInterval( slideInterval );

  switch( e.direction ) {
    case 'left':
      // stop if at the bounds
      if (this.currSlide >= slideCount - 1) {
        // rubberband it
        var thisPosLeft = slideWidth * -1 * (slideCount - 1);
        $slideWrap.css('left', thisPosLeft + slideWidth / 3 * -1);

        setTimeout(function() {
          $slideWrap.css('left', thisPosLeft);
        }, 200);

        return false;
      }

      this.currSlide++;
      this.changeSlide();
    break;

    case 'right':
      // stop if at the bounds
      if (this.currSlide <= 0) {
        // rubberband it
        $slideWrap.css('left', slideWidth / 3);

        setTimeout(function() {
          $slideWrap.css('left', 0);
        }, 200);

        return false;
      }

      this.currSlide--;
      this.changeSlide();
```

```
        break;
     }

     // prevent default behavior
     return false;
   }, this);
};

var slideshow = new Slideshow( $('.slideshow') );
```

To recap what's going on here:

1. The script first defines a `changeSlide()` function, which sets a new horizontal position for the `.slides` wrapper. This position is in turn animated by the transitions in the CSS.

2. An interval is set up to show the slides in a reel in all browsers, mobile and desktop.

3. Hammer.js is instantiated on the slideshow, and a swipe gesture is bound, with a switch for left and right swipes.

4. In each swipe direction, a rubber banding animation is triggered if the swipe is past the bounds of the slideshow. Otherwise, it uses the `changeSlide()` function to switch to the new slide.

Hammer.js's Transform Gestures

In addition to swiping, iOS users have become familiar with a few more gestures, such as pinching and rotating. Typically, the pinch gesture is used to scale elements larger or smaller, and the rotate gesture is used to rotate them. iOS provides native events for these gestures, but you can enable cross-platform support using Hammer.js.

Creating a Box That Scales and Rotates

First, adjust the meta viewport of the page to disable any erroneous scaling:

```
<meta name="viewport" content="width=500, user-scalable=no"/>
```

Then start with a simple element:

```
<div id="transformer"></div>
```

And apply some basic styling:

```
#transformer {
    background: tomato;
    width: 300px;
    height: 300px;
    margin: 50px auto;
}
```

Next attach Hammer.js to this element and define a transform handler:

```
var wrapper = document.getElementById('transformer');
var hammer = new Hammer( wrapper );
```

```
hammer.ontransform = function(e) {
  wrapper.style.webkitTransform = 'rotate(' + e.rotation + 'deg)' + '
scale(' + e.scale + ')';

  return false;
};
```

Here the transform handler uses the CSS property `-webkit-transform` to apply the scale and rotation changes, which are accessed with `e.rotation` and `e.scale`. Now when you load this page in a mobile device, the element scales and rotates with your finger gestures.

> Don't worry about other vendor prefixes for the `transform` CSS. The devices Hammer.js supports all use WebKit.

Caching Transformation Changes

However, if you try another gesture it gets a bit wonky. Since the script doesn't cache the new scale and rotation values after each gesture, it restarts each gesture from the beginning. Fortunately, that's easily solved:

```
// cache rotation and scale
var rotation = 0;
var scale = 1;

// bind hammer.js
var wrapper = document.getElementById('transformer');
var hammer = new Hammer( wrapper );

// transform event - modify CSS
hammer.ontransform = function(e) {
  wrapper.style.webkitTransform = 'rotate(' + (e.rotation + rotation) +
  'deg)' + ' scale(' + (e.scale * scale) + ')';

  return false;
};

// transform end event - cache new values
hammer.ontransformend = function(e) {
  rotation += e.rotation;
  scale *= e.scale;
};
```

Here the script starts by caching `rotation` and `scale` variables. Then it uses these to adjust the values in the `ontransform` handler. Finally, it caches the new values in the `ontransformend` handler, which fires at the end of the gesture. It can't simply change the cached values in the normal `ontransform` handler, or they'll pile up too fast. Now the script saves any previous transformations, so multiple gestures work as expected.

Geolocation

One advantage to mobile sites is that they can provide specific information based on the user's physical location in the world. For instance, if you're trying to find the nearest pizza shop, why should you enter in your zip code when your device already knows exactly where you are?

Finding the User's Location

Fortunately, tapping into the geolocation API is easy with JavaScript:

```
if ( navigator.geolocation ) {
  navigator.geolocation.getCurrentPosition(function(position) {
    console.log('Location: ' + position.coords.latitude + ' ' + position.
coords.longitude);
  });
}
```

Here the script first checks whether geolocation is available and then uses `getCurrentPosition()` to return the user's latitude and longitude. Of course, there are inherent privacy issues with geolocation, so whenever you make a call to the API, the user's browser or device will prompt them to accept it, as you can see in Figure 10-1.

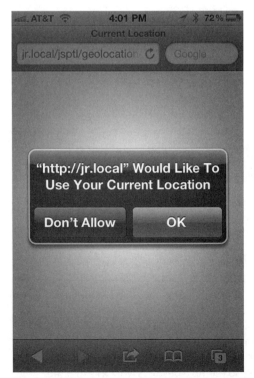

Figure 10-1 The user must grant access to geolocation data, as you can see from this iOS device.

Bear in mind that even in non-mobile devices, geolocation calls will return something based on the user's IP.

Connecting with Google Maps

Once you have the user's latitude and longitude, you can do a number of things with it—for instance, tap into an API to get his or her city name or relaying the data to the Google Maps API.

First, obtain a Google Maps API key by following the instructions here: `https://developers.google.com/maps/documentation/javascript/tutorial#api_key`. Then, to show a map of the user's current location, use the following code:

```
<!DOCTYPE html>
<html>
<head>
  <title>Current Location</title>
  <meta name="viewport" content="initial-scale=1.0, user-scalable=no" />

  <style type="text/css">
  html, body, #map_canvas { height: 100% }
  body { margin: 0; padding: 0 }
  </style>
</head>

<body>
  <div id="map_canvas" style="width:100%; height:100%"></div>

  <script src="https://maps.googleapis.com/maps/api/js?key=YOUR_API_KEY&
  sensor=true">
  </script>
  <script>

  // get current position
  if ( navigator.geolocation ) {
    navigator.geolocation.getCurrentPosition(function(position) {
      displayMap( position.coords.latitude, position.coords.longitude );
    });
  }

  // show map
  function displayMap(latitude, longitude) {
    // define map options
    var mapOptions = {
      center: new google.maps.LatLng(latitude, longitude),
      zoom: 10,
      mapTypeId: google.maps.MapTypeId.ROADMAP
    };

    // pull the map from the Google API
```

```
        var map = new google.maps.Map(document.getElementById("map_canvas"),
            mapOptions );
    }
    </script>
</body>
</html>
```

This script first sets up some basic styling and markup and then references the Google Maps API script. Make sure to fill your API key into the `YOUR_API_KEY` value. Next, the script uses `navigator.geolocation.getCurrentPosition()` to pull the user's latitude and longitude. It then relays that information to a `displayMap()` function. The `displayMap()` function simply passes the latitude and longitude values into the Google Maps API and renders the map. That's all there is to it.

Now, fire up this page in your mobile device (or desktop browser), and you should see something similar to Figure 10-2.

Figure 10-2 The geolocation script is displaying a map of my current location in Portland, OR.

As this example demonstrates, interfacing with the API is pretty straightforward. You can then take it to the next level, creating a custom map to your business location or placing pins for relevant locations close to the user.

Tracking Geolocation Changes

You can also track changes to the user's position over time using `watchCurrentPosition()`:

```
if ( navigator.geolocation ) {
  navigator.geolocation.watchCurrentPosition(function(position) {
    console.log('Location: ' + position.coords.latitude + ' ' + position.
coords.longitude);
  });
}
```

This script sets up an event handler to track changes in geolocation. It's a lot better than simply setting up `getCurrentPosition()` with an interval, since it fires only when the location changes. `watchCurrentPosition()` can also be useful even when you don't need to track a moving target. Mobile devices often return a rough geolocation as soon as one is available and then refine it as more precise data becomes available.

Using `watchCurrentPosition()` ensures that you pull the most accurate location data once it's available. But to save resources, you should remove the handler after it fires a few times:

```
var watchCount = 0;
var positionTimer = navigator.geolocation.watchPosition(function
(position) {
    // increment the count
    watchCount++;

    // clear the watch on the third attempt
    if ( watchCount > 2 ) {
      navigator.geolocation.clearWatch(positionTimer);
    }
});
```

Using `clearWatch()` allows you to save resources when you want a refined geolocation but don't need to actually track changes over time.

Phone Numbers and SMS

With JavaScript, you can even dial phone numbers and send text messages on certain devices. Don't get too excited; it won't start the call directly in the browser. But you can use JavaScript to route users into the phone or messaging app in their device.

Static Phone Numbers and SMS Links

The trick to dialing phone numbers and sending texts is built upon the HTML5 markup standard for phone links:

```
<a href="tel:+12125551234">(212) 555 - 1234</a>
```

This code dials the given phone number if the user clicks the link from a capable device. Additionally, you can set up links for text messaging:

```
<a href="sms:+12125551234">Text me</a>
```

When a user clicks this link, his or her text-messaging client opens with the given number. You can even set up texts to multiple recipients:

```
<a href="sms:+12125551234,+12125556789">Text us</a>
```

Dialing Phone Numbers and Texting with JavaScript

You can also use the `tel:` and `sms:` protocols to interface with phone features directly from JavaScript. It's really simple; you just call these links with `window.location`:

```
// call (212) 555-1234
window.location = 'tel:+12125551234';
```

Now, when you call this script, it interfaces with the user's phone. For instance, in iOS, it triggers a prompt the user can accept or cancel, as shown in Figure 10-3.

Figure 10-3 Dialing a number with JavaScript causes this prompt in iOS. The prompt avoids any malicious use of the protocol.

Likewise, you can send text messages:

```
// text (212) 555-1234
window.location = 'sms:+12125551234';
```

However, when interfacing with the device's phone functionality, you need to make sure that you're on a capable device. It's not enough to simply detect mobile because many mobile devices such as tablets and iPod Touches do not include a phone.

PhoneGap

So far in this chapter, you've learned how to build a mobile web app that users can access through their device's browser. However, sometimes you want to build an app they can install directly on the device. Previously, that meant writing a different app in native code for each platform: Objective-C for iOS, Java for Android, and so on. Wouldn't it be nicer if you could just roll out a single app across a number of mobile platforms?

PhoneGap makes that possible, allowing you to write a dedicated mobile app with the HTML, CSS, and JavaScript skills you already have. PhoneGap then packages that app into code that can run natively on a variety of devices, including iOS, Android, Blackberry, Windows Phone 7, Symbian, and more.

Best of all, since the code runs as a native app, PhoneGap is able to expose device functionality that is not available at the browser level because of security issues. PhoneGap provides JavaScript APIs for a number of native features, such as:

- Accelerometer
- Geolocation and compass
- Media capture (photo, audio, and video)
- Media playback
- Notifications (alert popups as well as sound and vibration notifications)
- File structure and storage
- Contact list
- Connection type (WiFi, 2G, 3G, and so on)

To see more native features, go to `http://docs.phonegap.com`.

> The open source arm of PhoneGap is called Apache Cordova.

Pros and Cons of PhoneGap

While PhoneGap supports a wide variety of functionality, it's important to remember that it's not for every project.

PhoneGap Versus Native Code

PhoneGap renders apps using web views instead of each platform's native UI framework. That's decidedly worse for performance than building an actual native app. The fact is that PhoneGap makes it easy to roll out native apps. It's great for projects that already have a web app that you want to convert to a native device app, which means that you have to do very little programming to release your dedicated app.

As always, you get what you pay for. Natively coded apps are always going to be better than PhoneGap apps, but they also tend to cost a lot more to develop, especially if you're planning on releasing on multiple platforms.

Native Apps Versus Web Apps

You also have to decide whether you need a native app at all. Depending on your situation, a standard web app might be a better fit. Web apps are less commitment for users because they don't have to download and install something new to their device. Ask yourself: *Would I want to download this app or simply access it through the browser?*

Another piece of this decision is whether you want to involve the iOS App Store or Android Market. These can be a blessing when it comes to distribution or a curse when it comes to the 30 percent in fees they take (which is not to mention the enigmatic approval process).

> Keep in mind that web apps can still be saved to the homescreen on many devices, which means the user can still click on an icon from his or her phone to pull up your app.

Getting Started with PhoneGap

Although PhoneGap can roll out your code to a number of different mobile platforms, the roll-out process isn't as simple as flipping a switch. Each platform deployment works a bit differently and must be performed separately. But it's still a lot easier than writing each app from scratch. For more information about how to get started for each platform you want to support, visit `http://docs.phonegap.com/en/2.2.0/guide_getting-started_index.md.html`.

Also, keep in mind that not all of the APIs are available in every device or platform. For a compatibility table, visit `http://phonegap.com/about/feature`.

Connecting with the Camera

Once you have PhoneGap set up, using device functionality is easy because PhoneGap exposes native device features with simple JavaScript APIs. For instance, you can access the device's camera using the `getPicture()` method:

```
navigator.camera.getPicture(onSuccess, onError, {
  quality: 60,
  destinationType: Camera.DestinationType.DATA_URL
});

function onSuccess(imageData) {
  // create a new image
  var img = new Image();
  img.src = "data:image/jpeg;base64," + imageData;
```

```
    // append it to the DOM
    document.body.appendChild( img );
  }

  function onError(message) {
    alert(message);
  }
```

When the app runs this script, it opens up the native camera dialog on the device and then passes that data back into the app. The `getPicture()` method accepts both a success and error callback, along with an options object. In this example, the camera relays the image as a data URI, which is then appended to the DOM.

Alternatively, you could save this data on a server or even tap into the file system of the device to store the image.

> Although most devices don't provide camera access at the browser level, Android supports the Media Capture API, which you can use to take pictures even without PhoneGap.

Connecting with the Contact List

It's unlikely that mobile devices will ever provide browser-level access to the data in the contact list. The information is just too sensitive. However, native apps are able to access this data, and PhoneGap apps are no exception. Simply take advantage of the `contacts` API:

```
navigator.contacts.find('*', function(contacts) {
  console.log(contacts);
}, function(error) {
  alert(error);
}, {
  multiple: true
});
```

Here the `find()` method returns a list of all contacts. Similarly to the camera API, this method accepts success and error callbacks, as well as an options array.

Getting contact information can be very useful for certain apps, for instance if the user wants to find friends to play games against, or share a photo.

Other APIs

Hopefully, these quick examples have given you an idea of how easy it is to use PhoneGap's APIs. But they're really just the tip of the iceberg. PhoneGap includes a variety of additional APIs you can leverage in your mobile app.

You can access the accelerometer and gyroscope, record audio and video, save and load files in the device's storage, and much more. For more information, visit the PhoneGap Docs: `http://docs.phonegap.com/en/2.2.0/index.html`.

Summary

In this chapter, you discovered a variety of mobile development skills. You first learned how to detect mobile devices and create responsive layouts that scale for different screen sizes and device orientations. Then you looked into a couple of easy scripts that you can use to handle mobile viewports and deliver responsive content and images.

Next you learned about multi-touch devices and how to set up gesture handlers with Hammer.js. Then you learned about localized content using the geolocation API as well as how to use the device's phone features—sending phone calls and text messages using JavaScript.

Finally you read about PhoneGap and how to build native mobile apps using the JavaScript skills you already have.

I'm sure you understand the importance of developing a mobile app. Now you have the skills to make it happen.

Additional Resources

Mobile Usage Stats

Google Mobile Planet: `www.thinkwithgoogle.com/mobileplanet/en`

Ofcom Report: `www.smartinsights.com/marketplace-analysis/customer-analysis/new-internet-usage-report`

Pingdom Report: `http://royal.pingdom.com/2012/05/08/mobile-web-traffic-asia-tripled`

Mobile Detection

Detect Mobile Browsers: `http://detectmobilebrowsers.com`

WURFL: `http://wurfl.sourceforge.net`

Tera-WURFL Remote Client: `http://dbapi.scientiamobile.com/wiki/index.php/Remote_Webservice`

Mobile Frameworks

SenchaTouch: `http://www.sencha.com/products/touch`

jQuery Mobile: `www.jquerymobile.com`

Mobile Libraries

Hammer.js: `http://eightmedia.github.com/hammer.js`

Zepto.js: `http://zeptojs.com`

jQTouch: `http://jqtouch.com`

Mobile Styling Tools

Viewporter (Zynga): `https://github.com/zynga/viewporter`

Ish: `https://github.com/bradfrost/ish.`

Responsive Images (Filament Group): `https://github.com/filamentgroup/Responsive-Images`

Which Responsive Images Solution Should You Use?: `http://css-tricks.com/which-responsive-images-solution-should-you-use`

Additional Mobile Tools

iOS Gyroscope and Accelerometer: `www.peterfriese.de/how-to-use-the-gyroscope-of-your-iphone-in-a-mobile-web-app`

PhoneGap Docs: `http://docs.phonegap.com`

Chapter 11

JavaScript Graphics

One of the most impressive features introduced in HTML5 is the capability to render graphics directly in the browser. Not only can you generate static images with JavaScript, but also you can leverage these techniques to create stunning interactive applications such as video games. In fact, these apps aren't limited to only two dimensions. With the integration of the WebGL engine, you can now create 3D applications that run natively in the browser.

In this chapter, you first discover how to draw 2D scenes in canvas, integrating animation as well as mouse events. You then learn how to render similar scenes with scalable vector graphics (SVG), which are much easier to animate and make interactive. Next, you discover the library Raphaël.js, which will streamline your SVG development with intuitive APIs. You're then introduced to Raphaël's charting libraries, and you find out how to customize these charts with your own code.

After you understand the different two-dimensional techniques, you'll be ready to dive in and work with 3D rendering using canvas and WebGL. You find out why to avoid the low-level WebGL API and instead use the library Three.js, which you leverage to build and animate some basic three-dimensional scenes. Finally, you consider another 3D rendering option, CSS3 transforms, which can be an attractive alternative for more basic apps. By the end of this chapter, you'll know enough JavaScript drawing techniques to render just about any scene you want directly in the browser. This chapter is a jumping-off point for developing a rich visual application based in JavaScript.

Canvas Basics

HTML5 canvas allows you to dynamically render just about any shape or scene you can imagine. It all starts by defining a canvas element in the markup:

```
<canvas id="my-canvas" width="200" height="150"></canvas>
```

Next, you use JavaScript to hook into this element and render whatever scene you want to draw. Start by setting the context using the element's ID hook:

```
var canvas = document.getElementById('my-canvas');

if ( canvas.getContext ) {
  var ctx = canvas.getContext('2d');
}
```

The context of the canvas element tells the browser which type of rendering engine you want to use—in this case, basic two-dimensional rendering. But before setting the context, it's important to check for canvas support. Some users have older browsers that don't support canvas, and you can avoid throwing errors in these browsers by first verifying that `canvas.getContext` is available. Fortunately, canvas support is pretty decent these days, with the exception of IE8 and earlier, as you can see here: `http://caniuse.com/#feat=canvas`.

Later in the "3D Canvas with WebGL" section, you learn how to use a different context to render 3D scenes.

Drawing Basic Shapes

Now, you're ready to dive in and start drawing on the canvas. The canvas API provides a number of different methods you can use to render shapes and lines, along with a variety of methods for styling these objects. For example, this script draws a rectangle on the canvas:

```
var canvas = document.getElementById('my-canvas');

if ( canvas.getContext ) {
  var ctx = canvas.getContext('2d');

  ctx.fillStyle = '#d64e34';
  ctx.fillRect(10, 15, 80, 50);
}
```

Here the `fillStyle` first defines the color of the rectangle (and the color of any subsequent shapes you draw). Then `fillRect()` renders a solid rectangle at coordinates (10,15) with a size of 80px by 50px, which means the rectangle is drawn 10 pixels from the top of the canvas element and 15 pixels from the left, as shown in Figure 11-1.

Figure 11-1 fillRect draws a rectangle on the canvas.

`fillRect` is easy shorthand for drawing boxes, but you can also build your own shapes by drawing paths. For example, you can draw a triangle:

```
ctx.beginPath();
ctx.moveTo(20, 90);
ctx.lineTo(140, 90);
ctx.lineTo(80, 25);
ctx.fill();
```

Drawing your own shapes is a little more complicated:

1. `beginPath()` starts a new path.

2. `moveTo()` defines the start point of the path, in this case 20px from the left and 90px from the top.

3. `lineTo()` draws lines to coordinates, in this case a first line is drawn from the start point to (140,90). Then another line is drawn to (80,25).

4. Finally, the shape is colored in using `fill()`, which draws the triangle shown in Figure 11-2.

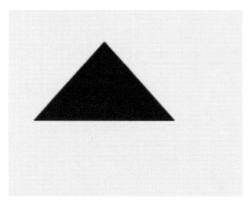

Figure 11-2 This triangle was drawn using paths.

In addition to drawing filled shapes, you can draw lines. For example, draw the same triangle with a stroke instead of a fill:

```
ctx.beginPath();
ctx.moveTo(20, 90);
ctx.lineTo(140, 90);
ctx.lineTo(80, 25);
ctx.stroke();
```

However, this code produces a bit of an unexpected result. As shown in Figure 11-3, only two lines of the triangle have been drawn.

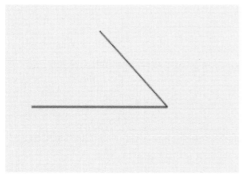

Figure 11-3 When you apply a stroke to the same triangle, it only draws two of the three arms.

While `fill()` automatically filled in the rest of the triangle, in this case, only two lines were drawn, so the canvas appropriately renders exactly that. To connect the last two points of the triangle, simply add a `closePath()`:

```
ctx.beginPath();
ctx.moveTo(20, 90);
ctx.lineTo(140, 90);
ctx.lineTo(80, 25);
ctx.closePath();
ctx.stroke();
```

As shown in Figure 11-4, the canvas renders the completed triangle.

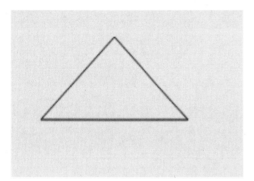

Figure 11-4 closePath() finishes off the last arm of the triangle.

Now you know how to draw a few basic shapes, but this is just the tip of the iceberg when it comes to what is possible in HTML5 canvas. The API also allows for drawing arcs and complex Bézier curves, styling elements with gradients, drop shadows and stroke styles, and much more. The API is pretty easy to use, but I don't want to bore you with a manual of different API options. A number of resources are listed at the end of this chapter if you want to dig deeper.

Animating the Canvas

Animating the canvas isn't much more complicated than drawing on it. The trick is simply to draw and redraw elements that you want to move on the screen. Start with a simple two-frame animation. First, draw a rectangle for the first frame:

```
ctx.fillRect(10, 10, 50, 50);
```

Then clear the entire contents of the canvas using `clearRect()` and draw the next frame of the rectangle:

```
ctx.clearRect(0, 0, 200, 150);
ctx.fillRect(11, 11, 50, 50);
```

That's all there is to it. Of course, you shouldn't hard-code every single frame of an animation. Instead, you can script the frames and apply them over time using an interval:

```
var posX = 0;

var drawInterval = setInterval(function(){
  posX++;

  // stop when it gets to the edge
  if ( posX > 150 ) {
    clearInterval(drawInterval);
    return;
  }

  ctx.clearRect(0, 0, 200, 150);
  ctx.fillRect(posX, 10, 50, 50);
}, 1000/60);
```

Here, you're using `setInterval` to redraw the square every 60th of a second, which moves it across the screen to the right (stopping when it reaches the bounds).

You might worry that this practice of drawing and redrawing the canvas is really resource-intensive. But, you'd be surprised: Browsers handle canvas rendering well, and these types of animations are typically smooth. And in the next chapter, you learn how to use `requestAnimationFrame` to make them even smoother.

Canvas Mouse Events

HTML5 canvas is often used to create interactive elements, which means that you need to set up an interface to manipulate these elements. However, adding mouse interaction to the canvas isn't as intuitive as you'd expect. You can't set up click listeners on the elements you draw to the canvas. Instead, you have to set up generalized listeners that determine whether the location of a click event lines up with the position of the elements that are rendered on the canvas. For example, take the rectangle from the earlier example:

```
ctx.fillRect(10, 15, 80, 50);
```

Unfortunately, you can't get a DOM reference to this rectangle and use it to apply a click handler because the canvas is just a static rendering of everything that has been drawn to it. Thus you'll have to be a little more creative when setting up mouse handlers with canvas. First, set up a generalized click listener on the canvas element and determine the location of the click event relative to the canvas:

```
$('#my-canvas').click(function(e) {
  var offsetX = e.pageX - this.offsetLeft;
  var offsetY = e.pageY - this.offsetTop;
});
```

Next, determine whether this point exists within the boundaries of the rectangle:

```
$('#my-canvas').click(function(e) {
  var offsetX = e.pageX - this.offsetLeft;
  var offsetY = e.pageY - this.offsetTop;

  if ( (offsetX > 10 && offsetX < 90) && (offsetY > 15 && offsetY < 65) )
  {
```

```
        alert('Rectangle clicked');
    }
});
```

Here, the script compares the coordinates of the click event against the coordinates of the rectangle. For instance, the x points of the rectangle go from 10 (the start point) to 90 (the start point plus the width). While this may seem complicated, calculating the click points for a rectangle is relatively simple. Imagine how much harder this math would be for a complex polygon or curve!

Unless you're really into linear algebra, you're going to want to use a library to handle this sort of behavior. Or read on to the next section, where you learn about SVGs, which are a lot friendlier to mouse interactions.

SVG Basics

Unlike canvas, you can actually define SVG images using only markup and no JavaScript. For example, this markup draws a rectangle:

```
<svg height="200" xmlns="http://www.w3.org/2000/svg">
  <rect width="150" height="100" fill="blue" />
</svg>
```

Here, SVG markup first starts with an <svg> wrapper. Then the markup declares a rectangle element, with dimensions and a fill color.

You can add as many shapes as you want to your SVG. For example, add a circle and a triangle:

```
<svg height="200" xmlns="http://www.w3.org/2000/svg">
  <rect width="150" height="100" fill="blue" />
  <circle r="50" cx="50" cy="50" fill="red" />
  <polygon points="0,0 50,50 100,0" fill="orange" />
</svg>
```

Here, the circle and polygon (triangle) are stacked on top of the rectangle, as shown in Figure 11-5.

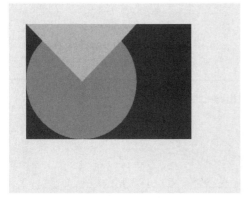

Figure 11-5 Three shapes have been drawn in this SVG using simple markup. Shapes in an SVG pile up in the order they are added.

Animating the SVG

You already know that it can be difficult to work with canvas, since everything drawn to the canvas is completely static. Well, you'll be happy to know that SVG is precisely the opposite. You don't have to draw and redraw everything in the SVG whenever you want to move something; you can just grab the node from the DOM and move it with JavaScript:

```
$('svg circle').attr('cx', 60).attr('cy', 60);
```

This example uses jQuery to select the circle and move its center point to (60,60). You can use a similar technique for anything else you want to manipulate: the color, dimensions, and so on. You can even set up simple animation—for instance, to increase the size of the circle:

```
var circle = $('svg circle'),
    radius = 50;

var svgInterval = setInterval(function() {
  radius += .2;

  if ( radius > 70 ) {
    clearInterval(svgInterval);
    return;
  }

  circle.attr('r', radius);
}, 1000/60);
```

SVG Mouse Events

Likewise, setting up mouse event handlers for SVGs is significantly easier than it is for canvas drawings. Simply grab a DOM reference and attach the listener:

```
$('svg circle').click(function() {
  alert('Circle clicked!');
});
```

There's no need to calculate the clickable area of complex shapes or handle overlapping content; the DOM takes care of all those issues for you. Indeed, if you run the example code, you'll see that the event fires only when you click the exposed area of the circle, and not the shape on top or behind it.

If you have a number of shapes in your SVG, you can set up class and ID hooks to help you grab the appropriate reference.

Scripting SVG

Creating SVGs with markup is great for static images, but not really that versatile or useful for dynamic content. Fortunately, you can create SVGs with JavaScript as well. But again, much like with canvas, the SVG API runs pretty deep and I don't want to write a manual. I've listed a number of resources at the end of this chapter if you want to dig any deeper.

Additionally, while it's a good idea to understand the fundamentals of the SVG API, you don't necessarily have to work with it. There are libraries out there that can handle all the SVG heavy lifting for you and streamline your development process—namely, Raphaël.js.

Raphaël.js

Raphaël.js is an SVG JavaScript library that makes it much easier to generate vectored graphics in the browser. It provides an intuitive API for developing rich SVG applications, and getting started with Raphaël is relatively easy. First download the library from `http://raphaeljs.com` and then create a wrapper for your drawing:

```
<div id="my-svg"></div>
```

Next, you need to create a drawing canvas that Raphaël can use to add SVGs. In Raphaël, that's called the *paper*, which you can add to your wrapper element:

```
var paper = Raphael(document.getElementById('my-svg'), 600, 400);
```

Here, the code references the `my-svg` wrapper and creates a drawing canvas with a width of 600px and a height of 400px. Now, you can begin adding shapes to the paper:

```
var rect = paper.rect(0, 0, 600, 400);
rect.attr('fill', '#FFF');

var circle = paper.circle(300, 200, 120);
circle.attr('fill', '#F00');
circle.attr('stroke-width', 0);
```

This code adds two shapes to the drawing (shown in Figure 11-6):

1. The `rect()` method adds a rectangle to the canvas—in this case, it starts at the top-left corner (0, 0) of the paper and has a width of 600px and a height of 400px. Then a fill color is defined for the rectangle (`#FFF`).

2. The `circle()` method adds a circle centered at (300, 200) with a radius of 120px. The script then defines a red fill color and sets the `stroke-width` to zero to remove the default 1px black stroke.

Figure 11-6 This simple Japanese flag was drawn with Raphaël.

Drawing Paths

In addition to using Raphaël's basic built-in shapes, you can draw more complex shapes using paths. Although it is quite powerful, the API for drawing paths is a bit strange because everything is defined in a path string. For example, this code draws a simple triangle:

```
var triangle = paper.path('M300,50 L100,350 L500,350 L300,50');
```

While the string passed into the `path()` method might seem a bit intimidating, it's not actually all that complicated:

1. It starts with the move operation, `M300,50`, which moves the start point of the path to (300,50), which is similar to the `moveTo()` method you learned about earlier in the "Canvas Basics" section.

2. Next, `L100,350` draws a line to (100,350), similar to the `lineTo()` method in canvas.

3. Then `L500,350`, and `L300,50` draw two more lines to complete the triangle, as shown in Figure 11-7.

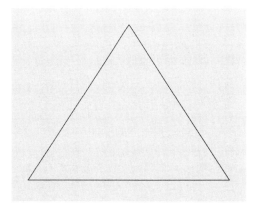

Figure 11-7 This triangle is drawn using a complex path string.

Next, the path string can be simplified a bit:

```
var triangle = paper.path('M300,50 L100,350 L500,350 Z');
```

Here, the last line command has been replaced with Z, which closes the path, thereby drawing the third line of the triangle.

Path strings in Raphaël are built upon the standardized SVG path strings from the W3C spec. You can read more about path strings here: www.w3.org/TR/SVG/paths.html#PathData.

Drawing Curves

So far, I've shown you how to draw only straight lines, but you can also use path strings to draw a number of curves, from basic arcs to complex Béziers. However, manually generating path strings for complex curves can be challenging. Sure, you can draw any type of curve you want; the only problem is that getting there is difficult. It's generally a better idea to use a visual editor to create the curves you need and then export SVG strings for your JavaScript. For example, Adobe Illustrator offers a SaveDocsAsSVG option, as shown in Figure 11-8. With this tool, you can draw complex shapes in Illustrator, and then save them as an SVG.

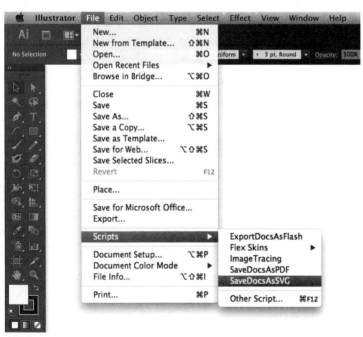

Figure 11-8 Adobe Illustrator allows you to export your vectored graphics as an SVG.

Once you save the SVG, open it up in a text editor and extract the pieces you need. For example, here's the output from a simple curve:

```
<?xml version="1.0" encoding="iso-8859-1"?>
<!-- Generator: Adobe Illustrator 16.0.4, SVG Export Plug-In . SVG
Version:
6.00 Build 0)   -->
<!DOCTYPE svg PUBLIC "-//W3C//DTD SVG 1.1//EN"
"http://www.w3.org/Graphics/SVG/1.1/DTD/svg11.dtd">
<svg version="1.1" id="Layer_1" xmlns="http://www.w3.org/2000/svg"
xmlns:xlink="http://www.w3.org/1999/xlink" x="0px" y="0px" width="600px"
height="400px" viewBox="0 0 600 400" style="enable-background:new 0 0 600
400;" xml:space="preserve">
<path style="fill:none;stroke:#000000;stroke-width:2.1155;
stroke-miterlimit:10;" d="M251.742,85.146 C75.453,48.476,100.839,430.671,
309.565,250.152"/>
</svg>
```

I've highlighted the important piece here: `M251.742,85.146 C75.453,48.476,100.839,430.671,` `309.565,250.152`.

You can then pass this path string into Raphaël's `path()` API to generate the curve in your SVG. Depending on how you draw the path in Illustrator, you may need to adjust some of the values to get it to line up correctly on your drawing canvas.

This example is pretty easy to port into Raphaël by hand, but if you have a more complicated SVG, you can save yourself even more legwork. Just upload the exported SVG to `www.readysetraphael.com`, which automatically converts SVGs to Raphaël code.

Alternatively, to find out how to build curves yourself, go to `https://developer.mozilla.org/` `en-US/docs/SVG/Tutorial/Paths`, **where you can read up on a number of different curve types.**

Styling

Raphaël offers a variety of styling options for your SVGs that can be applied with the `attr()` method. You already saw some of these styles in the examples earlier, where `attr()` was used to apply fill colors and stroke widths. But those were just the tip of the iceberg in terms of the rich styling capabilities in Raphaël.js. For example, to apply a gradient to the triangle in the previous example, you write

```
triangle.attr({
   gradient: '90-#444-#EEE'
});
```

Here, the gradient string defines three different options. First, `90` is the angle of the gradient, in this case, a vertical gradient starting from the bottom (for top down, you use `270`). Next, two hex colors are defined for the gradient, which transitions from a dark gray to a lighter gray, as shown in Figure 11-9.

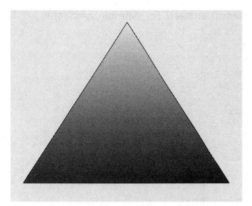

Figure 11-9 This gradient uses Raphaël's attr() method.

Raphaël also provides a wide variety of stroke options, as in this example:

```
triangle.attr({
    'gradient': '90-#444-#EEE',
    'stroke': 'green',
    'stroke-width': 20,
    'stroke-linejoin': 'round'
});
```

This code first changes the stroke color to green, demonstrating that Raphaël is able to parse color strings (in addition to hexadecimal colors, RGB, RGBa, HSL, and so on). Then the stroke width is increased to 20px, and the joins are set to round, which renders rounded corners like those in Figure 11-10.

Figure 11-10 A number of stroke styles have been added to the triangle.

Raphaël even includes some interesting options for dashed and dotted lines. You can use any combination of dashes and dots with the stroke-dasharray option:

```
var circle = paper.circle(300,200,120);

circle.attr({
```

```
    'stroke-width': 15,
    'stroke-dasharray': '-..'
});
```

As shown in Figure 11-11, this dash array creates a dash-and-two-dots pattern for the stroke.

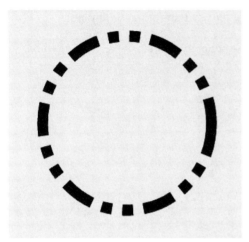

Figure 11-11 This custom stroke leverages the stroke-dasharray option.

These are just some of the many styling options you can use with Raphaël.js. To find more about its comprehensive styling capabilities, visit `http://raphaeljs.com/reference.html#Element.attr`.

Animation

One the best arguments for using Raphaël is its robust animation support, which allows you to accomplish a wide variety of animations with minimal effort. For example, you can rotate the triangle:

```
var triangle = paper.path('M300,100 L150,300 L450,300 Z');

triangle.animate({transform: 'r 360'}, 3000, 'bounce');
```

Here, `r 360` rotates the triangle 360° over the course of `3000` milliseconds using the `bounce` easing formula. However, the `bounce` timing function can be a bit jarring. It's a great option at times, but if you'd like something more conservative try < to ease in, > to ease out, or <> to ease in and out. You can also write your own cubic Bézier function or use one of the other defaults listed at `http://raphaeljs.com/reference.html#Raphael.easing_formulas`.

Also notice that the animation leverages another option string, this time to control the transformation. You can add more transformations to this string if you want—for instance, to control the scale:

```
triangle.animate({transform: 'r 360 s 0.2'}, 3000, '<>');
```

Here, the triangle rotates 360° and scales down to 20 percent of its original size. You can also add a callback to fire another animation after the first or execute any other JavaScript you want:

```
triangle.animate({transform: 'r 360 s 0.2'}, 3000, '<>', function() {
   triangle.animate({transform: 'r 0 s 1'}, 3000, '<>');
});
```

Here, the triangle animates back to its original size and position after the first transformation finishes.

In addition to transformations, you can animate just about any of the options you set in the `attr()` method. For example, you can animate a number of features of a circle:

```
var circle = paper.circle(300,200,120);

circle.attr({
   fill: '#FFF',
   'stroke-width': 20
});

circle.animate({
   fill: '#444',
   'stroke-width': 1,
   r: 60,
   cx: 500,
   cy: 100
}, 2000, '<>');
```

Here, the script animates several features of the circle: the `fill` color, `stroke-width`, radius (r), and center point (cx and cy).

Finally, you can animate the individual points of a path. Simply pass in a new path to the animation, and Raphaël will automatically set up a tween between the old and new points, animating smoothly between them:

```
var triangle = paper.path('M300,100 L150,300 L450,300 Z');

triangle.animate({path: 'M300,300 L150,100 L450,100 Z'}, 2000, '<>');
```

If you run this script, you'll see paths of the triangle flip over. But it doesn't have to stop there; you can use path animations to create a very complex animation:

```
var triangle = paper.path('M300,100 L150,300 L450,300 Z');

(function animationCycle() {
   triangle.animate({path: 'M300,300 L150,100 L450,100 Z'}, 1200, '<>',
   function() {
      triangle.animate({path: 'M300,300 L600,300 L450,100 Z'}, 1200, '<>',
      function() {
         triangle.animate({path: 'M450,100 L600,300 L300,300 Z'}, 1200,
         '<>', function() {
            triangle.animate({path: 'M300,100 L150,300 L450,300 Z'}, 1200,
            '<>', animationCycle);
```

```
         });
       });
     });
   })();
```

Here, the triangle flips over and over in a variety of directions in an endless loop. Animations in Raphaël are really limited only by your imagination.

Mouse Events

Earlier in the "SVG Mouse Events" section, you saw how easy it is to apply mouse interaction to SVGs, and SVGs built with Raphaël are no exception. But before you can apply mouse interaction, you have to get a DOM reference for the SVG. To do so, tap into the `node` property of the Raphaël object:

```
var triangle = paper.path('M300,100 L150,300 L450,300 Z');
triangle.attr('fill', 'white');

triangle.node.onclick = function() {
  triangle.attr('fill', 'red');
};
```

Here, a click event has been bound to the triangle node, which changes its fill color. If you prefer to avoid using the basic JavaScript event handlers, you can also pass this reference into jQuery or another library:

```
$(triangle.node).on('mouseover', function() {
  triangle.attr('fill', 'red');
}).on('mouseout', function() {
  triangle.attr('fill', 'white');
});
```

Here, jQuery binds `mouseover` and `mouseout` handlers to change the color of the triangle on hover.

> When binding mouse events, if your SVG doesn't have a fill color, be careful. Without a fill, the event fires only when the user clicks on the stroke, and won't fire in the interior of the shape. If that's not the behavior you want, you can apply a transparent fill of `rgba(0,0,0,0)` to get around the issue.

Charting with gRaphaël

In addition to the standard graphics library, the Raphaël project maintains a charting library called gRaphaël (`http://g.raphaeljs.com`). gRaphaël is built on top of Raphaël and provides a few charting options. Compared to other libraries, these charts are relatively lightweight, especially if you're already using Raphaël for other features. However, that filesize benefit comes at a price—gRaphaël's charts aren't as feature-rich as those in other charting libraries. That said, if you want something simple and elegant, gRaphaël is an excellent option.

Pie Charts

You can create a pie chart in gRaphaël with a single line of code:

```
paper.piechart(300, 200, 150, [65, 40, 13, 32, 5, 1, 2]);
```

This script creates a pie chart centered at (300,200) with a radius of 150px and showing the data in the array (as shown in Figure 11-12).

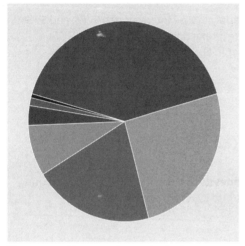

Figure 11-12 A basic pie chart in gRaphaël.

To add a legend to the chart, as shown in Figure 11-13, pass the legend as part of an options object in the fifth argument:

```
paper.piechart(300, 200, 150, [65, 40, 13, 32, 5, 1, 2], {
  legend: ['Donkeys', 'Monkeys', 'Llamas', 'Pandas', 'Giraffes', 'Rhinos',
'Gorillas']
});
```

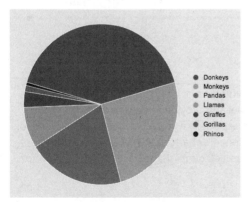

Figure 11-13 A pie chart with a legend.

You can also tweak the legend array to show values by including ##.## in your legend key, such as '##.## – Monkeys' ('40 Monkeys'), or use %%.%% to convert the value to a percent.

Finally, to convert the different slices in the chart to links, simply pass the links as a href array:

```
paper.piechart(300, 200, 150, [65, 40, 13, 32, 5, 1, 2], {
  legend: ['Donkeys', 'Monkeys', 'Llamas', 'Pandas', 'Giraffes', 'Rhinos',
'Gorillas'],
  href: ['url-1.html', 'url-2.html', 'url-3.html', 'url-4.html',
'url-5.html', 'url-6.html', 'url-7.html']
});
```

These are just some of the options available in gRaphaël's pie chart. To learn more about other capabilities, visit http://g.raphaeljs.com/reference.html#Paper.piechart.

Bar Chart

gRaphaël also supports basic bar graphs. For example:

```
paper.barchart(0, 0, 600, 400, [[63, 86, 26, 15, 36, 62, 18, 78]]);
```

Here, the first two arguments are the start point (0, 0), and the next two are the width and height, respectively. Finally, an array of values is passed to generate the chart shown in Figure 11-14.

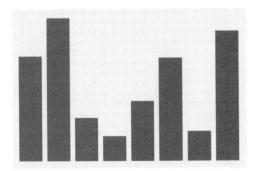

Figure 11-14 A basic bar chart in gRaphaël.

Notice that the values array is contained in another array. That's because you can pass multiple sets of values to the chart to compare different values:

```
var data1 = [63, 86, 26, 15, 36, 62, 18, 78],
    data2 = [12, 47, 75, 84, 7, 41, 29, 4],
    data3 = [39, 91, 78, 4, 80, 54, 43, 49];

paper.barchart(0, 0, 600, 400, [data1, data2, data3]);
```

Here, the three different arrays are compared across the chart, as shown in Figure 11-15.

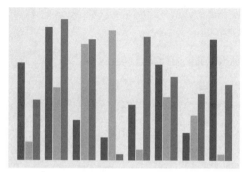

Figure 11-15 A bar chart with three different value sets.

You can also stack the value sets by setting the `stacked` option (shown in Figure 11-16):

```
paper.barchart(0, 0, 600, 400, [data1, data2, data3], {stacked: true});
```

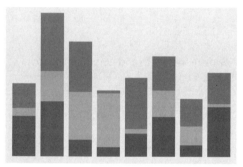

Figure 11-16 A bar chart with stacked values.

Unfortunately, gRaphaël's bar chart does not provide an easy way to add labels, which makes it somewhat limited. A number of hacks for adding labels have been suggested, but they no longer work in the more recent versions of the library. You can, however, add your own labels using Raphaël's `text()` method. Here's a function that you can leverage to create the labels:

```
Raphael.fn.labelBarChart = function(opt) {
  var paper = this;

  // offset x_start and width for bar chart gutters
  opt.x_start += 10;
  opt.width -= 20;

  var labelWidth = opt.width / opt.labels.length;

  // offset x_start to center under each column
  opt.x_start += labelWidth / 2;
```

```
    for ( var i = 0, len = opt.labels.length; i < len; i++ ) {
      paper.text( opt.x_start + ( i * labelWidth ), opt.y_start,
    opt.labels[i] ).attr( opt.textAttr );
    }
};
```

Don't worry too much about the code in here. It just calculates a position for each column's label and then writes it to the SVG. Here's how to use it:

```
var chart = paper.barchart(0, 0, 600, 380, [[63, 86, 26, 15, 36, 62, 18,
78]]);

var labels = ['Col 1', 'Col 2', 'Col 3', 'Col 4', 'Col 5', 'Col 6',
    'Col 7', 'Col 8'];

paper.labelBarChart({
  x_start: 0,
  y_start: 390,
  width: 600,
  labels: labels,
  textAttr: {'font-size': 14}
});
```

In this implementation, an object of settings is passed to `labelBarChart`, defining the start coordinates for the labels (0,390), as well as the width of the chart. Additionally, it defines the labels for each column, along with optional settings for the text. As shown in Figure 11-17, this labels the x-axis of the bar chart.

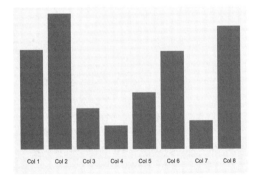

Figure 11-17 The bar chart with custom labels.

Labeling the y-axis is a bit more challenging, but certainly not impossible. Write it as an exercise, following the example for the x-axis. Alternatively, if you need y-axis labels and don't want to write this bit of code, consider using a different library for your bar chart, such as Raphy Charts: `http://softwarebyjosh.com/raphy-charts/`.

Line Chart

Fortunately, gRaphaël's line charts are a little more robust than its bar charts. The API is also fairly similar, the main difference being that you need to pass two value arrays for the x and y values:

```
var xVals = [0, 5, 10, 15, 20, 25, 30, 35, 40, 45, 50, 55],
    yVals = [63, 84, 75, 91, 62, 75, 35, 53, 47, 75, 78, 54];

var chart = paper.linechart(0, 0, 600, 380, xVals, yVals);
```

Here, the first two arguments are the start coordinates (0,0), followed by the width and height of the chart, and then the two value arrays. It generates a very basic line graph as shown in Figure 11-18.

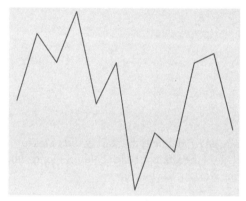

Figure 11-18 gRaphaël's basic line chart.

You can also pass multiple sets of values to add lines to the chart:

```
var xVals = [0, 5, 10, 15, 20, 25, 30, 35, 40, 45, 50, 55],
    yVals1 = [63, 84, 75, 91, 62, 75, 35, 53, 47, 75, 78, 54],
    yVals2 = [24, 45, 31, 42, 88, 85, 67, 88, 72, 37, 54, 48];

var chart = paper.linechart(0, 0, 600, 380, xVals, [yVals1, yVals2]);
```

Here, a second set of y values has been added, which uses the same set of x values as shown in Figure 11-19.

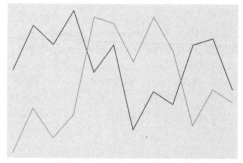

Figure 11-19 You can add multiple lines to the chart.

Fortunately, unlike bar charts, gRaphaël provides native methods for adding axes to line charts. Axes can be added using the `axis` option:

```
var chart = paper.linechart(30, 0, 570, 380, xVals, [yVals1, yVals2],
{axis: '0 0 1 1'});
```

The `axis` string defines which axes to render in TRBL order (top right bottom left)—in this case, showing the bottom and left axes (see Figure 11-20). Also notice how the `x_start` and `width` arguments have been adjusted to allow for 30px of room for the y-axis.

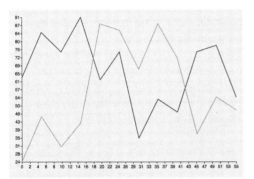

Figure 11-20 A line chart with axes.

Finally, you may have noticed that the step values on the axes are a bit strange. Since the x values are all evenly spaced, labeling them accordingly is good practice. You can set up more natural labeling using the `axisxstep` option:

```
var chart = paper.linechart(30, 0, 570, 380, xVals, [yVals1, yVals2],
{axis:
'0 0 1 1', axisxstep: 11});
```

Now the x-axis is labeled much more intuitively, as you can see in Figure 11-21.

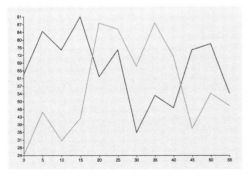

Figure 11-21 The axisxstep value has been adjusted in this chart.

The `axisxstep` value is a bit confusing since it is one less than the number of steps you want to show. In this case, the value of 11 shows the 12 steps on the axis.

> gRaphaël's axis-labeling options leave a lot to be desired. The documentation states that `axisxstep` and `axisystep` define the distance between values in axes x and y. However, in actuality, they define the number of steps on each axis, which is considerably less useful. Hopefully, this shortcoming will be resolved soon.

3D Canvas with WebGL

One of the most exciting aspects of writing JavaScript today is the ability to build full-scale 3D applications directly in the browser. These apps are possible thanks to the WebGL engine, which has been integrated as a special context of the HTML5 canvas element. However, writing code with WebGL is challenging because the API is really low level—meaning that it was designed for power rather than ease of use. Therefore you can accomplish just about anything you want with the API, provided you are willing to navigate large blocks of code for even the smallest tasks. In fact, the WebGL API is so low-level that working with it pretty much requires creating a library. Fortunately, a number of other developers have paved the way with some really great WebGL libraries for JavaScript. In this section, you learn how to use one of the best WebGL libraries, Three.js.

Introducing Three.js

Although Three.js streamlines WebGL development, it still uses a few concepts that may be foreign if you haven't worked with 3D programming. In this subsection, I introduce you to all the techniques you need to render a basic 3D scene—such as cameras, geometry, materials, and lighting.

Setting Up the Scene

To get started, download the latest version of Three.js (`https://github.com/mrdoob/three.js`) and include it on your page along with a container element:

```
<div id="container" style="background-color: #000; width: 600px;
height: 400px;"></div>
```

Now, set up the scene with some basic JS:

```
// get the wrapper
var container = document.getElementById('container'),
    width = container.offsetWidth,
    height = container.offsetHeight;

// create renderer and add it to the container
var renderer = new THREE.WebGLRenderer();
renderer.setSize( width, height );
container.appendChild( renderer.domElement );

// create a new scene
var scene = new THREE.Scene();
```

WebGL Caveats

Before you get too excited about using WebGL in the browser, it's important to remember a few caveats. First, browser support isn't entirely there yet. While WebGL canvas is supported in most desktop browsers, it's not supported in any version of IE at the time of this writing. Additionally, mobile coverage is very poor, with support existing only in the latest version of Blackberry Browser. Fortunately, Three.js provides a 2D canvas fallback that you learn about at the end of this section.

Furthermore, performance is still an issue with WebGL canvas. While performance is improving, don't expect the same capabilities as with desktop applications.

This snippet references the container for the scene and creates a WebGL renderer and scene in Three.js. Make sure to call this script sometime after the container is added to the DOM.

Adding a Camera

Next, create an integral part of any 3D scene—the camera. By itself, a 3D scene in WebGL is just a conceptual model of how shapes exist in 3D space. The camera is used to render that information and relay it to the user:

```
// create a camera, position it and add it to the scene
var camera = new THREE.PerspectiveCamera( 45, width/height, 0.1, 1000 );
camera.position.z = 400;
scene.add( camera );
```

Here, a new camera is added to the scene.

- The first argument in `THREE.PerspectiveCamera` is the angle of view for the camera lens. Generally, a good option is 45°, but you can increase it to 80° for a wide-angle lens effect (like the fish-eye lens in skateboarding videos).

- The next argument is the aspect ratio; in this case, it uses the aspect ratio of the container element.

- The last two values are the near and far boundaries that you want to render in the scene. WebGL conserves resources by limiting the scope of the scene that is rendered in the camera. Thus you can improve performance by using intelligent defaults for the scene area to allow the engine to ignore irrelevant distances.

After the camera is created, you then position it in the scene. Much like the shapes that make up a scene, the camera also exists in 3D space. You can think of this position as where you want the cameraman to stand and film the scene that will eventually unfold. In this example, `camera.position.z` moves the camera 400 units along the z-axis.

Adding a Mesh

In WebGL, any shape you add to the scene is called a *mesh*. Meshes are made up of two components:

- Geometry, which defines the vertices that shape the object
- Material, which defines how the surface of the material is lit and rendered

To add a simple sphere to the scene, the script needs to create these components:

```
// add a sphere
var geometry = new THREE.SphereGeometry( 100, 24, 24 ),
    material = new THREE.MeshPhongMaterial({
      color: 0x00FF00
    }),
    sphere = new THREE.Mesh( geometry, material );

scene.add( sphere );
```

This code first creates some sphere geometry. The first argument defines a radius of 100 units, and the second two define the number of segments and rings to use when creating the model. The more segments and rings you use, the smoother the surface of the model will appear when rendered. That's because a sphere in WebGL isn't a true sphere: It's an approximation made up of polygons. To get an idea of how this works, see Figure 11-22.

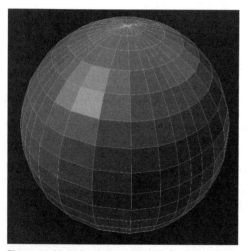

Figure 11-22 A 3D sphere comprised of polygons. The jagged edges are smoothed by the renderer at runtime. This sphere was rendered using the 3D graphics program Blender, but WebGL uses the same concept.

Next, a Phong material is defined with a color of #00FF00. Phong is a type of shader that defines how light affects the object in the renderer. Don't worry too much about shaders just yet. Finally, the geometry and the material are put together to create the mesh, which is added to the scene.

Another common material option in Three.js is `MeshLambertMaterial`, **which is similar to Phong except that Lambert is less reflective and tends to show less shadow.**

Adding a Light

Now that the camera and sphere have been added to the scene, it's just about finished. However, if you try rendering it as is, Three.js shows a black screen because you still have to add lighting:

```
// add a light
var light = new THREE.DirectionalLight( 0xFFFFFF, 1 );
light.position.set( 0, 0.5, 1 );
scene.add( light );
```

This code adds a directional light to the scene. The first argument specifies the color of light, and the second specifies the intensity. Directional lights are one of a handful of different lighting options in Three.js, including ambient light (which lights the whole scene evenly) and point light (which emanates from an individual point like a candle). Directional lights, on the other hand, light evenly in a given direction, much like the parallel rays of the sun beating down on the earth (okay, practically parallel).

To set the angle of the directional light, you just have to position it. Here, the light is positioned 0.5 units up on the y-axis and 1 unit toward the camera on the z-axis. The light then automatically orients its angle to point into the origin (0,0,0). In this case, the result is a 30° angle down and away from the camera.

Rendering the Scene

Last but not least, you need to render the scene:

```
renderer.render( scene, camera );
```

As shown in Figure 11-23, this script creates a simple sphere.

Figure 11-23 This sphere has been rendered with Three.js and WebGL.

Just to recap, here's the entire example:

```
// get the wrapper
var container = document.getElementById('container'),
    width = container.offsetWidth,
    height = container.offsetHeight;

// create renderer and add it to the container
var renderer = new THREE.WebGLRenderer();
```

```
renderer.setSize( width, height );
container.appendChild( renderer.domElement );

// create a new scene
var scene = new THREE.Scene();

// create a camera, position it and add it to the scene
var camera = new THREE.PerspectiveCamera( 45, width/height, 0.1, 1000 );
camera.position.z = 400;
scene.add( camera );

// add a sphere
var geometry = new THREE.SphereGeometry( 100, 24, 24 ),
    material = new THREE.MeshPhongMaterial({
      color: 0x00FF00
    }),
    sphere = new THREE.Mesh( geometry, material );

scene.add( sphere );

// add a light
var light = new THREE.DirectionalLight( 0xFFFFFF, 1 );
light.position.set( 0, 0.5, 1 );
scene.add( light );

// render it
renderer.render( scene, camera );
```

As shown in this example, you take four main steps to render this scene in Three.js:

1. Set up the renderer and the scene.

2. Add a camera and position it in 3D space.

3. Build the geometry and material to create a mesh for your shape.

4. Light the scene.

Creating Texture with Images

The previous example used a simple block color when creating the material for the sphere. But Three.js also allows you to use images to create custom textures for the models in your scene. For instance, you can add a realistic Earth texture to the sphere from the previous example. First, go to www.3dstudio-max.com/download.php?id=57 and download the Earth texture, which is shown in Figure 11-24.

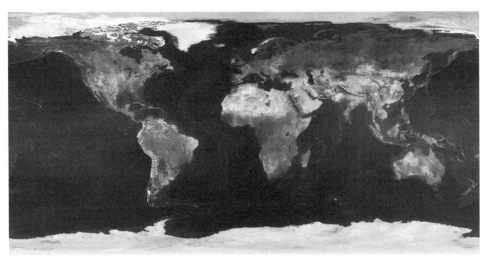

Figure 11-24 The Earth texture will be mapped to the sphere.

Next, add this texture to the mesh:

```
// add image map
var map = THREE.ImageUtils.loadTexture( 'images/earth.jpg' );

// add the earth
var geometry = new THREE.SphereGeometry( 100, 24, 24 ),
    material = new THREE.MeshPhongMaterial({
        map: map
    }),
    earth = new THREE.Mesh( geometry, material );

scene.add( earth );
```

Here, `THREE.ImageUtils.loadTexture()` is used to load the texture into Three.js. That texture is then assigned to the Phong material as an image map. However, if you try to render the scene now, you will most likely have problems because the image takes a little while to load. To get around this issue, make sure to render it after the window loads:

```
window.onload = function() {
  renderer.render( scene, camera );
};
```

In Figure 11-25, the image map positions the texture correctly around the sphere to make it look like the planet Earth. This calculation is actually very complex under the hood, so be thankful that Three.js handles it for you and that you aren't writing vanilla WebGL.

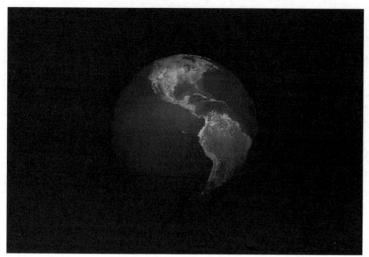

Figure 11-25 A sphere with a photorealistic image map.

Animating 3D Canvas

You now know how to render static 3D scenes with WebGL. But if you needed only static images, you could just render them in a 3D graphics program and include a basic <image> on the page. The real reason to use WebGL is to create interactive, animated 3D scenes, which is precisely what you learn in this subsection.

Animation in the WebGL canvas works similarly to that in the 2D canvas: You simply draw and redraw the scene for each frame in the animation. For example, the following script rotates the Earth:

```
window.onload = function() {
  var rotation = 0;

  var animationLoop = setInterval(function() {
    rotation += 0.05;
    earth.rotation.y = rotation;
    renderer.render( scene, camera );
  }, 100);
};
```

This example uses a basic interval to adjust the rotation of the earth mesh every 100 milliseconds. If you run the script in your browser, you'll see the Earth slowly rotating around its axis.

> In the next chapter, you discover how to use HTM5's `requestAnimationFrame`, an alternative to animating with a simple interval. `requestAnimationFrame` produces smoother animations with better performance.

Adding Mouse Events

Earlier in the "Canvas Mouse Events" section, you saw that applying event listeners to canvas drawings is tricky since the drawn shapes can't be referenced in the DOM. Unfortunately, WebGL canvas is no exception. You can, however, use a technique to add mouse interactivity to your 3D scenes. The trick is essentially to create a ray from the camera to the mouse position and see if that intersects the object:

```
var projector = new THREE.Projector();

container.onmousedown = function(e) {
  e.preventDefault();

  var vector = new THREE.Vector3( ( e.pageX - this.offsetLeft ) /
this.offsetWidth * 2 - 1, - ( e.pageY - this.offsetTop ) /
this.offsetHeight *  2 + 1, 0.5 );
  projector.unprojectVector( vector, camera );

  var raycaster = new THREE.Raycaster( camera.position, vector.sub(
camera.position ).normalize() );

  var intersects = raycaster.intersectObject( earth );

  if ( intersects.length > 0 ) {
    console.log('Earth');
  }
};
```

The script first uses `Three.Vector3()` to create a vector from the mouse position relative to its container. That vector is then "unprojected" (projected in reverse) toward the camera. Next, a ray is cast from the camera toward the unprojected vector. If that ray intersects the object, the user is clicking that object.

> Don't worry about following the code in THREE.Vector3—you can simply reuse this snippet to unproject vectors and calculate intersection.

You can also use this technique with layered objects to ensure that the mouse event applies to only the topmost object. For example, you can add a moon to this scene:

```
var moonGeometry = new THREE.SphereGeometry( 20, 24, 24 ),
    moonMaterial = new THREE.MeshPhongMaterial({
      color: 0xDDDDDD
    }),
    moon = new THREE.Mesh( moonGeometry, moonMaterial );
moon.position.z = 150;
moon.position.x = 50;

scene.add( moon );
```

Now, instead of using `intersectObject` in the click handler, use `intersectObjects` with an array of objects:

```
var intersects = raycaster.intersectObjects( [earth, moon] );

if ( intersects.length > 0 ) {
  var topObjectId = intersects[0].object.id;

  if ( topObjectId == earth.id ) {
    console.log('Earth');
  }
  else if ( topObjectId == moon.id ) {
    console.log('Moon');
  }
}
```

This script first passes both the `earth` and `moon` mesh references into `intersectsObjects`. Then it determines the `id` of the topmost object that intersects the click event, which is the first item in the `intersects` array. Finally, it compares that `id` to those of the two objects to determine which is the top layer.

Using a 2D Canvas Fallback

Unfortunately, browser support for WebGL canvas is still lacking, with no IE support and very limited mobile coverage at the time of this writing (details here: `http://caniuse.com/#feat=webgl`). However, one of the nicest features of the Three.js library is its built-in fallback to 2D canvas. Although the fallback doesn't look as nice as the WebGL renderer, it provides a certain amount of coverage for non-supportive browsers. Setting up the 2D renderer works just like it does with the WebGL counterpart:

```
var renderer = new THREE.CanvasRenderer();
```

To use the fallback, simply set up detection for WebGL support, using either Modernizr or Three.js' built-in detector:

```
var renderer = Detector.webgl ? new THREE.WebGLRenderer():
  new THREE.CanvasRenderer();
```

The 2D canvas renderer certainly isn't as pretty, but it's a decent fallback, as you can see in Figure 11-26.

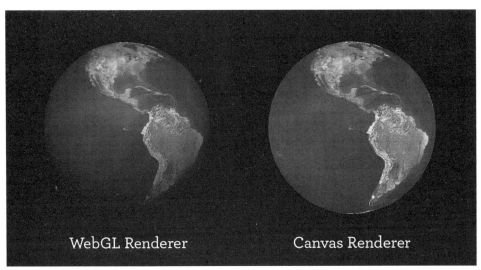

Figure 11-26 Comparison of Three.js' WebGL and Canvas renderers. The WebGL version on the left has better shading and lighting. Additionally, the canvas version shows some artifacts of the polygons used to create the image map.

3D Transforms in CSS

You don't necessarily need WebGL to create interactive 3D graphics on the web. Provided that the functionality you need is simple enough, you may be able to accomplish the same features using 3D transforms in CSS3.

While browser support still isn't perfect for 3D transforms, they are supported in the current versions of all major desktop and mobile browsers (details provided at `http://caniuse.com/#feat=transforms3d`). That's a good deal better than WebGL canvas, which isn't supported in IE10, iOS Safari, or Android Browser at the time of this writing.

Of course, CSS3's capabilities are a lot more limited than those of WebGL, being confined to basic manipulations of flat objects, such as rotating a card or line of text in 3D space. To see how this works, start with the following markup:

```
<div class="container">
  <div class="card">CSS3 Transform</div>
</div>
```

Then style it with 3D transforms (relevant parts in bold):

```
.container {
  width: 400px;
  height: 250px;
  position: relative;
```

```
    -webkit-perspective: 500px;
       -moz-perspective: 500px;
            perspective: 500px;
}

.card {
  position: absolute;
  top: 0;
  right: 0;
  bottom: 0;
  left: 0;
  padding: 50px;
  font-size: 50px;
  background: tomato;
  color: #FFF;
  -webkit-transform: rotateY( 45deg );
     -moz-transform: rotateY( 45deg );
          transform: rotateY( 45deg );

}
```

The first step for 3D transforms is defining the perspective on the parent element. That's similar to setting the angle of view for the camera in WebGL—it alters how the 3D view is rendered. Next, the CSS applies the actual 3D transforms to the `.card`. These rotate it 45º around the y-axis, producing the slightly angled card shown in Figure 11-27.

Figure 11-27 This card has been rotated using CSS3 transforms.

By default, perspective applies to only the direct descendants of an element. To extend it to all descendants, add `transform-style: preserve-3d` to the `.card` element (along with the `-webkit` and `-moz` extensions).

To animate the transform, you have a couple options. First, you can use a CSS3 transition:

```
.card {
  position: absolute;
  top: 0;
  right: 0;
  bottom: 0;
  left: 0;
  padding: 50px;
  font-size: 48px;
  background: tomato;
  color: #FFF;
  -webkit-transform: rotateY( 45deg );
     -moz-transform: rotateY( 45deg );
          transform: rotateY( 45deg );
  -webkit-transition: -webkit-transform .5s ease;
     -moz-transition:    -moz-transform .5s ease;
          transition:         transform .5s ease;
}

.card:hover {
  -webkit-transform: rotateY( -45deg );
     -moz-transform: rotateY( -45deg );
          transform: rotateY( -45deg );
}
```

Here, CSS applies a transition to the element, which will smoothly animate between style changes. Then a `:hover` pseudo class is added to the card, to rotate it backward to –45°. Alternatively, you can use CSS keyframe animation (the next chapter has more about transitions and keyframe animations).

Another option is to animate the change with JavaScript. However, doing so generally isn't a good idea since the CSS3 animations tend to outperform JavaScript alternatives. That said, you can take advantage of the CSS3's animation performance, while still triggering the actual change using JavaScript. Simply apply a new class to alter the style of the transform, and then let the previously applied transition handle the animation for you.

Summary

In this chapter, you discovered a number of techniques for rendering graphics in the browser. First, you learned about canvas and SVG and how to use both technologies to render basic shapes. You then animated these shapes and applied mouse interactivity.

Next, you jump-started your 2D drawing capabilities with the SVG library Raphaël.js. With Raphaël, you examined how to draw more complex shapes and how to add a variety of styling options and take advantage of the built-in animation support. Then you extended your knowledge of Raphaël on to gRaphaël, a simple charting library.

After solidifying your skills for 2D graphics, you moved on to 3D canvas with WebGL. You learned how to use the Three.js library to render a basic scene using cameras, lighting, geometry and materials. Then you discovered image maps and used them to create a photorealistic texture for the scene. Next ,you learned how to animate the 3D canvas, as well as a technique for adding mouse event handlers to the scene. Finally, you considered an alternative to WebGL: 3D transforms in CSS3. These transforms aren't nearly as powerful as WebGL but can provide a more elegant solution to simple problems.

Now that you are able to draw custom 2D and 3D graphics in the browser, the possibilities are practically endless for what you can achieve on the front end. Use these techniques to create a rich, interactive app that will delight and impress your users.

Additional Resources

Inspiration

Chrome Experiments: `www.chromeexperiments.com`

21 Ridiculously Impressive HTML5 Canvas Experiments: `http://net.tutsplus.com/articles/web-roundups/21-ridiculously-impressive-html5-canvas-experiments`

Interactive Experiments Focused on HTML5: `http://hakim.se/experiments`

Canvas

Canvas Tutorial: `https://developer.mozilla.org/en-US/docs/HTML/Canvas/Tutorial`

Fulten, Steve, and Jeff Fulton. *HTML5 Canvas* (O'Reilly Media, Inc., 2011): `http://shop.oreilly.com/product/0636920013327.do`

SVG

SVG Tutorial: `https://developer.mozilla.org/en-US/docs/SVG/Tutorial`

SVG Path String Specifications: `www.w3.org/TR/SVG/paths.html#PathData`

Raphaël.js

Raphaël.js Documentation: `http://raphaeljs.com/reference.html`

gRaphaël Documentation: `http://g.raphaeljs.com/reference.html`

SVG with a Little Help from Raphaël: `www.alistapart.com/articles/svg-with-a-little-help-from-raphael`

Ready Set Raphaël (SVG Converter): `www.readysetraphael.com`

WebGL

WebGL Fundamentals: `www.html5rocks.com/en/tutorials/webgl/webgl_fundamentals`

Cantor, Diego, and Brandon Jones. *WebGL Beginner's Guide* (Packt Publishing, 2012): `www.packtpub.com/webgl-javascript-beginners-guide/book`

Three.js

Three.js Documentation: `http://mrdoob.github.com/three.js/docs`

Parisi, Tony. *WebGL: Up and Running* (O'Reilly Media, Inc., 2012): `http://shop.oreilly.com/product/0636920024729.do`

Take a Whirlwind Look at Three.js: `http://2011.12devsofxmas.co.uk/2012/01/webgl-and-three-js`

Three.js Click Event Example: `http://mrdoob.github.com/three.js/examples/canvas_interactive_cubes.html`

3D Transforms in CSS3

Intro to CSS 3D Transforms: `http://desandro.github.com/3dtransforms`

20 Stunning Examples of CSS 3D Transforms: `www.netmagazine.com/features/20-stunning-examples-css-3d-transforms`

Chapter 12
Launching Your App

At this point, you're just about ready to launch your app. However, the development process may have introduced performance issues. Now that the majority of the code has been written, it's an excellent time to step back and assess the overall performance of the app.

In this chapter, you discover performance testing techniques that complement the Test Driven Development (TDD) approach you established in Chapter 1. These tests help you identify problem areas and create a solid optimization plan.

Next, you learn the differences between perceived and actual performance, as well as how to compress files properly for the smallest filesizes. Then you hear about techniques for optimizing animation. These include dipping into CSS3 animation techniques, as well as HTML5's cutting edge `requestAnimationFrame` API. Afterwards, you discover some more general optimization approaches such as reducing tasks and minimizing browser reflows. Finally, you explore different deployment options, such as Content Delivery Networks (CDNs) and scalable server clouds.

Performance Checklist

One of the most important features of any app is how quickly it runs. In the past, optimization efforts were focused primarily on the server: improving latency issues and increasing capabilities to handle more concurrent requests. However, in recent years, developers have begun to focus much more on client-side performance, which comes primarily down to JavaScript. Although you can throw money at server-side performance (by purchasing better servers), you really can't do anything about client-side performance, other than optimize the code. That's because you have no control over the devices used to access your app. You may think that this becomes less of an issue because computers are constantly improving, but as more users move to browsing the web on mobile devices, your app needs to be compatible with much slower processors. Additionally, even on desktop computers, users have higher expectations for the level of interactivity an app should provide.

Where to Focus

That said, it doesn't make much sense to optimize all the code in your app. Sure, you should make efforts to optimize code as you write it, but it's not really worthwhile to go in afterward and refactor every line. Instead, you should test the code and determine where performance bottlenecks arise.

Testing Performance

If you've set up unit tests with QUnit, you should already be getting data about the test execution time. But there's another way to test performance when you want to compare two different approaches: the benchmark testing at `http://jsperf.com`.

jsPerf makes it easy to compare the performance of short scripts and to compare them across different browsers, as you can see in Figure 12-1.

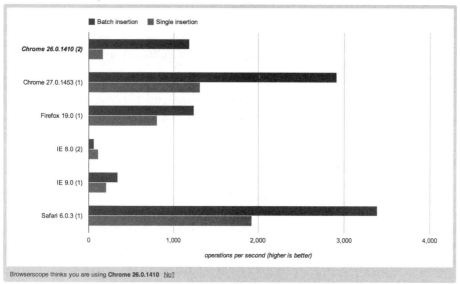

Figure 12-1 jsPerf caches all the browsers you use to run the benchmarks, and provides them for easy comparison.

Although jsPerf is great for testing individual micro-optimizations, it's not very useful for testing the speed of an entire app. For that, use either QUnit or the profiler tool in Chrome or Firefox.

Another useful tool for performance testing is the profiler in the WebKit developer tools. You can use the JavaScript profiler to gather data as to what parts of your code are executing most and what parts are demanding more resources, as you can see in Figure 12-2.

Repeated Code

Beyond testing, it's also a good idea to focus on optimizing code that is executed repeatedly. The more often a function runs, the larger the gains will be when optimizing. So take a look at your loops and any reused functions first.

You can also do yourself a favor ahead of time and follow the practice referred to as Don't Repeat Yourself (DRY) by abstracting the commonly used parts into their own functions so that they can be shared throughout your app. The benefit of doing this is that your code is easier to maintain and test in addition to reducing the total filesize.

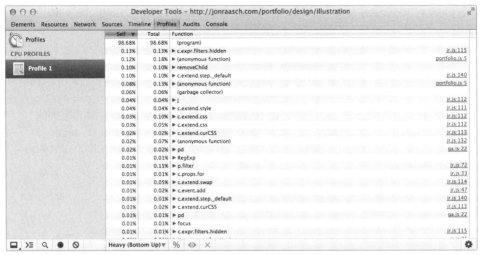

Figure 12-2: The JavaScript profiler from WebKit's built-in developer tools.

Actual Versus Perceived Performance

Finally, note that there are two different types of performance: actual and perceived. It ultimately doesn't matter how fast a benchmark test thinks your app is running; what matters is the user's perception.

The classic case for perceived performance is offloading certain tasks for later, so that the user sees something happen on the page as soon as possible. For instance, say you have a JavaScript chart that is really resource-intensive. It doesn't make sense to block the rest of the page while the chart loads. Instead, first load the entire page with a "loading" gif and then load the chart at the end.

Even though the script takes the same amount of time to load (or even slightly longer), users will perceive better performance because they will be able to interact with the other parts of the page while the slower component finishes loading.

> The perceived performance improvements in this example don't have to stop with the chart—you can set up the page to load the bare minimum you need to display the smallest amount of relevant data, then load the rest on demand.

Asset Management

When it comes to optimization, you can see the largest gains in the way you're serving assets like `.js` files. You can use a number of techniques to reduce the size of these files, and thereby reduce the bandwidth requirements of your site or app.

Sure, users have more bandwidth and download files faster these days. But faster speeds also lead to increased expectations, so you had better do everything you can to reduce the size of files. After all, many mobile networks are still comparatively slow, and you can never be sure how a user is connecting to your app.

In this section, I cover a three-pronged approach: minification, gzip compression, and hosting. These techniques can reduce the size of files dramatically; it's not uncommon to see reductions of 90 percent or more when using these methods. Chances are that you're already doing some of this, but making sure you're following all of these guidelines will ensure that your JavaScript will load as quickly as possible.

Minification

This one is pretty much a no-brainer. Before you go to production, make sure you run your code through a minifier or packer to strip out any whitespace and comments, and reduce the characters in local variables. Depending on how many of these characters can be removed, you will see substantial gains when minifying— for instance, a 100K file shrinking to 30K.

But keep in mind that not all minifiers are the same. They handle things a bit differently and produce different sized files. My personal favorite is the Google Closure Compiler (`http://code.google.com/p/closure-compiler`), because it consistently provides some of the smallest minified files. For example, see this comparison: `http://coderjournal.com/2010/01/yahoo-yui-compressor-vs-microsoft-ajax-minifier-vs-google-closure-compiler/`.

You can download the compiler and run it in your computer's terminal, or use the online version here: `http://closure-compiler.appspot.com`. If you're running Node, take a look at the Uber-Compiler module (which also compiles LESS): `https://github.com/kennberg/node-uber-compiler`.

> You should also minify your CSS and consider minifying markup as well.

Gzip Compression

In addition to minifying, you should also gzip files. Gzipping will further reduce the size of files, with substantial gains. Gzipped files are typically a third of the size of their non-compressed counterparts. For instance, take a look at jQuery 2.0. The uncompressed, non-minified core is 240K. That gets minified down to 83K, which is further compressed with gzip to under 30K. That's an 88 percent difference from the original!

Best of all, gzipping can be done dynamically on the server. If you're using Node, simply install one of these compression modules: `https://github.com/joyent/node/wiki/modules#wiki-compression`.

Or if you're on an Apache server, gzipping can be done from the `.htaccess` file:

```
# compress text, html, javascript, css, xml:
AddOutputFilterByType DEFLATE text/plain
AddOutputFilterByType DEFLATE text/html
AddOutputFilterByType DEFLATE text/xml
AddOutputFilterByType DEFLATE text/css
AddOutputFilterByType DEFLATE application/xml
AddOutputFilterByType DEFLATE application/xhtml+xml
AddOutputFilterByType DEFLATE application/rss+xml
AddOutputFilterByType DEFLATE application/javascript
AddOutputFilterByType DEFLATE application/x-javascript
```

> Also gzip `.css` and `.html` files (or output gzipped markup from a dynamic page).

Hosting

After you've prepared the `.js` file by minifying and gzipping, it's time to host it. But rather than host it on your main server, it's best to upload it to a CDN, for a number of reasons. I discuss these advantages later in this chapter in the "Deployment" section.

Animation Optimization

Another place you can see substantial gains in performance is within your app's animations. Animation is one of the heaviest processes for the browser because it has to draw and redraw the page repeatedly for each frame of the animation.

Additionally, performance is particularly *noticeable* in animation. That's because the better an animation performs, the more frames the browser can render per second. Poorly optimized animations look choppy because the browser has to drop too many frames, whereas high performance animations appear smooth and seamless to viewers.

> Before you start optimizing an animation, decide whether you need it at all. Sure, animation can provide a better user experience, but bad performance will outweigh any of that. So pick your battles when it comes to animation and animate only important areas. Remember: Too much animation can be a bad experience because users have to wait for each animation to complete.

CSS3 Animation

CSS3 introduces transition and keyframe animations, both of which can be used as an alternative to JavaScript. Because these animations can be optimized by the browser and take advantage of hardware acceleration, it's a good idea to do this wherever possible. As a result, in capable devices, the graphics processing unit (GPU) rather than the central processing unit (CPU) will be used to render the animation. The GPU is not only better suited for rendering, but it also frees up the CPU to focus on other tasks.

Combining CSS3 Animation with JavaScript

Using CSS3 animation doesn't mean you have to handle everything in the stylesheet. You can still start the animation with JavaScript; simply add a transition to a class name and then apply that class using JS.

First, start with the CSS:

```
.my-element {
  position: absolute;
  top: 0;
  left: 0;
```

```
        -webkit-transition: left 500ms ease;
          -moz-transition: left 500ms ease;
               transition: left 500ms ease;
}

.my-element.slide-left {
  left: 200px;
}
```

Next, attach the `slide-left` class to your element with jQuery:

```
$('.my-element').addClass('slide-left');
```

When this class is applied, it animates the element 200px to the left over the course of 500 milliseconds.

Downsides of CSS3 Animation

Unfortunately, CSS3 animation can be more difficult to work with than the JavaScript techniques you're already used to. For example, jQuery animations have an intuitive callback function that is called whenever the animation completes. Although you can accomplish the same thing using CSS3's `transitionend` handler, this event fires whenever any transition completes, and it can be difficult to discern which transition triggered it. To make matters worse, it fires multiple times if you are transitioning multiple properties (for example, both `height` and `width` on the same transition).

More importantly, CSS3 animation creates an organizational issue because animation is often more of a scripting task than a styling one, so it doesn't make sense to have that code in the stylesheet. Sometimes it's not a big deal; for instance, if you want to transition the color of a link on hover, that animation is just a styling thing. But once you start using JavaScript to apply CSS3 animation and then try to handle the `transitionend` event in the JS, you'll have pieces of the same script running from completely different locations. That doesn't mean you should avoid this practice altogether. Sometimes you need to use CSS3 animation; for example, on underpowered mobile devices, it can be a lifesaver. But you also need to understand the drawbacks to this development pattern.

Finally, keep in mind that browser support is still lacking for CSS3 animation. Fortunately, as of IE10, the latest A-list browsers all support transition and keyframe animation (with the exception of Opera Mini). However, earlier versions of IE don't support it, and that still represents a considerable market share at the time of this writing. With transitions, it's typically not a major issue, since they simply fall back to immediate, non-animated style changes. On the other hand, keyframe animation is a different story. Of course if any of these animations are mission-critical, you can always write a JavaScript fallback or use a polyfill.

Request Animation Frame

Alternatively, if you'd like to avoid the rat's nest of interfacing with CSS3 transitions, you can get a best-of-both-worlds solution using the HTML5 `requestAnimationFrame` API. This API provides a more performance-friendly way for the browser to render each frame of an animation.

Why You Should Use Request Animation Frame

Typically when animating in JavaScript, you use a timer loop like `setTimeout` to make CSS changes every few milliseconds. But that isn't necessarily the best approach because it's impossible to figure out the best frame rate to use on each user's machine. Make changes too slowly, and your animation appears choppier than it has to. Make changes too quickly, and the browser chokes on extra rendering tasks that it ultimately won't perform (because the timer will have moved on to the next frame of the animation).

Additionally, even if the CPU can handle the extra frames, they have to be timed to match the refresh rate of the user's screen—the rate at which the screen displays a new frame. Different devices have different refresh rates. The standard is 60 Hz, but a laptop in power-saving mode might use a refresh rate of 50 Hz, and some desktop monitors are 70 Hz.

That's where `requestAnimationFrame` comes in. It provides a better way to animate in the browser, by providing an API to render frames according to the capabilities of the device, rather than setting them to an arbitrary timer. Then the browser can render frames as quickly as it is able, potentially dropping that rate to better align with the screen's refresh rate.

> You might think that it doesn't make much difference, but our eyes are finely tuned to motion and notice even the slightest change in frame rate. Thus it's better to be consistently lower in your frame rate than to drop frames at random. The former appears smooth, and the latter appears choppy.

Request Animation Frame Polyfill

Before you get started with `requestAnimationFrame`, make sure you're using this polyfill from Paul Irish:

```
(function() {
 var lastTime = 0;
 var vendors = ['ms', 'moz', 'webkit', 'o'];
 for(var x = 0; x < vendors.length && !window.requestAnimationFrame; ++x)
{
    window.requestAnimationFrame = window[vendors[x]+'RequestAnimationFra
me'];
    window.cancelAnimationFrame =
      window[vendors[x]+'CancelAnimationFrame'] || window[vendors[x]+'Canc
elRequestAnimationFrame'];
  }

  if (!window.requestAnimationFrame)
    window.requestAnimationFrame = function(callback, element) {
      var currTime = new Date().getTime();
      var timeToCall = Math.max(0, 16 - (currTime - lastTime));
      var id = window.setTimeout(function() { callback(currTime +
timeToCall); },
        timeToCall);
      lastTime = currTime + timeToCall;
```

```
      return id;
    };

  if (!window.cancelAnimationFrame)
    window.cancelAnimationFrame = function(id) {
      clearTimeout(id);
    };
}());
```

This polyfill aligns the different browser extensions and also provides a fallback for non-supportive browsers using timeouts. You can read more about it here: http://paulirish.com/2011/ requestanimationframe-for-smart-animating.

How to Use Request Animation Frame

After you include the polyfill, you're ready to get started. First, create some markup to work with:

```
<div id="my-element">Click to start</div>
```

And add some basic styling:

```
#my-element {
  position: absolute;
  left: 0;
  width: 200px;
  height: 200px;
  padding: 1em;
  background: tomato;
  color: #FFF;
  font-size: 2em;
  text-align: center;
}
```

Now here's the JavaScript:

```
var elem = document.getElementById('my-element'),
    startTime = null,
    endPos = 500, // in pixels
    duration = 2000; // in milliseconds

function render(time) {
  if (time === undefined) {
    time = newDate().getTime()
  }
  if (startTime === null) {
    startTime = time;
  }
```

```
    elem.style.left = ((time - startTime) / duration * endPos % endPos) +
  'px';
  }

  elem.onclick = function() {
    (function animationLoop(){
      render();
      requestAnimationFrame(animationLoop, elem);
    })();
  };
```

This script adds a click handler to the element, which will animate it 500 pixels to the right over the course of two seconds and then loop around to the beginning.

First, the `render()` function compares the current time against the start time to figure out the right position to render in the animation, similar to way you might handle it with a standard JavaScript timer.

Next, the `animationLoop()` function renders the current frame of the animation. It then calls `request AnimationFrame()`, passing itself and the element you want to animate, which sets up a loop that renders a new frame in the element's animation whenever the browser is ready to do so.

Running this script in your browser results in a decidedly smooth animation, even if you increase the speed substantially.

> Another advantage of `requestAnimationFrame` **is that it stops the animation when the current tab loses focus, conserving resources like power consumption.**

Doing Less

You can further optimize other parts of your app by following the mantra of "doing less." In this sense, optimization is really very simple. The more the browser has to do, the slower that work will be completed. Therefore, if you reduce the number of tasks, you improve speed. One easy way to reduce tasks is by caching anything you're reusing.

This technique is especially important when it comes to jQuery DOM references, since CSS selectors can be particularly resource-intensive even with the super-fast Sizzle engine. For example, you should avoid selecting DOM elements within a loop, unless the loop somehow changes what those selectors reference.

Take a look at the jsPerf test here: `http://jsperf.com/caching-jquery-dom-refs/2` (shown in Figure 12-3). As you can see, the cached selector is considerably faster than the selector that is called repeatedly in the loop.

Testing in Chrome 26.0.1410.43 on Mac OS X 10.8.3		
	Test	**Ops/sec**
Uncached Reference	```for (var i = 0; i < 10; i++) {\n $('h1').length;\n}```	17,871 ±0.92% 90% slower
Cached Reference	```var $h1 = $('h1');\n\nfor (var i = 0; i < 10; i++) {\n $h1.length;\n}```	177,663 ±0.33% fastest

Figure 12-3: The cached reference to $('h1') is much faster in Chrome.

Avoiding Reflows

Additionally, you can optimize client-side JavaScript by minimizing the amount of reflows on the page. A reflow occurs whenever the layout of an element changes. For instance, if you make a floated element wider, it pushes other floated elements down to the next line and then pushes the following elements downward in turn.

> **To get an idea of how reflows work, take a look at this visualization of reflows in action on a Gecko browser:** http://youtube/ZTnIxIA5KGw.

The best way to avoid reflows is to avoid unnecessary manipulation of the DOM. Whenever possible, batch any DOM changes and insert them at once.

See this jsPerf test, which appends images to the page either one at a time or all at once: http://jsperf.com/individual-vs-batch-jquery-insertion/6. As shown in Figure 12-4, the batched changes run considerably faster.

Testing in Chrome 26.0.1410.43 on Mac OS X 10.8.3		
	Test	**Ops/sec**
Single insertion	```// Times 10\nfixture.append(nyanImg);\nfixture.append(nyanImg);\nfixture.append(nyanImg);\nfixture.append(nyanImg);\nfixture.append(nyanImg);\nfixture.append(nyanImg);\nfixture.append(nyanImg);\nfixture.append(nyanImg);\nfixture.append(nyanImg);\nfixture.append(nyanImg);```	169 ±0.29% 86% slower
Batch insertion	```// Batch of 10\nvar batch = $(new Array(11).join(nyanImg));\nfixture.append(batch);```	1,231 ±3.22% fastest

Figure 12-4 Batching ten Nyan cat images is faster than appending them one at a time.

Deployment

After you've tested your app thoroughly and are happy with both the functionality and performance, it's time to deploy.

Deploying Static Assets on a CDN

There are a variety of performance advantages to deploying your app's static scripts to a CDN such as Amazon Simple Storage Service (S3).

Advantages of CDNs

First, CDNs distribute your files throughout the world, which reduces latency and increases availability because the files live closer to wherever users are requesting them. Remember, the Internet isn't magic; files still have to come from and go to somewhere—a trip that is limited by the speed of the electrical signal.

Second, CDNs are optimized to deliver static assets. For instance, on your site, you're probably using cookies in one way or another, if only for analytics. Every time a user requests a file from your server—be it HTML, JS, CSS, or an image—this cookie data is passed as part of the header.

Although cookies are relatively small (usually less than 1K), this extra data can really add up when you consider that it's being sent along with every single request. For that reason it's a good idea to host all static assets (JS, CSS, and images) on a CDN because CDNs don't pass any cookies along with the header. Third, CDNs provide aggressive HTTP caching capabilities, which reduce latency and increase output, allowing the CDN to handle massive traffic spikes. That, combined with a high level of redundancy contributes to an availability level that is difficult to match on your own server.

Disadvantages of CDNs

The only downside with using a CDN is that it introduces a new point of failure, which means that your site won't work if either your server or the CDN goes down. But you shouldn't worry about this issue too much. Most CDNs provide a high degree of redundancy, which ensures an extremely high uptime. I'm not saying CDNs will never go down, but that risk is far outweighed by the performance benefits it provides.

Just bear in mind that it's not unheard of for CDNs to go down, even popular CDNs that are considered extremely stable. For example, Amazon Web Service (AWS) has gone down in the past, which is always a highly publicized event because of the number of sites that depend on it. In October 2012, AWS went down, bringing down major sites like Reddit and Netflix with it.

Deploying Node Server on EC2

In addition to deploying the static front-end resources to a CDN, you can also deploy your Node implementation to a server cloud such as Amazon's Elastic Computer Cloud (EC2). EC2 servers are great because they are scalable, meaning that you can ramp up resources when you need them, and avoid paying for them when you don't. Thus you get a best-of-both-worlds solution: one that is cheap during slow periods but can handle just about any amount of load you throw at it. Of course, the more resources you use, the more you spend on hosting. But don't worry; you can set up limits that you're comfortable with.

To learn more about how to deploy your Node server to EC2, visit `http://rsms.me/2011/03/23/ec2-wep-app-template.html`.

The Launch

After all is said and done, you're finally ready to launch. So pat yourself on the back, take a break, grab a drink. However, don't get too comfortable, because issues always occur. Fires have to be put out, extreme edge cases crop up, and users won't understand certain features. But if you've done your due diligence pre-launch, you'll be able to limit the issues that come up afterward. No launch is perfect, but you'd better try to get close.

Hopefully, you haven't made the common release mistake of including too many features. From a business perspective, features are easier to add than they are to eliminate. You can always add features as users request them. But if you start with too many, you'll end up with a two-fold problem. First, your app will be exponentially more complicated and therefore more susceptible to bugs. Second, you'll end up supporting underused features forever.

I hope you discovered some new techniques in this book, but more importantly, I hope the book got you excited about JavaScript development. There's so much fun stuff going on in JavaScript, and it's only the beginning of this ever-evolving language.

You can always find new libraries to streamline new aspects of your development, as well as all the new DOM APIs that are increasing the capabilities of what you can achieve with JavaScript. Moreover, if you can't find a browser-level API for a feature you want, you can bet there will be one at some point—after all, you can suggest one yourself.

So keep learning and keep coding!

Additional Resources

Performance Testing

jsPerf. "JavaScript Performance Playground": `http://jsperf.com`

WebKit's JavaScript Profiler Explained: `http://fuelyourcoding.com/webkits-javascript-profiler-explained/`

File Compression

Online Closure Compiler Service: `http://closure-compiler.appspot.com`

Github. Kennberg: Node Uber-Compiler: `https://github.com/kennberg/node-uber-compiler`

Other Node Compression Modules: `https://github.com/joyent/node/wiki/modules#wiki-compression`

Compression Comparison: `http://coderjournal.com/2010/01/yahoo-yui-compressor-vs-microsoft-ajax-minifier-vs-google-closure-compiler/`

Animation Performance

Jank Busting for Better Rendering Performance: `www.html5rocks.com/en/tutorials/speed/rendering`

`requestAnimationFrame` for Smart Animating: `http://paulirish.com/2011/requestanimationframe-for-smart-animating`

CSS-Tricks. "A Tale of Animation Performance": `http://css-tricks.com/tale-of-animation-performance`

General Performance

Zakas, Nicholas C. *High Performance JavaScript*. (O'Reilly Media, Inc., 2010)

Smashing Magazine. "Writing Fast, Memory-Efficient JavaScript": `http://coding.smashingmagazine.com/2012/11/05/writing-fast-memory-efficient-javascript`

HTML5 Rocks. Chris Wilson. "Performance Tips for JavaScript in V8": `www.html5rocks.com/en/tutorials/speed/v8`

SlideShare Inc. Jake Archibald. "JavaScript—Optimising Where It Hurts": `www.slideshare.net/jaffathecake/optimising-where-it-hurts-jake-archibald`

SlideShare Inc. Steve Souders. "JavaScript Performance (at SFJS)": `www.slideshare.net/souders/javascript-performance-at-sfjs`

YouTube. "Gecko Reflow Visualization": `http://youtube/ZTnIxIA5KGw`

Deployment

Amazon S3: `http://aws.amazon.com/s3`

Amazon EC2: `http://aws.amazon.com/ec2`

Amazon AWS Goes Down Again, Takes Reddit with It: `www.forbes.com/sites/kellyclay/2012/10/22/amazon-aws-goes-down-again-takes-reddit-with-it`

A Template for Setting Up Node.js-Backed Web Apps on EC2: `http://rsms.me/2011/03/23/ec2-wep-app-template.html`

CSS Preprocessing with LESS

It may seem a bit strange to talk about CSS in a JavaScript book, but preprocessing with LESS is hardly your standard CSS. LESS adds some of the familiar traits of a dynamic language that you can use to write efficient CSS, allowing you to compile your app's CSS with JavaScript. This preprocessor enables you to build CSS with variables, functions, and all the other features you've always wanted to use in CSS. LESS speeds up the development process and also makes stylesheets more organized and easier to maintain.

In this appendix, you find out why you should be using CSS preprocessing and how to install an automated LESS compiler. Then you learn the basics of LESS, including variables, operators, and nesting. You also discover how to use functions and custom mixins. Finally, you structure your LESS and organize it into separate files.

Introducing LESS

LESS allows you to script your CSS with custom variables and functions. Then the scripted LESS file is compiled to static CSS before it ever reaches the browser, which means you can use scripting in your CSS development efforts but still serve regular old browser-friendly CSS to your users. Additionally, if you decide to move away from LESS, you can simply start developing with the generated CSS file. Thus, there's really no loss to using a preprocessor.

What's So Good About Preprocessing?

CSS preprocessing has a number of advantages, all of which boil down to speeding up development and organizing stylesheets. The most impressive use case for preprocessing is how it handles CSS3 vendor prefixes. Without a preprocessor, you must memorize a number of different prefixes, some of which may use entirely different syntaxes. For example, take a cross-browser linear gradient:

```
.my-element {
  background-image:  -khtml-gradient(linear, left top, left bottom,
from(#444), to(#000));
  background-image: -webkit-gradient(linear, left top, left bottom,
color-stop(0%,#444), color-stop(100%,#000));
  background-image: -webkit-linear-gradient(top, #444, #000);
  background-image:    -moz-linear-gradient(top, #444, #000);
  background-image:     -o-linear-gradient(top, #444, #000);
  background-image:        linear-gradient(top, #444, #000);
  filter: progid:DXImageTransform.Microsoft.gradient(
startColorstr='#444444', endColorstr='#000000', GradientType=0 );
}
```

Here you see three different formats for the gradient: the older `-webkit-gradient`, the newer `linear-gradient`, and an IE fallback using `filter`. However, rather than memorize and type these different syntaxes, you can use a simple LESS mixin:

```
.my-element {
  .vertical-gradient(#444, #000);
}
```

As you can see, the LESS version is much easier to write. Of course, this is an exaggerated example, and you probably wouldn't include the `-khtml-gradient` for Konqueror or `-o-linear-gradient` for older versions of Opera. But chances are that you're using at least some vendor prefixes in your stylesheets. Think about how much faster and easier it would be to use LESS.

LESS isn't the only CSS preprocessor. Other popular options include SASS and Stylus.

Installing a LESS Compiler

Browsers don't understand the LESS syntax, so you need to compile it to standard CSS before deploying your stylesheets. Fortunately, a number of different compilers work on each operating system:

- **LESS.app for Mac OS X:** First, if you're using Mac OS X, LESS.app is a very simple solution for LESS compilation. Download LESS.app from `http://incident57.com/less`. Open it and drag any LESS files/directories you want to watch into the app. Now, when you save a `.less` file, LESS.app automatically recompiles static CSS files.

- **SimpLESS for Windows and Linux:** If you're using Windows or Linux, you can download SimpLESS, which works across all operating systems (including Mac OS X if you'd prefer it over LESS.app). Simply download the app here: `http://wearekiss.com/simpless`. Just like with LESS.app, all you have to do is drag and drop LESS files into the app, and it automatically compiles them to static CSS when a change is made.

Compiling on the Server

You can also set up your server to compile LESS at runtime or whenever a LESS file changes. In Chapter 7, you learn how to use the Express framework to compile LESS files automatically on a Node server. Otherwise, if you're using PHP you can leverage lessphp: `http://leafo.net/lessphp/`, or simply search for a compiler for any other platform you're using.

LESS Basics

Now that you have a compiler installed, you can start writing LESS. Open a file called `style.less` and add it to your compiler. In this section you'll learn how to use some of the most basic features of less: variables, operators, and nesting.

Variables

One of the simplest and most powerful features of LESS is the ability to use variables. Variables are defined with @—for example, you can create a variable for padding:

```
@padding: 25px;

.my-element {
  width: 250px;
  padding: @padding;
}
```

When this LESS file is compiled to CSS, the @padding variable will be inserted into the rule for .my-element.

When you define variables in LESS, you can also take advantage of scope. The previous example defined a variable at the top level, but you can also define local variables within any { } brackets. For example, you can overwrite the @padding variable:

```
@padding: 25px;

.my-element {
  width: 250px;
  padding: @padding;
}

.less-padding {
  @padding: 10px;

  padding: @padding;
}

.another-element {
  padding: @padding;
}
```

Here the original @padding is overwritten in the block for .less-padding, giving it a padding of 10px. But this doesn't overwrite the global @padding variable of 25px, which will still be used later in the .another-element block.

Operators

You can also use basic math operators in LESS; for example, you can combine the @padding variable with some basic math:

```
@padding: 25px;

.more-padding {
  padding: @padding + 10;
}
```

Here the `.more-padding` block gets a padding of 35px, or 25px + 10px. You can use any math operator you want: +, −, *, and /. And don't be shy about using operators with numbers—they're not only for calculating variable changes. Because the LESS file will be compiled to CSS, there's no loss in using these basic operators when you're too lazy to do basic math.

In fact, this can often be a better idea because the stylesheet will show why a particular number is that way—for example, when handling box-model issues:

```
.bordered-element {
  border-left: 1px solid black;
  border-right: 1px solid black;
  width: 250px - 1 - 1;
}
```

Here, instead of writing the ambiguous 248px, the block uses operators to show that the width is compensating for the two border widths.

Nesting

My personal favorite part of LESS is also the simplest. Nesting allows you to organize selectors under parent elements, making the stylesheet faster to write and a whole lot more organized. For example, without LESS, you might have a number of different rules for your site's header:

```
header {
  min-width: 800px;
}

header nav {
  width: 800px;
  margin: 0 auto;
}

header nav li {
  list-style: none;
}

header a {
  text-decoration: none;
}
```

But your LESS file can clean this up a lot by nesting each rule within its parent:

```
header {
  min-width: 800px;

  nav {
    width: 800px;
    margin: 0 auto;

    li {
      list-style: none;
```

```
    }
  }

  a {
    text-decoration: none;
  }
}
```

When this LESS file compiles, it looks exactly like the previous example, with all the parent rules written out explicitly. But nesting saves you the hassle of constantly having to retype parent selectors. Furthermore, it organizes the rules into more meaningful blocks, such as the `header` section in this example.

> **The new CSS3 spec allows for nesting in actual CSS files. But with cross-browser support still a long way off, it would be foolish to use this in your compiled stylesheets.**

The & Symbol

So far you've seen nesting with parent-child relationships, but it can also be more versatile. You can use the & symbol to nest rules that are grouped, for example, without LESS you write this:

```
p {
  color: gray;
  padding: 10px;
}

p.more-padding {
  padding: 25px;
}
```

But you can use the & symbol to simplify this:

```
p {
  color: gray;
  padding: 10px;

  &.more-padding {
    padding: 25px;
  }
}
```

You can also use this with pseudo-classes—for example, to define a hover state for a link:

```
a {
  text-decoration: none;

  &:hover {
    text-decoration: underline;
  }
}
```

Furthermore, you can place the & symbol after a selector to reverse the parent-child order:

```
.child {
  color: blue;

  .parent & {
    color: red;
  }
}
```

This compiles as:

```
.child {
  color: blue;
}

.parent .child {
  color: red;
}
```

Nesting and Variable Scope

Variable scope becomes especially powerful with nesting because you can define a variable that is confined to the given block:

```
.contact-form {
  @labelWidth: 100px;
  @formPadding: 5px;

  padding: 5px 0;

  label {
    display: inline-block;
    width: @labelWidth - 10px;
    padding-right: 10px;
    text-align: right;
    vertical-align: top;
  }

  input[type=text], input[type=email] {
    width: 250px;
    padding: @formPadding;
  }

  textarea {
    width: 400px;
    height: 150px;
    padding: @formPadding;
  }

  input[type=submit] {
    margin-left: @labelWidth;
    font-size: 36px;
```

```
    }
}
```

Here the two variables `@labelWidth` and `@formPadding` are confined to the scope of this `.contact-form` block. This way, you can have site-wide `@labelWidth` and `@formPadding` variables that are set differently for this particular form.

Functions and Mixins

In addition to variables and basic operators, LESS supports a variety of more advanced functions you can use to streamline your CSS workflow. And where LESS doesn't have a built-in function, you can write your own.

Functions

LESS includes a number of prebuilt functions you can use to script CSS properties. For example, you can use the `darken()` function to darken the text of a link on hover:

```
a {
    @linkColor: #DDD;
    color: @linkColor;

    &:hover {
        color: darken(@linkColor, 20%);
    }
}
```

This will make the `@linkColor` 20 percent darker. Likewise, you can `lighten()` the color with `lighten (@linkColor, 20%)`.

Most of the built-in LESS functions are color operations, but there are also some math functions, such as `round()`, `floor()`, and `ceil()`, as well as some miscellaneous functions. For a complete list of the functions available in LESS, visit: `http://lesscss.org/#reference`.

Mixins

Besides the standard LESS functions, you can create your own functions, called *mixins*. Writing your own mixins is really easy, and there are also a number of third-party mixins you can incorporate into your build.

Writing Mixins

One of the most common applications of mixins is handling browser prefixes for experimental CSS properties. For instance, even though `border-radius` is supported in most modern browsers, you can create a mixin to support older versions:

```
.border-radius(@radius) {
    -webkit-border-radius: @radius;
        -moz-border-radius: @radius;
            border-radius: @radius;
}
```

Next, call this mixin in a CSS rule:

```
.my-element {
  .border-radius(5px);
}
```

This will compile as:

```
.my-element {
  -webkit-border-radius: 5px;
    -moz-border-radius: 5px;
         border-radius: 5px;
}
```

You can also add a default to the argument that is passed into the mixin:

```
.border-radius( @radius: 10px ) {
  -webkit-border-radius: @radius;
    -moz-border-radius: @radius;
         border-radius: @radius;
}
```

Now, if you don't pass a radius value into the `.border-radius()` mixin, it will default to `10px`. For more information on mixin-building techniques, visit `http://lesscss.org/#-mixins`.

Using Third-Party Mixins

Writing mixins is relatively simple, but that doesn't mean you should write them all yourself. LESS has been around for a while, and there are several free mixins you can use to jumpstart your LESS development. You can find these mixins through a search engine, or turn to the end of this chapter where I list a number of free mixins in the Further Resources section. Even if you'd rather write all your own mixins, these examples can be great starting points.

File Structure

Now that you know how to use the basic features of LESS, you're ready to put that knowledge into practice. But just like with other development efforts, it's a good idea to structure your LESS into separate files.

Using Imports

For example, you'll probably be reusing a set of standard mixins on every project. Copying and pasting these at the top of each LESS file doesn't make sense. Instead, place them in their own `mixins.less` file. Including the external file in your main `style.less` file is easy. Simply use `@import`:

```
@import "mixins.less"
```

This imports the LESS code in `mixins.less` into the current document.

Additionally, to import a file only if it hasn't been imported yet, use `@import-once`:

```
@import-once "mixins.less"
```

Finally, don't worry about HTTP requests when using `@import`—so long as the imported file has the `.less` extension, it will be concatenated into the parent file when LESS compiles.

Example File Structure

It's a good idea to use `@import` to break your LESS files into logical pieces. For example, your main `style.less` might look like this:

```
/**
 * Import base variables
 */

@import "variables.less";

/**
 * Import mixins
 */

@import "mixins.less";

/**
 * Import other stylesheets
 */

@import "reset.less";
@import "site.less";
@import "media-queries.less";
```

Here the LESS file starts with base variables, a file that includes all the global variables you want to use throughout the stylesheets. Then it imports a standard set of mixins—for instance, those found on `http://lesselements.com`. It imports various stylesheets: a CSS reset such as the YUI reset, a set of main styles called `site.less`, and a set of modifications to the styles based on media queries.

Furthermore, note that there are no actual styles in the main `style.less` file. By storing all the styles in subfiles, you ensure that you can just copy `style.less` into any new project (as well as `mixins.less` and `reset.less`).

Customizing the Structure

You should customize the file structure to suit your individual needs and workflow. If you're embedding a number of different fonts with `@font-face`, include these in a separate `fonts.less` file. If a portion of your styling is pretty encapsulated, put it in its own file to make collaborative development easier.

Finally, match any organizational methods you're already using. For example, if you like to divide your styles into type, color, and layout, you can do so with separate files:

- `type.less` for typography properties such as `font-size`
- `color.less` for color and image properties such as `background`
- `layout.less` for box-model properties such as `width` and `padding`

Summary

LESS streamlines front end development by bringing scripting into stylesheets. It not only speeds up the development process but also leads to better organized, easier-to-maintain stylesheets. In this appendix, you learned how preprocessing works and how to install a LESS compiler. Then you discovered the basics of LESS, including variables, basic operators, and nesting. Next you read about the LESS built-in functions as well as how to write custom mixins. Finally you found out how to structure the files in your LESS app to complement the organizational techniques you're already using. After seeing how LESS works, I'm sure you agree that it's a good idea to use CSS preprocessing for all your projects.

Additional Resources

LESS Documentation

http://lesscss.org

LESS Function Reference

http://lesscss.org/#reference

LESS Compilers

LESS.app (Mac OS X): http://incident57.com/less

SimpLESS (Cross-platform): http://wearekiss.com/simpless

Mod-less Apache Module: https://github.com/waleedq/libapache2-mod-less_beta1

Free Mixins

LESS Elements: http://lesselements.com

Useful CSS3 LESS Mixins: http://css-tricks.com/snippets/css/useful-css3-less-mixins

10 LESS CSS Examples You Should Steal for Your Projects: http://designshack.net/articles/css/10-less-css-examples-you-should-steal-for-your-projects

Tutorials

A Comprehensive Introduction to LESS Mixins: `http://www.sitepoint.com/a-comprehensive-introduction-to-less-mixins/`

How To Squeeze the Most out of LESS: `http://net.tutsplus.com/tutorials/php/how-to-squeeze-the-most-out-of-less/`

Mixins and Nesting: `http://blog.lynda.com/2012/08/27/css-pre-processors-part-two-mixins-and-nesting/`

Index

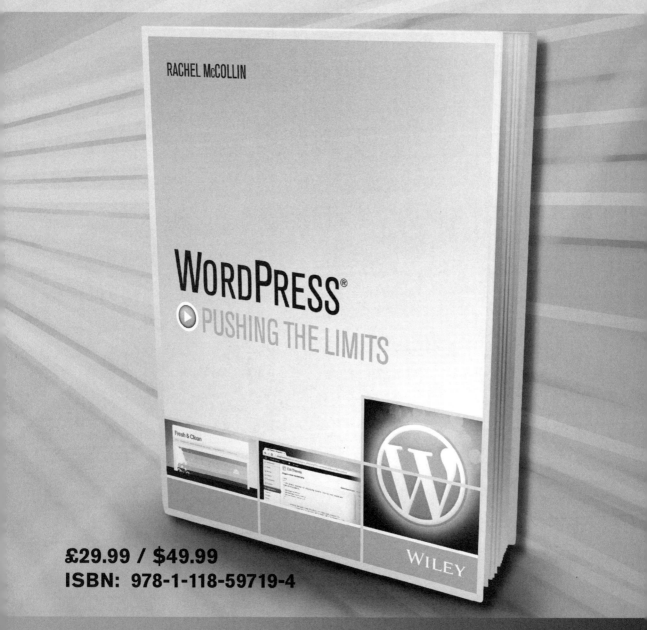

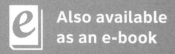

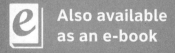